WATER RESOURCES MANAGEMENT

MONITORING AND ASSESSMENT

ENV BOOKS SERIES

WATER RESOURCES MANAGEMENT

MONITORING AND ASSESSMENT

Editors

Dr. Sandeep Gupta
Assistant Professor
Department of Applied Science and Humanities
Ajay Kumar Garg Engineering College
Adhyatmik Nagar, Ghaziabad (UP) (India)

&

Dr. Pawan Kumar 'Bharti'
Vice President
Society for Environment, Health, Awareness of Nutrition & Toxicology (SEHAT)
1775, Sohan Ganj, Near Clock Tower
Delhi - 110 007 (India)
E-mail: *gurupawanbharti@rediffmail.com*

DPH

DISCOVERY PUBLISHING HOUSE PVT. LTD.
NEW DELHI-110 002

Published by:
Namit Wasan
DISCOVERY PUBLISHING HOUSE PVT. LTD.
4383/4B, Ansari Road, Darya Ganj
New Delhi-110 002 (India)
Phone : +91-11-23279245, 43596064-65
Fax : +91-11-23253475
E-mail : discoverypublishinghouse@gmail.com
namitwasan9@gmail.com
sales@discoverypublishinggroup.com
web : www.discoverypublishinggroup.com

***First Edition:* 2016**

ISBN: 978-93-5056-799-9

Water Resources Management: *Monitoring and Assessment*

Printed at:
Infinity Imaging Systems
Delhi

ENV Books Series, India

Calls lengthy and error free chapters for further volumes of books on various environmental issues. (Send your manuscripts to envbooks@gmail.com)

Founding Editor (Editor-in-Chief)

Dr. Pawan Kumar 'Bharti'

Society for Environment, Health, Awareness of Nutrition & Toxicology (SEHAT-India)
1775, Sohanganj, Near Clock Tower, Delhi-7, (India)
E-mail:*gurupawanbharti@rediffmail.com*

Other Titles by Editor-in-Chief:

1. **Advances in Biotechnology and Ecological Sciences (2013)**
   Bharti, P.K., Chauhan, A. and Ray, J. (eds.)
   (ISBN: 978-93-5056-358-8).
2. **Advances in Agriculture and Ecology (2013)**
   Bharti, P.K.; Chauhan, A. and Ezeaku Peter Ikemefuna (eds.)
   (ISBN: 978-93-5056-362-5).
3. **Agriculture and Environmental Biotechnology (2014)**
   Bharti, P.K. and Chauhan, A. (eds.)
   (ISBN: 978-93-5056-479-0).
4. **Agriculture Development and Sustainable Environment (2015)**
   Ray, J. and Bharti, P. K. (eds.)
   (ISBN: 978-93-5056-759-3)
5. **Agriculture Ecology and Environment (2014)**
   Bharti, P.K. and Olubukola O. Babalola (eds.)
   (ISBN: 978-93-5056-480-6).
6. **Agriculture, Environment and Nano-science (2015)**
   Bharti, Pawan K. (ed.)
   (ISBN: 978-93-5056-760-5)
7. **Agro-biodiversity: *Conservation & Sustainable Development* (2016)**
   Sharma, Pankaj; Singh, Narayan; and Bharti, P.K. (eds.)
   (ISBN: 978-93-505-782-1)
8. **Agro-forestry and Climate Change (2014)**
   Bharti, Pawan K. and Singh, Narayan (eds.)
   (ISBN: 978-93-5056-514-8).

9. **Agro-forestry and Sustainable Agriculture (2016)**
Sharma, Pankaj; Bharti, P.K. (eds.)
(ISBN: 978-93-5056-786-9).

10. **Aquaculture and Fisheries Environment (2014)**
Gupta, S.K. and Pawan K. Bharti (eds.)
(ISBN: 978-93-5056-408-0).

11. **Aquatic Biodiversity and Pollution (2013)**
Bharti, P.K.; Chauhan, A. and Kaoud, H.A.H. (eds.)
(ISBN: 978-93-5056-359-5).

12. **Aquatic Ecology and Biotechnology (2014)**
Bharti, P.K. and Zaki, M.S.A. (eds.)
(ISBN: 978-93-5056-451-6).

13. **Aquatic Environment and Toxicology (2013)**
Bharti, Pawan K. (ed.)
(ISBN: 978-93-5056-236-9).

14. **Biodiversity, Biotechnology and Environmental Conservation (2015)**
Bharti, P.K. and Bhandari, G. (eds.)
(ISBN: 978-93-5056-750-0).

15. **Biodiversity of Aquatic Ecosystem: *Significance, Threat and Conservation* (2013)**
Bharti, P.K. and Kaoud, H.A.H. (eds.)
(ISBN: 978-93-5056-297-0).

16. **Biological Diversity and Ecology (2016)**
Arya, M.K.; Bharti, P.K. and Ritesh Joshi (eds.)
(ISBN: 978-93-5056-785-2).

17. **Bioremediation and Microbial Biotechnology (2016)**
Gupta, Sandeep; and Bharti, P.K. (eds.)
(ISBN: 978-93-5056-783-8)

18. **Biotechnological Approaches & Water Ecosystem (2016)**
Zaki, M.S.A.; and Bharti, P.K. (eds.)
(ISBN: 978-93-5056-779-1)

19. **Biotechnology, Agro-ecology and Environment (2015)**
Chauhan, Avnish and Bharti, P.K. (eds.)
(ISBN: 978-93-5056-757-9).

20. **Clean Technologies and Environmental Protection (2015)**
Chauhan, A.; Sharma, S. and Bharti, P.K. (eds.)
(ISBN: 978-93-5056-731-9).

21. **Climate Change and Agriculture (2012)**
Bharti, P.K. and Chauhan, Avnish (eds.)
(ISBN: 978-93-5056-148-5).

22. **Climate Change and Biodiversity (2013)**
Bharti, P.K. and Chauhan, Avnish (eds.)
(ISBN: 978-93-5056-360-1).

23. **Climate Change, Disaster Management and Environment (2016)**
Chauhan, Alka; Bharti, P.K. (eds.)
(ISBN: 978-93-5056-784-5).

24. **Conservation and Cultivation of Medicinal Plants (2015)**
Bharti, P.K. and Singh Narayan (eds.)
(ISBN: 978-93-5056-740-1).

25. **Crop Productivity and Plant Disease Management (2016)**
Chauhan, Alka; Bharti, P.K. and Sadana, Deepti (eds.)
(ISBN: 978-93-5056-791-3)

26. **Eco-toxicology and Eco-technology (2013)**
Bharti, P.K. and Zaki, M. (eds.)
(ISBN: 978-93-5056-313-7).

27. **Environmental Biotechnology and Application (2013)**
Bharti, P.K. and Chauhan, Avnish (eds.)
(ISBN: 978-93-5056-262-8).

28. **Environmental Conservation and Biotechnology (2014)**
Chauhan, A. and P.K. Bharti (eds.)
(ISBN: 978-93-5056-512-4).

29. **Environmental Health and Problems (2013)**
Bharti, P.K. and Gajananda, Kh. (eds.)
(ISBN: 978-93-5056-263-5).

30. **Environmental Pollution and Biodiversity (2012)**
Bharti, P.K.; Chauhan, Avnish and Kumar, P. (eds.)
(ISBN: 978-93-5056-149-2).

31. **Fisheries and Sustainable Aquaculture (2016)**
Gupta, S.K.; Bharti, P.K (eds.)
(ISBN: 978-93-5056-797-5).

32. **Fisheries and Toxicology (2014)**
Zaki, M.S.A.; Bharti, P.K. and Chauhan, A. (eds.)
(ISBN: 978-93-5056-452-3).

33. **Fish Habitat and Aquaculture (2015)**
Bharti, P.K.; Gupta Kr. Sanjay (eds.)
(ISBN: 978-93-5056-744-9).

34. **Food Processing, Management and Nanotechnology (2016)**
Chauhan, Avnish; Bharti, P.K. (eds.)
(ISBN: 978-93-5056-796-8).

35. **Freshwater Ecosystem and Xenobiotics (2013)**
Bharti, P.K.; Zaki, M. and Chauhan, A. (eds.)
(ISBN: 978-93-5056-299-4).

36. **Limnology and Aquatic Science (2015)**
Sharma, S. and Bharti, P.K. (eds.)
(ISBN: 978-93-5056-735-7).

37. **Medicinal Plants: *Distribution, Utilization and Significance* (2015)**
Sharma, P.; Bharti, P.K. and Narayan Singh (eds.)
(ISBN: 978-93-5056-734-0).

38. **Microbial Applications and Environment (2014)**
Bharti, Pawan K. (ed.)
(ISBN: 978-93-5056-515-5).

39. **Microbial Ecology and Habitat (2014)**
Bharti, Pawan K. (ed.)
(ISBN: 978-93-5056-514-8).

40. **Natural Ecosystem and Climate Change (2015)**
Bharti, P.K., and Kh. Gajananda (ed.)
(ISBN: 978-93-5056-745-6).

41. **Pest Management and Agro-Techniques (2016)**
Biswas Asim; Bharti, P.K., and Chauhan Avnish (eds.)
(ISBN: 978-93-5056-794-4).

42. **Prakriti me Aushadhi (*in Hindi*) (2012)**
Singh, J.R.; Bharti, P.K. and Bharti, B.
(ISBN: 978-93-5056-200-0).

43. **Seed Technology, Plant Growth and Cropping System (2015)**
Tyagi, P.K. and Bharti, P.K. (eds.)
(ISBN: 978-93-5056-738-8).

44. **Soil Characteristics and Agro-ecology (2015)**
Avnish Chauhan and Bharti, P.K. (eds.)
(ISBN: 978-93-5056-758-6)

45. **Soil Contamination and Conservation (2015)**
Ezeaku, P.I. and Bharti, P.K. (eds.)
(ISBN: 978-93-5056-737-1).

46. **Soil Quality and Contamination (2013)**
Bharti, P.K. and Chauhan, Avnish (eds.)
(ISBN: 978-93-5056-361-8).

47. **Waste Disposal and Management (2015)**
Bharti, P.K.; Tabassum, B. and Bajaj, P. (eds.)
(ISBN: 978-93-5056-729-6).

48. **Waste Generation and Utilization (2016)**
Bajaj Priya; Tabassum, B., and Bharti, P.K. (eds.)
(ISBN: 978-93-5056-792-0).

49. **Waste Management and Environmental Health (2016)**
Tabassum, B., Bajaj Priya, and Bharti, P.K. (eds.)
(ISBN: 978-93-5056-777-7).

50. **Water Resources and Agriculture (2014)**
Bharti, P.K. and Ezeaku Peter Ikemefuna (eds.)
(ISBN: 978-93-5056-481-3).

Preface

Water is an essential resource for all life on the planet. Of the water resources on Earth only three percent of it is fresh and two-thirds of the freshwater is locked up in ice caps and glaciers. Of the remaining one percent, a fifth is in remote, inaccessible areas and much seasonal rainfall in monsoonal deluges and floods cannot easily be used. At present only about 0.08 percent of all the world's fresh water is exploited by mankind in ever increasing demand for sanitation, drinking, manufacturing, leisure and agriculture.

Water resource management is the activity of planning, developing, distributing and managing the optimum use of water resources. It is a sub-set of water cycle management. Ideally, water resource management planning has regard to all the competing demands for water and seeks to allocate water on an equitable basis to satisfy all uses and demands. As with other resource management, this is rarely possible in practice.

Much efforts in water resource management is directed at optimising the use of water and in minimising the environmental impact of water use on the natural environment.

Successful management of any resources requires accurate knowledge of the resource available, the uses to which it may be put, the competing demands for the resource, measures to and processes to evaluate the significance and worth of competing demands and mechanisms to translate policy decisions into actions on the ground.

For water as a resource this is particularly difficult since sources of water can cross many national boundaries and the uses of water include many that are difficult to assign financial value to and may also be difficult to manage in conventional terms. Examples include rare species or ecosystems or the very long term value of ancient ground water reserves.

Water resources are sources of water that are useful or potentially useful. Uses of water include agricultural, industrial, household, recreational and environmental activities. The majority of human uses require fresh water.

97 percent of the water on the Earth is salt water and only three percent is fresh water; slightly over two thirds of this is frozen in glaciers and polar ice caps. The remaining unfrozen freshwater is found mainly as groundwater, with only a small fraction present above ground or in the air. Fresh water is a renewable resource, yet the world's supply of groundwater is steadily decreasing, with depletion occurring most prominently in Asia and North America, although it is still unclear how much natural renewal balances this usage, and whether ecosystems are threatened.

Ambient water quality, relates to water bodies such as lakes, rivers, and oceans. Water quality standards for surface waters vary significantly due to different environmental conditions, ecosystems, and intended human uses. Toxic substances and high populations of certain microorganisms can present a health hazard for non-drinking purposes such as irrigation, swimming, fishing, rafting, boating, and industrial uses. These conditions may also affect wildlife, which use the water for drinking or as a habitat. Modern water quality laws generally specify protection of fisheries and recreational use and require, as a minimum, retention of current quality standards.

There is some desire among the public to return water bodies to pristine or pre-industrial conditions. Most current environmental laws focus on the designation of particular uses of a water body. In some countries these designations allow for some water contamination as long as the particular type of contamination is not harmful to the designated uses. Given the landscape changes in the watersheds of many freshwater bodies, returning to pristine conditions would be a significant challenge. In these cases, environmental scientists focus on achieving goals for maintaining healthy ecosystems and may concentrate on the protection of populations of endangered species and protecting human health.

Water quality refers to the chemical, physical, biological, and radiological characteristics of water. It is a measure of the condition of water relative to the requirements of one or more biotic species and or to any human need or purpose. It is most frequently used by reference to a set of standards against which compliance can be assessed. The most common standards used to assess water quality relate to health of ecosystems, safety of human contact and drinking water.

Contaminants that may be in untreated water include microorganisms such as viruses, protozoa and bacteria; inorganic contaminants such as salts and metals; organic chemical contaminants from industrial processes and petroleum use; pesticides and herbicides; and radioactive contaminants. Water quality depends on the local geology and ecosystem, as well as human uses such as sewage dispersion, industrial pollution, use of water bodies as a heat sink, and overuse.

The present book updates the subject matter and issues related to water resources, water quality, aquatic resources and management, water quality monitoring and assessment. Thanks are due to contributors from various institutions and publisher for their interest in this book. The book will definitely provide a multidisciplinary forum to explore emerging areas in the field of water resources, water quality, aquatic resources and management, water quality monitoring and assessment.

–Editors

(envbooks@gmail.com)

Contents

Pages: 1-13

WATER RESOURCES MANAGEMENT: *MONITORING AND ASSESSMENT*

Edited by: Dr. Sandeep Gupta; Dr. Pawan Kumar 'Bharti'

ISBN: 978-93-5056-799-9

Edition: 2016

Published by: Discovery Publishing House Pvt. Ltd., New Delhi (India)

1

The Assessment of Water Quality at Narmada River Via Physico-Chemical and Benthic Macro Invertebrate Analysis

Kalpana Mimrot[1]; Shailendra Sharma[1*]; L.K.Mudgal[2]; Bhavna Dawar[1]

ABSTRACT

Benthic macro-invertebrate are best indicator for bio-assessment. This biotic environment of water body directly affects in the distribution of population density and diversity of macro benthic community. Benthic fauna are especially of great significance for fisheries. That they themselves act as food of bottom feeder fishes (Sharma, S. 2002). Macro benthic organism plays an important role in the energy cycle of fresh water bodies. The organisms associated with solid and liquid interface were ordinary termed as benthos and naturally two sub headings phytobanthos and zoobenthos were used. The present study deals with the populaton density and species diversity of Benthic macroinvertebrates of Narmada river at Maheshwar and their correlation coefficient. During the study period 7 sepecies of oloigochaeta, 10 species of insecta, 11 species of grastopoda and 8 species of pelecypoda were recorded.

1 Department of Biotechnology & Zoology, Adarsh Institute of Management & Science College, Dhamnod, Dhar - 454 552 (M.P), (India)

2 Department of Zoology, Mata Jijabai Govt Girls P.G. College, Indore (M.P.), (India)

INTRODUCTION

Water is necessary for the existence of man, who appeared on the earth in the early Pleistocene age above two to three million years ago. In the recent years rapid increase in growth of population took place. These have brought stress on agricultural and industrial sector to cope up with the demand. It is also true that for this factor water is critical factor. The origin of water in the planet is not clear. The current thinking is that the primordial earth has no ocean and perhaps very little atmosphere. It is believed that volatile constituents trapped inside the earth's surface came out through volcanic eruption, intensive rock moment and hard spring condensed to form ocean and the atmosphere. Water evaporates from oceans and returns to the earth in the form of precipitation resulting in "gigantic hydrological cycle" (Dar, H.A. 2011).

The macro-invertebrates are the most valuable indicators of environmental quality in aquatic ecosystem because of stable mode of life, their convenient size and distinct characters which offers an easy sorting and identification of these organisms (Krishnamoorthi and Sarkar 1979).

Macro-invertebrates community response to environmental changes are useful in assessing the impact of municipal, industrial and agricultural waste and impact of other land uses on surface water. The macro-invertebrates are highly popular as pollution indicators. (Sharma, S. *et al* 2008).

Correlation analysis is concerned with relationship between two variables. Workers have conducted many investigations in environmental science and engineering using correlation analysis. Other demonstrated the applications of this powerful mathematical tool to limnological studies. Only qualitative and quantitative estimation of living organism is not in so enough so physical and chemical parameters are also emphasized. With these parameters of water population dynamic is calculated (Dave, V. 2008).

MATERIAL AND METHODS

Narmada River

India is a land, which has been blessed with a large number of big and small rivers. River Narmada is considered one of the important rivers of the country. The Narmada basin extends over an area of 98.796 sq. km and lies between east longitudes 72°32′ to 81°45′ and north latitude 21°20′ to 23°45′.

Narmada is an important river in central India and the fifth largest river in Indian subcontinent. Narmada, a Sanskrit word, means 'one who endows with bliss'. After originating from Amarkantak, the river flows through the Mandla hills and enters the Narmada valley between the Vindhya and Satpura ranges. It forms the traditional boundary between North India and South India and flows westwards over a length of 1312 km before draining through the Gulf of Combay (Khambat) into the Arabian Sea, 50kms west of Bharuch city of Gujrat. It is one of only three major rivers in peninsular India that runs from east to west (largest west flowing river) along with the Tapti and the Mahi river. It is the only river in India that flows in a rift valley flowing west between the Satpura and Vindhya ranges. It flows through the states of Madhya Pradesh (1.077km), Maharashtra (74km-35km) border between Madhya Pradesh and Maharashtra and 39 km border between Madhya Pradesh and Gujarat 161km (NCA Narmada Control Authority).

About Maheshwar

The name Maheshwar comes from Mahesh, a name for Lord Shiva. The word Maheshwar in Hindi means *abode of Lord Mahesh.*

Maheshwar is a small town in Khargone district of Madhya Pradesh State in central India. It is located 91 km away from Indore, the commercial capital of the state. The town lies along the north bank of Narmada river.

It's Latitude (DMS) 22°18′60″N and Longitude (DMS) 75°34′60″ E.

Biological Analysis

Monthly samplings of this station was made (2009-2010). A hand net was used in collecting the sample and sieving them for isolation. The bigger animal species picked up by hand, where as the smaller forms were isolated by sugar floatation method and studied them under low power (x50) microscope. They were preserved by narcotizing them by Methanol and Chloral hydrate and late 70% Alcohol. The benthic organisms were identified with the help of APHA (2002), Willium & Feltmate (1992), Pennak (1989), Tonapi (1980), Needham & Needham (1969), etc.

Physico Chemical Analysis

The physico-chemical characteristics are the most influencing parameters which affect the life in water. Fluctuation in these constituents often creates an adverse environment to organism limiting their production and interfering in the physiological processes, while reduce their ability to compete with other populations within the environment.

The work of present study carried out during September 2009 to August 2010. Important physico-chemical parameters were estimated on the monthly basis. The physico-chemical analysis of water was performed as per methods given in APHA (2002), Welch (1998), Trivedi and Goel (1986) and Golterman (1978).

OBSERVATION AND RESULTS

The physico-chemical and Biological parameters and their correlation coefficient as reported in Table 1.1, 1.2 and 1.3.

Table 1.1: Monthly Fluctuations in Physico-chemical Parameters at Maheshwar Region in Narmada River during 2009-2010

Sl. No.	Parameters	September	October	November	December	January	February	March	April	May	June	July	August
1.	Water Temp. (°c)	27	26	23.5	21.5	18.5	20.5	26.5	28.5	28	30.5	24	22
2.	Transparency (cm)	28	22.0	29.0	42.5	54.0	57.0	47.5	49.5	55.0	59.5	24.5	14.0
3.	Hydrogen ion concentration	8.8	8.9	8.7	8.5	8.4	8.6	8.4	8.9	8.8	8.4	7.6	7.3
4.	D.O. (mg/l)	7.5	7.7	7.6	7.9	7.8	8.0	8.4	8.2	7.7	7.9	7.8	8.1
5.	B.O.D. (mg/l)	2.4	2.6	2.7	2.5	2.8	2.9	2.8	2.4	2.3	2.4	2.0	2.3
6.	Total hardness (mg/l)	120	125	130	140	155	160	170	180	165	145	130	110
7.	Chloride (mg/l)	30	35	40	50	46	49	50	53	55	45	30	35
8.	Phosphate (mg/l)	1.02	1.04	1.25	1.75	1.09	1.25	1.50	2.25	2.75	2.50	1.75	1.50
9.	Calcium (mg/l)	19.5	17.5	25.5	30.5	33.8	35.2	37.4	38.6	40.5	30.0	22.5	18.2
10.	Nitrate (mg/l)	0.50	0.75	1.50	1.50	1.95	2.50	2.90	3.50	3.75	2.25	1.55	1.00
11.	Sulphate (mg/l)	6.5	7.0	8.8	9.0	9.8	11.0	8.8	8.5	7.6	7.2	6.0	5.5

Table 1.2: Monthly Variation in Macro-invertebrates Diversity at Maheshwar in Narmada River during 2009-2010

Name of Group and Species	September	October	November	December	January	February	March	April	May	June	July	August
Oligochaeta (/M^2)												
Tubifex tubifex	10	15	20	10	15	15	14	18	22^	18	NIL	5*
Tubifex albicola	NIL	13	19	NIL	13	08	13	17	20^	13	NIL	4*
Limmodrilus hoffmeisteri	3	7	18^	3	7	10	7	6	9	5	NIL	2*
Dero dorsalis	7	9	10	7	9	11	4*	10	7	5	15^	10
Stylaria fossularis	3	5	7	3	5	10^	8	7	4	2*	5	8
Telmatodrilus multispinosus	8	14	22^	8	14	17	10	12	13	NIL	NIL	4*
Branchiodrillus hortensis	8	6	9	8	6	16^	9	4	10	7	8	3*
Insecta (/M^2) Baetidae -												
Baetiella ladakae	NIL	NIL	NIL	NIL	NIL	NIL	NIL	NIL	NIL	NIL	NIL	NIL
Baetis solangensis	NIL	NIL	11	16	19	24^	20	15	12	08	03*	NIL
Baetis simplex	NIL	NIL	13	19	25	30^	24	20	15	12	06*	NIL
Baetis festivus	NIL	NIL	NIL	NIL	NIL	NIL	NIL	NIL	NIL	NIL	NIL	NIL
Caenoidae -												
Caenis sp.	NIL	NIL	10	21	30	32^	28	21	17	14	08*	NIL
Ephemeridae -												
Ephemera nadinae	NIL	NIL	04*	08	12	15	13	10	17^	10	05	NIL
Heptageniidae -												
Epeorus gilliesi	NIL	NIL	04	09	15	19	23^	18	14	10	03*	NIL
Heptagenia nubila	NIL	NIL	NIL	NIL	NIL	NIL	NIL	NIL	NIL	NIL	NIL	NIL

(Table Contd…)

Name of Group and Species	September	October	November	December	January	February	March	April	May	June	July	August
Chironomidae-												
Chironomus chironomus	10	27	33^	20	18	22	15	12	15	18	05*	NIL
Chaoborus chaoborus	19	22	29	33^	25	21	18	14	12	10	08*	NIL
Gastropoda(/M²)												
Pila globosa	NIL	18	22	34	38^	29	22	19	17	12*	NIL	NIL
Bellamya bengalensis	NIL	30	39	47	38	30	46	52^	46	37	28*	NIL
Vivipara bengalensis	10*	22	30	34	27	19	33	40^	35	27	NIL	NIL
Thiara scabra	NIL	25*	35	42	49	58	40	55	61	69^	NIL	NIL
Thiara lineata	NIL	10*	18	23	29	33	40^	29	39	25	NIL	NIL
Thiara tuberculata	NIL	08*	15	27	35	52^	41	30	24	18	NIL	NIL
Melanoides tuberculates	NIL	NIL	10*	33	45	52	39	10*	40	55^	NIL	NIL
Lymnea acuminate	NIL	NIL	18*	28	52	59^	48	32	25	33	NIL	NIL
Lymnea auricularia	NIL	12	27	34	17	10	06*	37^	30	26	17	NIL
Digioniostoma pulchella	NIL	NIL	10*	19	26	39^	33	27	20	15	13	NIL
Gyraulus convexiusculus	NIL	NIL	09	16	21	28	33^	21	17	12	08*	NIL
Pelecypoda (/M²)												
Corbicula striatella	NIL	NIL	15*	22	29	35	39	43	49	55^	30	NIL
Musculium indicum	NIL	NIL	08	15	19	24	30^	22	15	10	07*	NIL
Pisidium clarkeanum	07*	20	22	29	32	36	40^	12	25	29	34	NIL
Parreysia caerulea	NIL	NIL	12	27	35^	20	18	12	15	10*	NIL	NIL
Parreysia favidens	NIL	NIL	08*	18	27	35^	24	17	10	30	NIL	NIL
Lamellidens corrianus	10	22	27	19	17	08*	NIL	NIL	34	37^	20	NIL
Lamellidens consobrinus	20*	33	45	50	57^	48	35	21	49	39	NIL	NIL
Lamellidens lamellatus	NIL	NIL	15*	22	29	35	39	43	49	55^	30	NIL

NIL = absent, * = minimum, ^ = maximum

Table 1.3: Correlation Between Physico-chemical Parameters and Benthic Macro-invertebrates at Maheshwar 2009-10

Serial Number	Parameters	Annelida (Oligochaeta)	Arthopoda (Insecta)	Mollusca (Gastropoda/ Pelecypoda)
1.	Temperature	-0.020	-0.256	-0.008
2.	Transparancy	0.383	0.798	0.931
3.	pH	0.610	0.465	0.423
4.	Dissolved Oxygen	-0.067	0.319	0.339
5.	Biological Oxygen Demand	0.614	0.716	0.514
6.	Hardness	0.473	0.784	0.847
7.	Chloride	0.500	0.798	0.886
8.	Phosphate	-0.005	0.064	0.394
9.	Calcium	0.476	0.817	0.897
10.	Nitrate	0.464	0.610	0.762
11.	Sulphate	0.627	0.953	0.798

Water Temperature

The range of temperature varies greatly in different environment conditions such as fresh water bodies, marine and terrestrial. The minimum temperature was recorded in the month of January 18.5° C while maximum in the month of June 30.5° C.

Transparency

It is mainly affected by the suspended particles and other factors like plankton growth, rain fall, nature of water and weather conditions. The minimum transparency was recorded in the month of August 14 cm while maximum in the month of June 59.5 cm.

pH

It is greatly affected by photosynthetic activity of aquatic plants by exposure of air temperature disposal of sewage and disposal of industrial water. The minimum pH was recorded in the month of August 7.3 while maximum in the month of October and April 8.9.

D.O.

It is important for aquatic system and also essential for the metabolism of organisms. There are two main source of D.O. in water i.e. by diffusion from air and photosynthetic activity. The minimum D.O. was recorded in the month of September 7.5 mg/l while maximum in the month of March 8.4 mg/l.

B.O.D.

It is an index of organic pollution and help in deciding the suitability for water consumption. The minimum B.O.D. was recorded in the month of July 2.0 mg/l while maximum in the month of February 2.9 mg/l.

Total Hardness

It shows the quality of water. Total hardness in water is the sum of the concentrations of alkaline earth metal cation (Ca++, Mg++) etc. The minimum total hardness was recorded in the month of August 110 mg/l while maximum in the month of April 180 mg/l.

Chloride

It is present in the form of Ca, Mg and Na salt. The concentration of chloride content is also used as an indicator of pollution in fresh water. The minimum chloride was recorded in the month of September and July 30 mg/l while maximum in the month of May 55 mg/l.

Phosphate

It is the important nutrient necessary for the production growth of aquatic organisms. The major source of phosphorus is the domestic sewage, detergents, agricultural effluents with fertilizer and industrial waste water. The minimum phosphate was recorded in the month of September 1.02 mg/l while maximum in the month of May 2.75 mg/l.

Calcium

It is an important micronutrient in aquatic ecosystem. Calcium is found in abundance in all natural water bodies. Being an important contributor to hardness in water and it also reduces the utility of water for domestic use. The minimum calcium was recorded in the month of October 17.5 mg/l while maximum in the month of May 40.5 mg/l.

Nitrate

Nitrogen is the basic constituent of all organisms and plays a vital role in metabolism, growth, reproduction and transmission of heritable character. In an aquatic ecosystem, it is present in the form of organic nitrogen compound ammonia, nitrate and nitrite. The minimum nitrate was recorded in the month of September 0.50 mg/l while maximum in the month of May 3.75 mg/l.

Sulphate

It is ecologically important for growth of plants and its short supply may inhibit the development of planktons. It is utilized by all living organisms in the form of both mineral and organic sulphate. The minimum sulphate was recorded in the month of August 5.5 mg/l while maximum in the month of February 11.0 mg/l.

Biological Analysis

Oligochaeta

During the study period, 7 species belongs to Oligochaeta group were recorded named *Tubifex tubifex, Tubifex albicola, Limmodrilus hoffmeisteri, Telmatodrilus multispinosus, Branchiodrilus hortensis, Dero dorsalis and Stylaria fossularis.*

Insecta

During the study period, 10 species belongs to Insecta group were recorded named *Baetiella ladakae, Baetis solangensis, Baetis simplex, Baetis festivus, Caenis sp., Ephemera nadinae, Epeorus gilliesi, Heptagenia nubila, Chironomus chironomus and Chaoborus chaoborus.*

Gastropoda

During the study period, 11 species belongs to Gastropoda group were recorded named *Pila globosa, Bellamya bengalensis, Vivipara bengalensis, Thiara scabra, Thiara lineata, Thiara tuberculata, Melanoides tuberculates, Lymnea acuminate, Lymnea auricularia, Digioniostoma pulchella and Gyraulus convexiusculus.*

Pelecypoda

During the study period, 8 species belongs to Pelecypoda group were recorded named *Corbicula striatella, Musculium indicum, Pisidium clarkeanum, Parreysia caerulea, Parreysia favidens, Lamellidens corrianus, Lamellidens consobrinus and Lamellidens lamellates.*

SPECIES OF OLIGOCHAETA

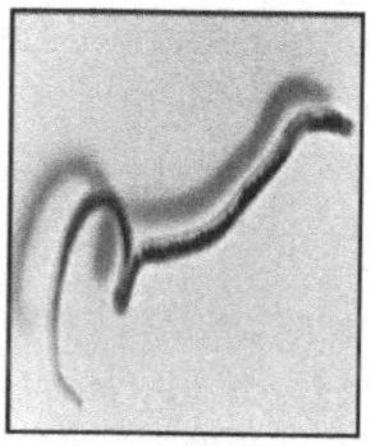

Tubifex tubifex

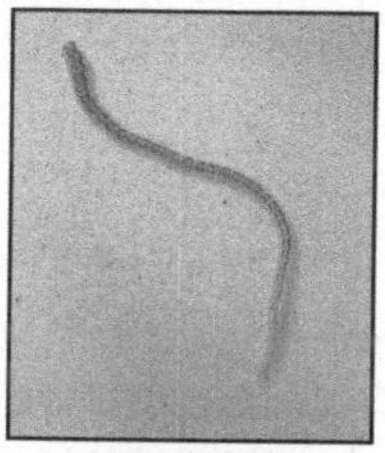

Limmodrilus hoffmeisteri

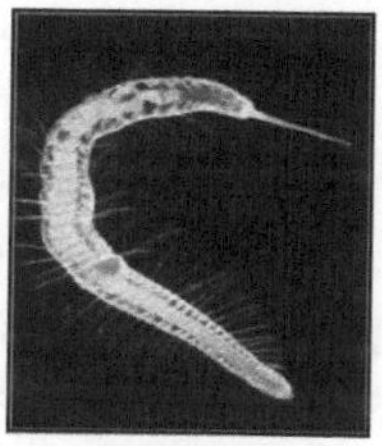

Stylaria foscularis

SPECIES OF INSECTA

Ladakae simplex

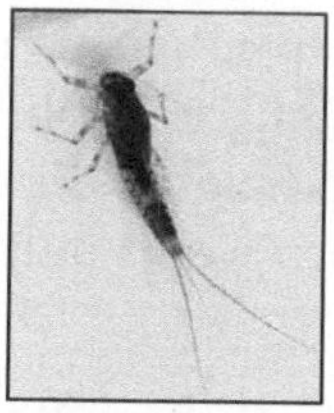

Chironomous chironomus

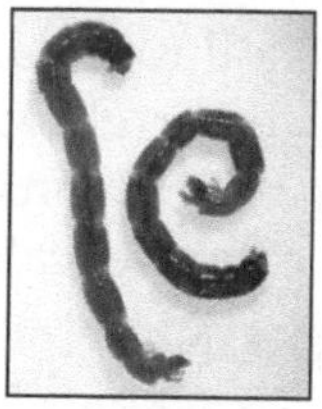

Baetiella Baetis

SPECIES OF GASTROPODA

Globosa lineata

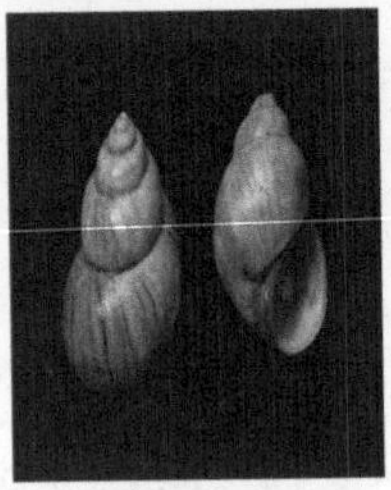

Thiara bengalensis

Pila Bellamya

SPECIES OF PELECYPODA

Corbicula striatella

Pisidium clarkeanum

Parreysia caerulea

Lamellidens corrianus

Correlation Coefficient Between Physico-chemical Parameters and Benthic Macro-invertebrates

To study the relationship between the physico-chemical parameters and benthic macro-invertebrates during study period (September 2009 - August 2010) Karl Pearson's correlation coefficient (r) method was used.

During the study period, annelida shows low negative correlation with tempreture, D.O. and phosphate while low positive correlation with transparency and moderate positive correlation with pH, BOD, hardness, chloride, calcium, nitrate and sulphate. Arthopoda shows low negative correlation with tempreture while low positive correlation with D.O. and moderate positive correlation with pH, phosphate and nitrate and high positive correlation with transparency, BOD, hardness, chloride, calcium and sulphate. Mollusca shows low negative correlation with tempreture, while low positive correlation with D.O. and phosphate, and moderate positive correlation with pH and BOD, and high positive correlation with transparency, hardness, chloride, calcium, nitrate and sulphate.

DISCUSSION

Nnaji et al (2010) observed nitrate value ranged between 1.6 to 2.4 mg/l in river Galma, Nigeria.

Chandra *et al* (2011) recorded temperature between 26° C to 31° C, BOD values between 1.6 to 7.2 mg/l, sulphate values ranged between 2 to 57 mg/l in various rivers of India. Murhekar (2011) recorded temperature ranging between 21° C to 29° C, nitrate value ranged between 0.19 to 7.1 mg/l in different locations around Akola city. Sharma and Chowdhary (2011) observed transparency ranged between 20cm to 112 cm, pH values between 6.8 to 9.4, DO variation between 0.4 to 8 mg/l, chloride ranged between 21.95 to 59.88 mg/l in the river Tawi.

Sharma and Chowdhary (2011) recorded the transparency ranged between 25 cm to 110 cm and pH value between 7.3 to 9.6, BOD variation between 2.3 to 4.7 mg/l, chloride between 9.8 to 16.51 mg/l, nitrate value ranged from 0.03 to 0.14 mg/l of the river Ganga at Ghaziabad. Sharma, S. et al (2011) observed DO variation between 4.2 to 4.6 mg/l, nitrate value in the range between 0.06 to 0.09 mg/l in Hoshangabad area of Narmada river.

Krishna, J.M. (2012) recorded total hardness value between 72.33 to 198.73 mg/l and calcium value between 12.13 to 54.73 mg/l in Kaveri river, Kudige, Kodagu, Karnataka. Sujitha, P.C. et al (2012) recorded total hardness varied between 32 to 71, phosphate varied between 0.06 to 1.52 mg/l and sulphate varied between 0.49 to 2.60 mg/l in Karamana river, Trivandram, Kerala.

Sharma, S. *et al* (2013) recorded water temperature varied between 25° C to 42° C, pH varied between 7.61 to 9.22, DO varied between 7.21 to 9.12 mg/l, BOD varied between 3.1 to 5.63mg/l, Total Hatrdness varied between 71 mg/l to 190 mg/l, Chloride varied between 0.3 mg/l to 53.4 mg/l, phosphate varied between 0.5 mg/l to 0.49 mg/l, nitrate varied between 0.11 mg/l to 0.131 mg/l in Kunda river, Khargone (M.P.). Hamaidi, C. F. et al (2013) observed phosphate ranged between 0 to 0.94 mg/l, calcium ranged between 90 to 104 mg/l in Chiffa river, Algeria.

Negi, *et al* (2008) studied the Hinval stream of Garhwal region and reported 29 genera of benthic fauna belonging to 7 orders. The most abundant order recorded was Ephemeroptera (11 genera), followed by Plecoptera, Coleoptera, Diptera with 4 genera each, Trichoptera, Odonata with 2 genera each and Megaloptera with 1 genus. Sharma, M.P. et al (2008) studied the macroinvertebrate diversity at two sampling sites of Ninglad stream (an important tributary of river Kosi) and collected a total of 36 families of macroinvertebrates.

Sharma, M.P. *et al* (2010) identified total 67 taxon of macro invertebrates belonging to 8 taxonomic groups during the study at various sampling locations on Kosi river. Panday, R.K. (2010) detected 53 families of benthic organisms under 13 orders of river Narmada in the Eastern Zone of M.P.

Sharma, K. K. and Chowdhary, S. (2011) were recorded 20 taxa of macrobenthic invertebrate fauna during the period of study belonging to 3 major phyla viz: Annelida, Arthropoda and Mollusca.Among these phyla, Arthropoda (70.54%) dominated and were followed by Annelida (28.11%) and Mollusca (0.95%) in Central Himalayan River, Tawi (Jammu and Kashmir).

Nautiyal and Mishra (2012) recorded the arthropod (Class Insecta, Crustacea), mollusc (Class astropoda, Pelecypoda) and annelid (Class Oligochaeta, Polychaeta) elements consisting of 22 taxa constitute the benthic macroinvertebrate fauna of the Ken river. The insects occur in high numbers at all the selected stations, the mayfly (Class Insecta, Order Ephemeroptera) occur in very high numbers in the river Ken.

Negi, R.K. and Mamgain, S. (2013) recorded total 31 benthos belonging to three phylum, 4 classes and 10 orders with Insecta emerging as the most dominant class. Sharma, S. et al (2013) reported forty-two species from Kunda river, Khargone (M.P.), India.

Present study is further supported by Chandra *et al* (2011), Murhekar (2011), Sharma and Chowdhary (2011), Sharma, S. *et al* (2011), Krishna, J.M. (2012), Sharma, S. *et al* (2013), Negi, *et al* (2008), Nautiyal and Mishra (2012) and Negi, R.K. and Mamgain, S. (2013).

REFERENCES

A.P.H.A. (2002): Standard Method for Examination of Water and Waste Water. American Public Health Association (22th Edition) APHA New York.

Chandra, S. Singh, A. Tomar, P.K. and Kumar, A. (2011): Evaluation of Physico-chemical Characteristics of Various River Water in India. *E Journal of Chemistry,* 8(4): 1546-1555.

Dar, H.A. (2011): Spatial Variation of Benthos in Upper Lake, Bhopal . *Dissertation Report Submitted for the Partial Fulfillment of Master's Degree in Environmental Science. Under the Supervision of Dr. Vipin Vyas. Department of Environmental Science and Limnology. Barkatullah University, Bhopal*

Dave, V. (2008): Limnological Studies of Krisnapura Lake with Special References to Population Dynamics. *Ph.D. Thesis, D.A.V.V. Indore (M.P.).*

Golterman, H.L. Clymo, R.S. and Ohnstad, M.A.M. (1978): Method for Physical and Chemical Analysis of Fresh Water. *IBP Hand Books No. 8 Black Well Scientific Publication,* Oxford 213pp.

Hamaidi-Chergui, F. Errahmani, M.B. Benouaklil, F. and Hamaidi, M.S. (2013): Preliminary Study on Physico-Chemical Parameters and Phytoplankton of Chiffa River (Blida, Algeria). *Journal of Ecosystems Volume 2013 Article ID* 148793.

Krishna, J.M. (2012): Physicochemical and Bacteriological Study of Kaveri River at Kudige, Kodagu District, Karnataka. *International Journal of Environmental Sciences Volume* 2, No. 4.

Krishnamoorthi, K.P. and Sarkar, R. (1979): Macro-invertebrates as Indicators of Water Quality. *National Environmental Engineering Research Institute, Nagur* - 440 020. (India).

Murhekar, G. H. (2011): Determination of Physico-Chemical Parameters of Surface Water Samples in and Around Akot City. *International Journal of Research in Chemistry and Environment. Vol. 1 (183-187)* ISSN 2248-9649.

Nautiyal, P. and Mishra, A.S. (2012): Longitudinal Distribution of Benthic Macroinvertebrate Fauna in a Vindhyan River, India. *International Journal of Environmental Sciences Vol. 1 No. 3. pp. 150-158.*

Needham, J.G. and Needham, P.R. (1969): A guide to the Study of Fresh Water Biology Holden – Day Inc. Sanfranhisco, 108.

Negi, R.K. and Mamgain, S. (2013): Seasonal Variation of Benthic Macro Invertebrates from Tons River of Garhwal Himalaya Uttarakhand. *Pakistan Journal of Biological Sciences, 16: 1510-1516.*

Negi, R.K. Negi, T. and Joshi, P.C. (2008): Study on Physico-chemical Parameters of Hinval Fresh Water Stream and Ganga River of Shivpuri in the Garhwal Region. *J. Env. Bio. Sci. Vol.* 22 (2) 203-212.

Nnaji, J.C. Uzairu, A. Harrison, G.F.S. and Balarabe, M.L. (2010): Effect of Pollution on the Physico-chemical Parameters of Water and Sediments of River Galma, Zaria, Nigeria. *Libyan Agriculture Research Center Journal International* 1 (2): 115-1, (ISSN 2219-4304).

Pandey, R.K. Kori, R. Akolkar, P. Saxena, A. Rajput, C.P. and Dutta, S. (2010): Benthic Macro-invertebrates of River Narmada in Eastern Zone of Madhya Pradesh. *Proceeding of IInd International River Festival* – March 2010: 78-86.

Pennak, Robert W. (1989): Fresh Water Invertebrates of the United States Protozoa to Mollusca. *3rd Edi.* John Wiley and Sons New York.

Ruttener, F: 1953. Fundamentals of Limnology. *Publ. E.E.J. Unic. Press,* Toronto 242.

Sharma, K.K. and Chowdhary, S. (2011): Macro-invertebrate Assemblages as Biological Indicators of Pollution in a Central Himalayan River, Tawi (J&K). *International Journal of Biodiversity and Conservation Vol.* 3(5), pp. 167-174.ISSN 2141-243X.

Sharma, S. Rakesh, V. Savita, D. and Praveen, J. (2011): Evaluation of Water Quality of Narmada River with Reference to Physico-chemical Parameters at Hoshangabad City, M.P. India. *Res. J. Chem. Sci.* 1(3): 40-48.

Sharma, M.P. Kumar, A. Sharma, P. Goel, V. And Sharma, S. (2010): Water Quality Assessment of Kosi River, Using Benthic Macro-invertebrates as Bioindicator. *Proceeding of IInd International River Festival* – March 2010: 41-42.

Sharma, M. P. Sharma, S. Goel, V. Sharma, P. Kumar, A. (2008): Water Quality Assessment of Ninglaad Nala Stream Using Benthic Mcro-invertebrates. *Life Sciences Journal (China)* (Vol. 5) No. 3. pp. 67-70.

Sharma, S. Dubey, S. and Chaurasia, R. (2013): Benthic Macro-invertebrate Abundance and its Correlations with Physico-chemical Parameters from Kunda River, Khargone (M.P.), India. *International Journal of Advanced Research,* Volume 1, Issue 2, 8-13. (ISSN NO 2320-5407)

Sujitha P.C. Mitra Dev D. Sowmya P.K. Mini Priya R. (2012): Physico-chemical Parameters of Karamana River Water in Trivandrum District, Kerala, India. *International journal of Environmental Sciences Volume* 2, No. 3.

Tonapi (1989): Fresh Water Animal of Indian Ecology Approach. *Oxford and IBH Publishing Co.* New Delhi, India p. 341.

Trivedi, R.K. and Goel, P.K. (1986): "Chemical and Biological Methods for Water Pollution Studies". *Environmental Publication,* Karad, India: 35-96.

Welch, P.S. (1998): Limnology. *Mcgrew Hill Book Co, New York,* p. 538.

William, D.P. and Feltmate, B.W. (1992): Aquatic Insects C.A.B. *International, Wallingford Oxon, UK.*

Yadav, R.C. and Srivastava, V.C. (2011): Physico-chemical Properties of the Water of River Ganga at Gazipur. *Indian J. Sci. Res.* 2(4): 41-44.

Pages: 14-30

WATER RESOURCES MANAGEMENT: *MONITORING AND ASSESSMENT*

Edited by: Dr. Sandeep Gupta; Dr. Pawan Kumar 'Bharti'

ISBN: 978-93-5056-799-9

Edition: 2016

Published by: Discovery Publishing House Pvt. Ltd., New Delhi (India)

2

Limnological Study of Traditionally Valued Jalikhora Wetland of Dimoria Tribal Block, Assam, India

Ratul Arya Baishya[1*] and **Chandra Sharma**[2]

ABSTRACT

The Jalikhora wetland situated at Dimoria Tribal Block, Khetri of Kamrup (M) District of Assam is an important wetland ecosystem in the region. It is famous for community fishing and is a valuable source for irrigation and animal feeding. An estimation of 14 imperative limnological parameters was investigated throughout the annual cycle. The samples were collected on the entire four seasons of the year for limonological parameters investigation. The study was carried out for a period of one year from January, 2013 to December, 2013. Correlation coefficients were calculated between different pairs of limnological variables to identify the highly correlated and interrelated water quality parameters and t-test and z-test were applied at 0.05 level of significance and 95% confidence interval for checking the significance. The Pearson (n) Correlation matrix between Water Temperature (°C) and pH, Water Temperature (°C) and FCO_2 (mg l^{-1}), Water Temperature (°C) and DO (mg l^{-1}), Water

[1] Research Scholar, Department of Zoology, Gauhati University, Guwahati – 781 014, (Assam), (India)

[2] Assistant Professor, Department of Environment Management, Dimoria College, Khetri – 782 403, Kamrup (R), (Assam), India

Temperature (°C) and Total Alkalinity (mg l^{-1}), Water Temperature (°C) and Turbidity (NTU) showed positive correlation (r = 0.445, 0.049, 0.706, 0.561 and 0.437) at 5% significance level respectively. Most of the parameters values were found within the permissible limit as laid down by WHO.

Keywords: Jalikhora wetland; Limnological features; Statistical analysis; Assam; India

INTRODUCTION

Water, which is most important element in the biosphere has a very vital role for the maintenance of all life-forms on one hand and on the other helps in the movement, circulation and cycling of nutrients in the biosphere. Water availability has become a great concern in our world today. Among the water bodies, wetlands (Ramsar Convention, 1971; Gosselink & Mitsch, 1986; U.S. Fish and Wildlife Service, 1989) have assumed high importance in the context of its water, soil, flora-fauna and ecosystem services. In the state of Assam, there are as many as 3513 wetlands and it is known differently in different parts of the North-Eastern regions. They are known as *beel* (Assam, Arunachal Pradesh, Meghalaya and Tripura), *boar* (Cachar District in Assam) and *pat* (Manipur). Among these, Assam has the largest area associated with the Brahmaputra and the Barak River.

Wetlands perform different functions such as Ground water recharge and discharge, Flood flow alternation, Sediment stabilization, Sediment/ toxicant retention, Nutrient removal/transformation, Carbon transformation, Recreation etc., and generates healthy wildlife, fisheries and forest resources. The combination of these functions and products, together with the value placed upon biological diversity and the cultural values of certain wetlands make these ecosystems invaluable to people all over the world.

Jalikhora beel (wetland) is one such wetland having its multi-utilities. It is traditionally very important and is situated at the Dimoria Tribal Development (T.D) Block under Khetri Gaon Panchayat of Kamrup District, Assam, India. The surrounding villages depend on this precious water resource as it helps in agricultural and economical sites taking role in community developments. The important significant of the wetland is that the local people use to cultivate in its fringe areas during winter season. The local people residing in the surrounding area are economically depended on the wetland because of the availability of diverse fish species. Community fishing in the middle part of January (paddy harvesting time) is the main cultural tradition of the surrounded villages of Jalikhora Wetland.

The demand of water resources is increasing day by day due to continuous growth of population. So far, very little information is available on the limnological attributes of the wetland. These resources for many people are the sources of employment and income activities. The human interventions thus have multiplied with the passage of time. Consequently, the very existence and continuity of the wetland as sources of livelihood and eco-system services are at stake. It is in this context of threats and management need, detail study on the limnological parameters of the wetland has been undertaken from January, 2013 to December, 2013 to find out the suitability of the water resources for irrigation, domestic needs, fishing & other purposes. The present study is an attempt towards that end.

DESCRIPTION OF STUDY AREA

Location

Dimoria T.D Block is located within the geographic limits of longitude 91°1′E to 92°3′E and latitude 25°88′N to 26°10′N with an elevation of 45-51 m MSL (Assam forest Department, 2004). It covers an area of approximately 26.16 ha with lush green vegetation. The Jalikhora Wetland falls under Helagog village, Khetri Gaon Panchayat under Dimoria T.D Block of Kamrup District (Metro), Assam, India (Fig 2.1). The total area of the wetland covers 13.17 acre (approximately) and is under the legitimate custodian of Bhoragoan village Community. The local people practice community fishing on occasion of paddy harvesting season (middle part of January) every year.

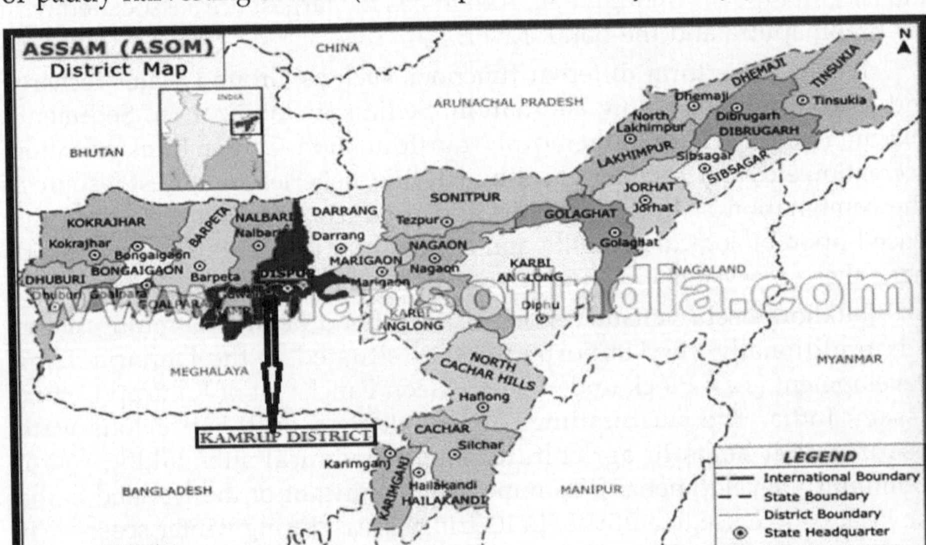

Fig. 2.1: Map of Assam Showing Kamrup District

Topography

The fluvial process under the tropical humid climatic regime has given rise to a plain topography in the area occasional marshes and swamps towards its north forming the huge natural reservoir and wetlands in the form of Jalikhora Wetland.

Climate

The climate of the area is humid tropical. It has a cold winter, pleasant spring and rainy summer. The minimum temperature varies from 10°C - 18°C during winter and 24°C - 34°C during summer. The monthly precipitation around the region ranges between 9.6 mm in December to 296 mm in June. Relative humidity varies from 70-85%.

METHODS AND METHODOLOGY

Selection of Sampling Station

The study was carried out over a period of one year from January, 2013 to December, 2013. In order to analysis the important physico-chemical parameters viz., Water Temperature (WT), pH, Free Carbon dioxide (FCO_2), Dissolve Oxygen (DO), Biochemical Oxygen Demand (BOD), Chemical Oxygen Demand (COD), Nitrate, Chloride, Sulphate and Phosphate, Total Alkalinity (TA), Total Hardness (TH), Total Dissolved Solids (TDS) and Turbidity, water samples were collected from four sampling stations of the wetland and were measured for the entire four seasons of the year followed after Trivedi & Goel (1986) and APHA (2005). A brief Description of these sampling points was summarized as follows:

Station 1: This sampling point is situated in the eastern part of the wetland. The GPS location is N 26°9/15.7//and E 92°4.0/53.4//, elevation is 47m.

Station 2: This sampling point is the middle part of the wetland. The station is about 1.5 km from Station 1. It is situated under the Maloibari bridge and GPS location is N 26°9/8.3//and E 92°4/48.0//, elevation is 51m.

Station 3: This sampling station is in the western part of the wetland and is about 3 km away from Station 1. The water of this part is mainly used for agricultural and irrigation purposes. GPS location of this station is N 26°9/22.2//and E 92°22.2//, elevation is 45m.

Station 4: This sampling point is located in the north western part of the wetland. GPS location of this station is N 26°9/12.6//and E 92°4.7/46.2//, elevation is 48m.

Collection of Samples and Storage

The water samples were collected from four different sampling stations at about 25cm depth on all the seasons of the year. The samples were collected in 1 liters capacity plastic bottles with stopper and washed a number of times with distilled water, dried thoroughly and labeled properly for identification before collecting. The collected samples were preserved immediately at low temperature because proper handling and adequate preservation of the samples were considered to protect the sample from any changes in chemical composition. For testing DO and BOD, samples were collected separately in 300 ml BOD bottle beneath the surface and fixed at the spot. Temperature, pH and FCO_2 were measured at the time of collection.

Statistical Analysis

The Agglomerative Hierarchical Clustering (AHC), Principal Component Analysis (PCA), One-sample t-test and z-test; and Pearson (n) Correlation matrix were estimated using software XLSTAT 2015 version 2015.1.02. The PCA for estimating the correlation among the limnological variables was followed after Gower (1966); Legendre & Legendre (1998).

RESULT

Keeping in mind about the importance of water body of traditionally valued Jalikhora Wetland for irrigation, domestic as well as animal feeding purposes, the present study has been undertaken in order to find out the suitability of water for such purposes. All together 14 important limnological parameters of the wetland were analyzed for the study purpose (Table 2.1). The results and subsequent discussions of the various parameters are summarized thoroughly below:

Water temperatures exert an important effect on chemical and biological activities of aquatic organisms. Rate of chemical reaction increases with the rise in temperature, but reduce solubility of the gases. The higher temperature favors the growth of blue-green algae. The water body of wetland shows a rapid fluctuation in temperature and ranged from 20.03°C to 29.18°C with mean ± SD (25.31 ± 4.14), the highest value was measured during monsoon season and the lowest being at winter period. The pH value of the water bodies has an important impact on fish species and other aquatic organisms. The pH value of the wetland is found to be in the range of 7.13 to 7.73 with mean ± SD (7.30 ± 0.29), showing slightly basic in nature. However, the pH value was estimated maximum in the monsoon period due to the heavy rainfall in this period of the year, while it was found minimum in the winter season. The Free Carbon dioxide (FCO_2) level of the wetland was found minimum in the winter season, while it was found maximum in the retreating monsoon period. The level of FCO_2 in all the sampling sites was estimated to be in the range of 2.2 mg l^{-1} to 8.8 mg l^{-1} with mean ± SD (5.84 ± 2.03). The levels of Dissolved Oxygen (DO) was estimated between the ranges of 7.65 mg l^{-1} and 10.18 mg l^{-1} with mean ± SD (8.66 ± 1.14). However, the level of DO estimated minimum in the winter season and maximum in the monsoon period.

The levels of BOD of the studied sites were found between the ranges of 2.15 mg l^{-1} and 2.94 mg l^{-1} with mean ± SD (2.42 ± 0.36), with minimum in the pre-monsoon season and maximum in the monsoon season which may be due to dilution factor. Similarly, the level of COD in all the sampling sites was estimated to be in the range of 14.78 mg l^{-1} to 17.40 mg l^{-1} with mean ± SD (15.79 ± 1.12). The value was found minimum in the winter season, while it was found maximum in the monsoon period.

Table 2.1: Range, Mean and Standard Deviation of Important Limnological Variables of Four Study Sites of Jalikhora Wetland, Assam

Limnological Variables	S1		S2		S3		S4	
	Range	Mean ± SD	Range	Mean ± SD	Range	Mean ± SD	Range	Mean ± SD
WT (°C)	19.9 - 29.1	25.20 ± 4.17	20.0 - 29.1	25.30 ± 4.13	20.0 - 29.2	25.30 ± 4.14	20.2 - 29.3	25.45 ± 4.12
pH	7.09 - 7.79	7.28 ± 0.34	7.18 - 7.55	7.31 ± 0.17	7.07 - 7.76	7.27 ± 0.33	7.13 - 7.81	7.33 ± 0.32
FCO_2 (mg l^{-1})	4.4 - 8.8	6.05 ± 2.11	4.4 - 6.6	4.95 ± 1.10	2.2 - 6.6	4.40 ± 1.80	3.3 - 6.6	5.23 ± 1.65
DO (mg l^{-1})	7.6 - 9.9	8.43 ± 1.04	7.3 - 10.7	8.68 ± 1.60	7.9 - 10.6	8.90 ± 1.19	7.8 - 9.5	8.65 ± 0.79
BOD (mg l^{-1})	2.0 - 2.79	2.32 ± 0.34	2.1 - 2.98	2.40 ± 0.41	2.2 - 3.12	2.53 ± 0.41	2.2 - 2.86	2.44± 0.29
COD (mg l^{-1})	14.2 - 16.8	15.10 ± 1.17	15.1 - 17.6	16.15 ± 1.05	15.2 - 18.4	16.48 ± 1.37	14.6 - 16.8	15.45 ± 0.97
Nitrate (mg l^{-1})	1.3 - 2.1	1.63 ± 0.36	1.0 - 1.9	1.45 ± 0.39	1.0 - 2.3	1.50 ± 0.57	1.1 - 2.0	1.55 ± 0.37
Phosphate (mg l^{-1})	0.26 - 0.48	0.35 ± 0.09	0.27 - 0.45	0.34 ± 0.08	0.27 - 0.49	0.34 ± 0.10	0.28 - 0.43	0.34 ± 0.06
Chloride (mg l^{-1})	16.52 - 23.02	20.40 ± 3.01	15.02 - 23.52	19.52 ± 3.76	16.02 - 22.02	19.52 ± 2.80	15.52 - 22.52	19.40 ± 3.42
Sulphate (mg l^{-1})	125 – 155	138.75 ± 12.5	130 - 160	143.75 ± 12.5	130 - 150	140.00 ± 9.13	125 - 160	140.00 ± 14.72
TA (mg l^{-1})	34 – 40	37.00 ± 2.58	32 - 48	38. 75 ± 7.27	33 - 52	41.00 ± 7.96	34 - 46	40.25 ± 5.32
TH (mg l^{-1})	20 – 38	30.75 ± 7.72	26 - 38	33.25 ± 5.12	24 - 44	36.75 ± 9.00	20 - 39	31.25 ± 8.06
TDS (mg l^{-1})	155 – 245	188.75 ± 39.45	165 - 230	191.25 ± 27.80	150 -240	186.25 ± 38.16	160 - 235	191.25 ± 31.46
Turbidity (NTU)	7.05 – 14	9.92 ± 3.02	6.94 - 16.4	10.49 ± 4.37	8.3 - 17	11.62 ± 3.75	7.67 - 15.76	11.01 ± 3.50

The estimated value of hardness in all the sampling stations was recorded between 22.50 mg l^{-1} and 38.25 mg l^{-1} with mean ± SD (33.0 ± 7.32), lowest estimated in monsoon and highest being in retreating-monsoon. The estimated values of Total Alkalinity (TA) in all sampling sites were found between the ranges of 33.25 mg l^{-1} and 46.50 mg l^{-1} with mean ± SD (39.25 ± 5.62) throughout the annual cycle. The highest value of alkalinity was recorded in the pre-monsoon period. Water transparency varied seasonally among all the study sites from 7.49 NTU to 15.79 NTU with mean ± SD (10.76 ± 3.63) NTU.

Similarly, the highest value of chloride was estimated in retreating monsoon period and whereas, the lowest value was recorded in the winter season. Highest value in retreating monsoon is due to the anthropogenic activity. However, the range of chloride was estimated between 15.77 mg l^{-} 1 and 22.40 mg l^{-1} with mean ± SD (19.71 ± 3.22). The estimated values of Total Dissolved Solids (TDS) in all sampling sites were found between the ranges of 157.50 mg l^{-1} and 237.50 mg l^{-1} with mean ± SD (189.38 ± 33.98) throughout the annual cycle. The highest value of TDS was recorded in the monsoon period, while the lowest value was estimated during winter season. The estimated value of sulphate was found between 127.50 mg l^{-1} to 156.25 mg l^{-1} with mean ± SD (140.63 ± 11.84) which is within the permissible limit. From the analysis the phosphate concentration is found to be in the range from 0.27 mg l^{-1} in to 0.46 mg l^{-1} with mean ± SD (0.34 ± 0.08), with minimum in the winter period and maximum in the monsoon season which may be due to surface run-off from the adjacent agricultural fields. The study shows greater nitrate concentration in monsoon season than the winter period. The overall concentration of nitrate ranges from 1.10 mg l^{-1} to 2.08 mg l^{-1} with mean ± SD (1.53 ± 0.41) which is under the permissible limits.

Among the important limnological attributes, pH, Water Temperature, DO, FCO_2 Total Alkalinity, Total Hardness and Turbidity were varying considerably from station to station (Fig. 2.2). The seasonal variations of the important limnological variables show a minor fluctuating trend in the entire selected stations in all the seasons.

The Pearson (n) Correlation matrix of the studied limnological variables shows that the relationship between Water Temperature (°C) with pH, FCO_2 (mg l^{-1}), DO (mg l^{-1}), BOD (mg l^{-1}), COD (mg l^{-1}), Total Alkalinity (mg l^{-1}), Nitrate (mg l^{-1}), Phosphate (mg l^{-1}), Sulphate (mg l^{-1}) and Turbidity (NTU) are positively correlated except with Total Hardness (mg l^{-1}), (r = -0.407) at 5% significance level respectively (Table 2.2). Similarly, pH and DO (mg l^{-1}), pH and BOD (mg l^{-1}), pH and COD (mg l^{-1}), pH and Nitrate (mg l^{-1}), pH and Phosphate (mg l^{-1}), pH and Sulphate (mg l^{-1}), pH and Turbidity (NTU) showed positive relationship (r = 0.896, r = 0.949, r = 0.969, r = 0.900, r = 0.976, r = 0.909 and r = 0.934).

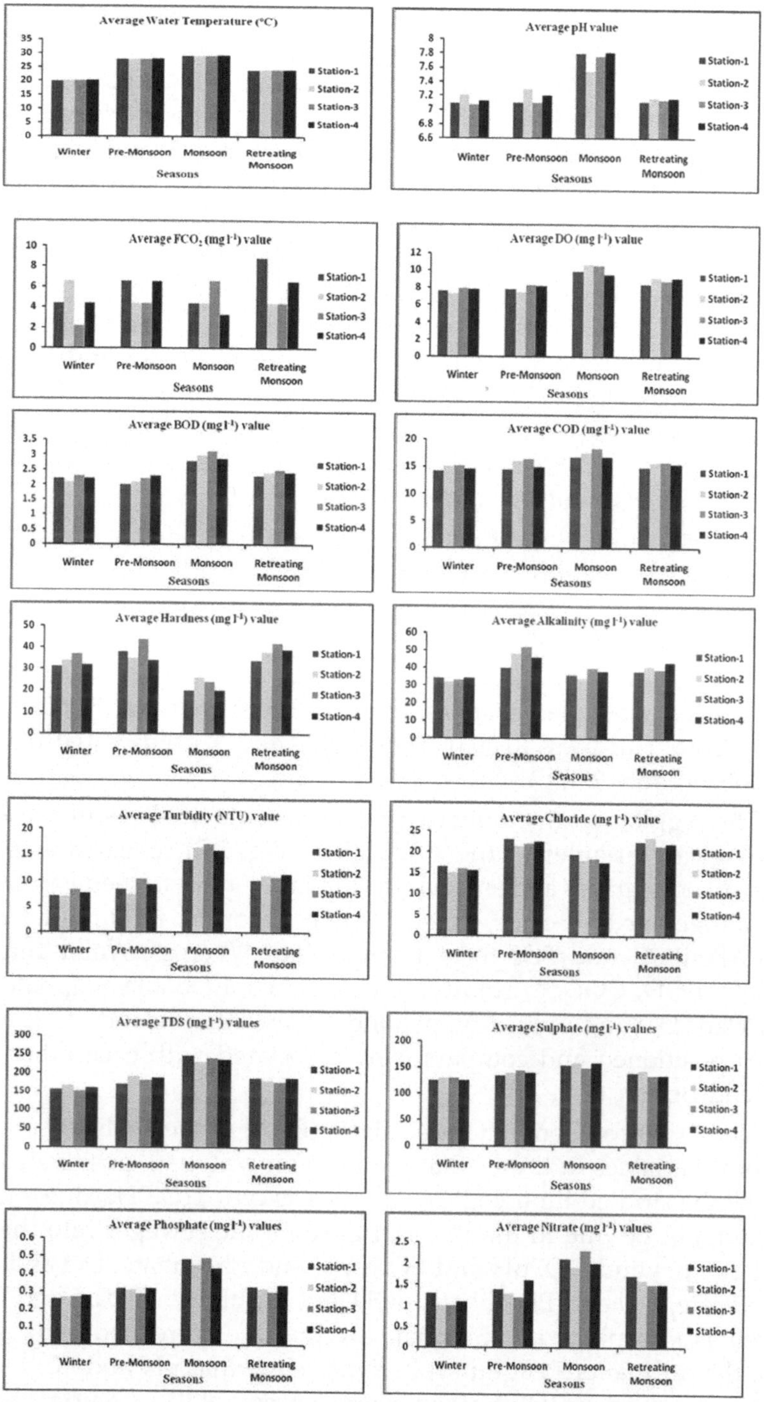

Fig. 2.2: Limnological Parameters Analysis of Jalikhora Wetland (Jan, 2013 to Dec, 2013)

DO (mg l^{-1}) and BOD (mg l^{-1}), DO (mg l^{-1}) and COD (mg l^{-1}), DO (mg l^{-1}) and Nitrate (mg l^{-1}), DO (mg l^{-1}) and Phosphate (mg l^{-1}), DO (mg l^{-1}) and Turbidity (NTU), BOD (mg l^{-1}) and Nitrate (mg l^{-1}), BOD (mg l^{-1}) and Phosphate (mg l^{-1}), BOD (mg l^{-1}) and Turbidity (NTU), Nitrate (mg l^{-1}) and Phosphate (mg l^{-1}), Nitrate (mg l^{-1}) and Sulphate (mg l^{-1}), Phosphate (mg l^{-1}) and Sulphate (mg l^{-1}), TDS (mg l^{-1}) and Turbidity (NTU) also showed positive relationship (r = 0.973, r = 0.948, r = 0.985, r = 0.954, r = 0.993, r = 0.939, r = 0.962, r = 0.975, r = 0.973, r = 0.970, r = 0.968, r = 0.975) respectively. Whereas, the association between measured pH and FCO_2 (mg l^{-1}), pH and Total Hardness (mg l^{-1}), FCO_2 (mg l^{-1}) and DO (mg l^{-1}), FCO_2 (mg l^{-1}) and BOD (mg l^{-1}), FCO_2 (mg l^{-1}) and Turbidity (NTU), DO (mg l^{-1}) and Total Hardness (mg l^{-1}), BOD (mg l^{-1}) and Total Alkalinity (mg l^{-1}), Total Alkalinity (mg l^{-1}) and Turbidity (NTU) as well as Total Hardness (mg l^{-1}) and Turbidity (NTU) showed insignificant negative relationship (r = -0.378, r = -0.937, r = -0.007, r = -0.236, r = -0.060, r = -0.749, r = -0.300, r = -0.085 and r = -0.788) respectively (Table 2.2).

The t-test and z-test of the mean value of studied physical and chemical variables at 0.05 level of significance and 95 % confidence interval shows a varied t (Observed) value for the individual parameters. The p-value for Water Temperature (WT), FCO_2, DO, BOD, Chloride and Total Alkalinity (TA) were found to be 0.001. The p-value for pH, and COD was found to be < 0.0001. Except these variables, the p-value for Nitrate (0.005), Phosphate (0.004), Total Hardness (0.003), TDS (0.002) and Turbidity (0.010) have been estimated (Table 2.3).

The Agglomerative Hierarchical Clustering analysis of the important limnological variables of the study sites (Fig. 2.3) revealed a comparable picture of similarities and associationship among the studied variables. There were altogether two clads, among which Chloride, FCO_2, Total Hardness, Total Alkalinity and TDS form a single clad. Whereas, Water Temperature, pH, DO, BOD, COD, Turbidity, Nitrate, Phosphate and Sulphate form the other clad. DO and Turbidity; pH and BOD; Chloride and FCO_2 were more closely positioned and comparatively associated with each other cluster in the dendrogram (Fig. 2.3).

The Principal Component Analysis (PCA) of the analyzed physical and chemical variables indicates that Water Temperature is positively correlated with all the studied limnological variables except Total Hardness (r = -0.407) which might be due to the released of domestic sewages into the wetland. Similarly, pH and DO, pH and BOD, pH and Phosphate, DO and BOD, DO and Nitrate, DO and Phosphate, BOD and Turbidity, Nitrate and Phosphate as well as Phosphate and Sulphate are positive correlated with each other. From the ordination diagram it becomes clear that pH and FCO_2, FCO_2 and BOD, FCO_2 and COD showed negative correlation among each other respectively (Fig. 2.4).

Table 2.2: The Pearson (n) Correlation Matrix of the Important Limnological Variables of Jalikhora Wetland, Assam

Limnological Variables	WT (°C)	pH	FCO_2	DO	BOD	COD	Nitrate	Phosphate	Chloride	Sulphate	TA	TH	TDS	Turbidity
WT (°C)	1													
pH	0.675	1												
FCO_2	0.207	-0.378	1											
DO	0.640	0.896	-0.007	1										
BOD	0.551	0.949	-0.236	0.973	1									
COD	0.793	0.969	-0.138	0.948	0.944	1								
Nitrate	0.765	0.900	0.053	0.985	0.939	0.973	1							
Phosphate	0.753	0.976	-0.168	0.959	0.962	0.998	0.973	1						
Chloride	0.482	-0.211	0.943	0.069	-0.160	0.034	0.177	-0.011	1					
Sulphate	0.886	0.909	0.019	0.917	0.874	0.981	0.970	0.968	0.215	1				
TA	0.589	-0.198	0.706	-0.119	-0.300	-0.004	0.040	-0.064	0.883	0.186	1			
TH	-0.407	-0.937	0.662	-0.749	-0.876	-0.823	-0.713	-0.845	0.539	-0.706	0.489	1		
TDS	0.812	0.963	-0.118	0.943	0.933	0.999	0.973	0.996	0.060	0.987	0.028	-0.808	1	
Turbidity	0.700	0.934	-0.060	0.993	0.975	0.978	0.992	0.985	0.050	0.950	-0.085	-0.788	0.975	1

Table 2.3: One-sample t-test and z-test with 5% Significance Level and 95% Confidence Interval on the Mean of Limnological Variables

Variable	Difference	t (Observed Value)	|t| (Critical Value)	DF	p-value (Two-tailed)	Alpha
WT	25.313	12.219	3.182	3	0.001	0.05
pH	7.295	50.474	3.182	3	< 0.0001	0.05
FCO_2	5.156	13.618	3.182	3	0.001	0.05
DO	8.663	15.262	3.182	3	0.001	0.05
BOD	2.422	13.443	3.182	3	0.001	0.05
COD	15.794	28.097	3.182	3	< 0.0001	0.05
Nitrate	1.531	7.442	3.182	3	0.005	0.05
Phosphate	0.341	8.137	3.182	3	0.004	0.05
Chloride	19.708	12.260	3.182	3	0.001	0.05
Sulphate	140.625	23.761	3.182	3	0.0001	0.05
TA	39.250	13.977	3.182	3	0.001	0.05
TH	33.000	9.020	3.182	3	0.003	0.05
TDS	189.375	11.146	3.182	3	0.002	0.05
Turbidity	10.758	5.926	3.182	3	0.010	0.05

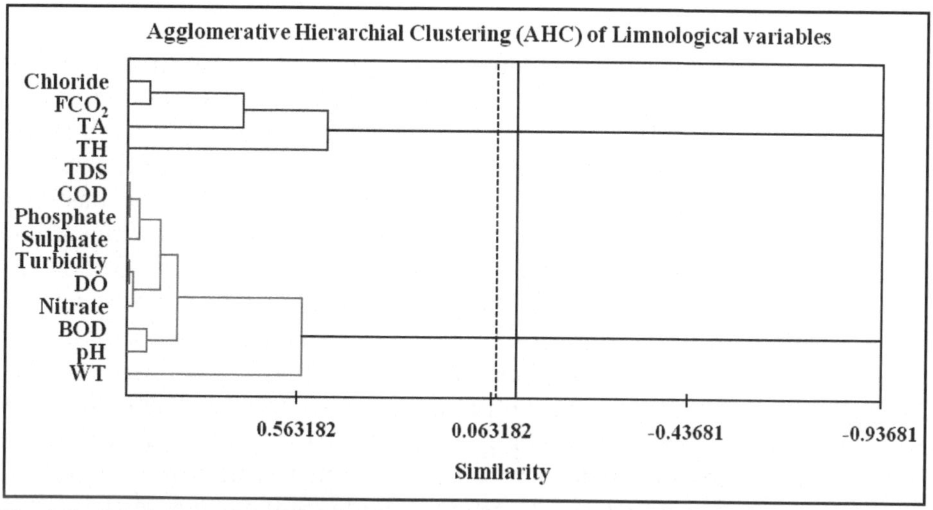

Fig. 2.3: Agglomerative Hierarchical Clustering (AHC) of Important Limnological Parameters of Jalikhora Wetland

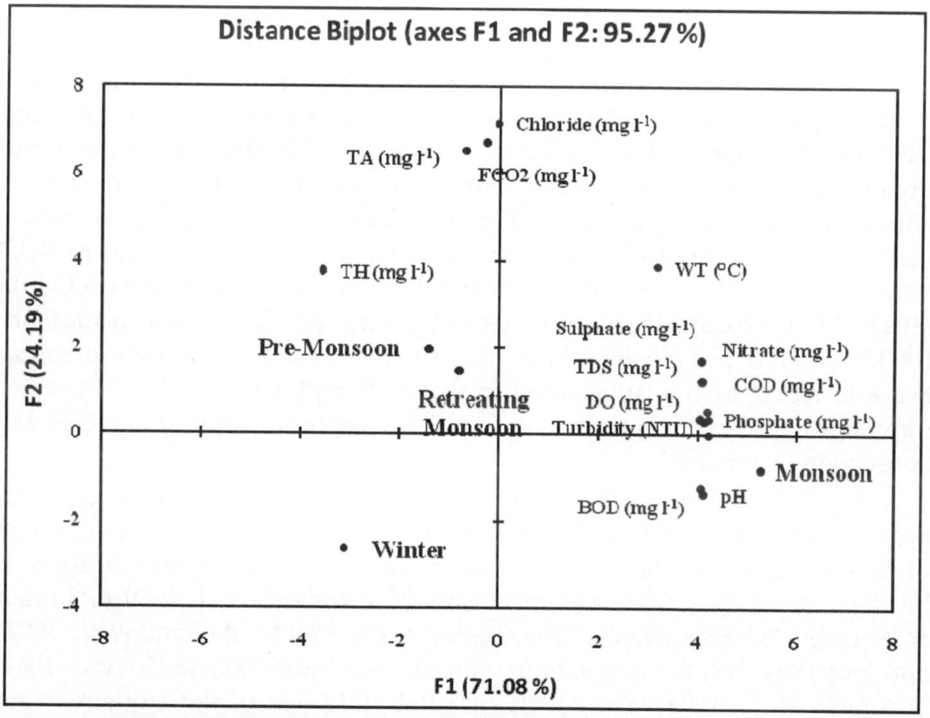

Fig. 2.4: PCA Ordination Showing the Relationship Among the Limnological Variables of Jalikhora Wetland

DISCUSSION

Water temperature is considered as a major and critical limiting factor for biotic components because most of the aquatic organisms often have a narrow thermal tolerance (Mudgal et al., 2009). According to Welch (1952) smaller the body of water, more quickly it reacts to changes in the atmospheric temperature. The pH value observed in the present investigation has been found in similar trend as observed by Sarwar & Wazir (1991); Kartha & Rao (1992); Kumar (1995). It virtually showed very little variation on monthly basis. The high pH value was associated with greater photosynthetic activity which resulted in utilization of CO_2 from bicarbonates and formation of carbonates (Baijot et al., 1994). Hutchinson et al. (1929) have asserted that the high pH is associated with the phytoplankton maxima. The observance of maximum FCO_2 in the retreating monsoon season in the present study might be due to high rate of decomposition of organic matters by the microbes resulting in rapid production of carbon dioxide (Sinha, 1988; Welch, 1952; Antwi & Ofori-Danson, 1993).

Highest concentration of oxygen during monsoon season may be due to abundant vegetation which took part in photosynthetic activities and subsequent release of oxygen. Dissolved oxygen concentrations of 5.0 mg l^{-1} or more are acceptable for most aquatic organisms (Stickney, 2000). The oxygen deficit during summer is a characteristic feature of a productive wetland (Sreenivasan, 1970; Timms, 1970). Biochemical Oxygen Demand (BOD) is the amount of dissolved oxygen required by the aerobic biological organisms in a water body. Water with BOD less than 3 mg l^{-1} are considered suitable for aquatic organisms and greater than 10 mg l^{-1} as polluted since it contains large amount of organic matters. The present observation of BOD values agrees with the findings of Pathak & Shastree (1993); Sharma & Gupta (1994); Maya (2003). Chemical Oxygen Demand (COD) is used to measure the total quantity of oxygen-consuming substances in the complete chemical breakdown of organic substances in water. A high COD-Cr load in water may signify oxygen deficiency, and fish and other aquatic species are consequently repelled.

The Total Hardness (TH) in water is derived largely from contact with the soil and rock formations. Rain water as it falls upon the earth is incapable of dissolving the solids found in natural waters. Generally the dilution of hardness depends with the advent of rains (Chakraborty *et al.*, 1959; Goldman & Wetzel, 1963; Sreenivasan 1964; Easley *et al.*, 1994; Mulholland *et al.*, 1997) and increases with the decrease in water levels (Subho Rao & Govind, 1964; D'Angelo *et al.*, 1994). The levels of Total Hardness of the wetland were estimated within the permissible limit. In the present investigation maximum Total alkalinity was recorded in pre-monsoon which might be due to the traditional fishing activities making the profundal zone of the wetland muddy in nature. Dilution plays an important factor in lessening the alkalinity values (Chakraborty *et al.*, 1959). The water body was slightly turbid in the monsoon season which may be due to surface and agricultural run-off, soil erosion and siltation. This has been well documented by Loffler (1969); Rodhe *et al.* (1966); Krishnyya & Laal (1990); Ramana & Sreeramulu (1994); Saijo *et al.* (1997); Sedamkar & Angadi (2003).

Thresh *et al.* (1994) in his study had made an observation on the value of chloride of fresh water ecosystem. Similar trend has been estimated in the present findings. Sulphate, which is an important constituent of hardness, was estimated highest in the monsoon period and lowest in the winter period. Increased value of sulphate during monsoon might be due to surface run off bringing more suspended solids along with organic and soluble salts (Sinha, 1986). The low value of sulphate during winter might be due to higher phytoplankton population. A small amount of phosphorous is an essential nutrient for all aquatic plants and algae but at high levels, phosphorous can be considered a pollutant. Phosphorous concentration determines the level of eutrophication. Most phosphorous in surface water is in the form of phosphates. Among the major nutrients, the importance of phosphates in water bodies is well documented (Vollenweider, 1968; Vaithiyanathan, 1993; Dortch, 1996; Chandrasekhar *et al.*, 2003). Phosphate concentration is little above the standards because of application of inorganic phosphate fertilizers in the nearby agricultural field. Nitrate ions (NO_3^-) found in freshwater samples result from a variety of natural and manmade sources. Nitrate levels in freshwater are usually less than 1 mg l^{-1} but manmade sources of nitrate may elevate levels above 3 mg l^{-1}. Levels above 10 mg l^{-1} in drinking water can cause a potentially fatal disease in infants called *methemoglobinemia* or Bluebaby Syndrome.

The Pearson (n) Correlation obtained among the studied limoogical attributes suggests that there was a minor fluctuation of Water Temperature, pH, DO, FCO_2 and BOD concentration during all the seasons of the year. It was clear from the Principal Component Biplot graph that among all the studied hydrological variables, Water Temperature, pH, DO, FCO_2, Turbidity, Nitrate, Phosphate and Chloride remains highly ideal for the physiological activities of all the aquatic organisms of the Jalikhora Wetland.

CONCLUSION

Wetlands are very important resource for the rural development as well as aquatic flora and fauna and also for the avifauna. Limnological quality of the Jalikhora wetland has been investigated to find out its suitability for the human as well as for domestic and other purposes. The study reveals that the physical and chemical variables of the wetland are still within the permissible limits of hydrological parameters and the water quality of the wetland is in optimum condition for both humans and other aquatic flora and fauna. It was observed that among all the habitat attributes, pH, DO, FCO_2, BOD and Total Alkalinity are the key habitat features that are found to be the important variables in determining the aquatic species distribution in the Jalikhora wetland. The variations in the habitat attributes like pH, dissolved oxygen, BOD and turbidity across these four sampling stations was attributed to different anthropogenic activities. The significance of habitat was endorsed by Peres-Neto (2004) with evidence suggesting species occurrence are driven more by relationship with abiotic factor than species interaction.

Despite the fact that the wetland are subjected to varied pressures (both anthropogenic and natural) but still it plays a key role in balancing the water quality of the wetland. For effective maintenance of the physical habitat of the wetland, a comprehensive annual abiotic assessment programme should be planned. Hence, for the conservation purposes varied strategies such as halting of siltation and control of water pollution are the need of the hour. The present hydrological approach may be applied to the entire wetlands of the state for identification of the other important hydrological factors which influences the wetland ecosystem of the region. Many active conservation organisations should come forward for formulating effective maintenance strategies for sustaining wetland ecosystem.

REFERENCES

Antwi, L.A.K. and Ofori-Danson, P.K. (1993): Limnology of a Tropical Reservoir (The Kpong Reservoir in Ghana). Tropical Ecology, 34: 75-87.

APHA. (2005): Standard Methods for Examination of Water and Waste Water. 17th Eds., Washington, D.C., USA.

Baijot, E., Moreau, J. and Bouda, S. (1994): Study of the Physicochemical Conditions of the Water Geographic and Hydrobiological Data EDE-Netherlands CTA CCE, 250: 830-886.

Chakraborty, R.D., Roy, P. and Singh, S.B. (1959): A Quantitative Study of Plankton and Physicochemical Study of the River Jamuna at Allahabad in 1954-55. Ind J Fish, 6: 186-203.

Chandrasekhar, J.S., Lenin, B.K. and Somasekher, R.K. (2003): Impact of Urbanization on Bellandur Lake, Bangalore- A Case Study. J Environ Bio, 24: 223-227.

D' Angelo, E. M. and Reddy, K. R. (1994): Diagenesis of Organic Matter in a Wetland Receiving Hypereutrophic Lake Water: I. Distribution of Dissolved Nutrients in the Soil and Water Column. J Environ Qual, 23: 928-936.

Dortch, M.S. (1996): Removal of Solids, Nitrogen and Phosphorus in the Cache River Wetland. Wetlands, 16: 358-365.

Easley, W.S., Barness-Walz, L.E., Neichter, P.L. and Bohannon, J.A. (1994): Evaluation of Water Quality in Taylorsville Lake, Eentucky, Using the CE-Qual-W2 Model. Lake Reserv Manage, 9: 71-72.

Gosselink, J.G. and Mitsch, W.J. (1986): WETLANDS. Van Nostrand Reinhold Co., Inc., New York, NY.

Goldmen, C.R. and Wetzel, R.G. (1963): A Study of the Primary Productivity of Clear Lake, Lake County, California. Ecology, 44: 283-294.

Gower, J.C. (1966): Some Distance Properties of Latent Root and Vector Methods Used in Multivariate Analysis. Biometrika, 53: 325-338.

Hutchinson, A.H., Lucas, S.C. and McPhail, M. (1929): Seasonal Variations in the Chemical and Physical Properties of the Culture of the Strait of Georgia in Relation to Phytoplankton. Trans Roy Soc Canada, 3: 177-183.

Hutchinson, G.E. (1967): A Treatise on Limnology. II. Introduction to Lake Biology and Limnoplankton. John Wiley and Sons. Inc., NewYork, USA.

Kartha, K.V. and Rao, K.S. (1992). Environmental Status of Gandhisagar Reservoir. Fish Technol, 29: 14-20.

Krishnayya, C.H.G. and Laal, A.K. (1990): Eutrophication, its Causes and Consequences with Particular Reference to Kolleru Lake. In Agarwal, V.P. & P. Das (eds.), Recent Trends in Limnology: 145-149.

Kumar, A. (1995): Some Limnological Aspect of the Fresh Water Tropical Wetlands of Santhal Pargana (Bihar) India. J Environ Poll, 2: 137-141.

Legendre, P. and Legendre, V. (1998): Numerical Ecology. Second English Edition. Elsevier, Amsterdam.

Loffler, H. (1969): High Altitude Lakes in Mount Everest Region. Verh Int Verin Limnol, 17: 373-385.

Maya, S. (2003): Pollution Assessment of Selected Temple Tanks of Kerala. Natur Env Poll Techno, 2: 289-294.

Mudgal, K.D., Kumari, M. and Sharma, D. K. (2009): Hydro-chemical Analysis of Drinking Water Quality of Alwar District, Rajasthan. Nature Sci, 7: 30-39.

Mulholland, P.J., Best, G.R., Coutant, C.C., Hornberger, G.M. and Wetzel, R.G. (1997): Effect of Climate Change on Freshwater Ecosystems of the South-eastern United States and the Gulf Coast of Maxico. 1994. Freshwat Ecosys Climat Chang, 11: 949-970.

Munawar, M. (1970): Limnological Studies on Freshwater Ponds of Hyderabad, India. II. The Biocenose Distribution of Unicellular and Colonial Phytoplankton in Polluted and Unpolluted Environments. Hydrobiology, 36: 105-128.

Pathak, S. and Shastree, N.K. (1993): Physicochemical Status of the Lentic Hydrosphere of Rukmini and Visar Sarovar of Gaya, Bihar. Environ Ecol, 11: 57-66.

Peres-Neto, P.R. (2004): Patterns in the Co-occurrence of Stream Fish Metacommunities: The Role of Site Suitability, Morphology and Phylogeny Versus Species Interactions. Oecologia, 140: 352-360.

Ramana, P.V. and Sreeramulu, K. (1994): Some Aspects of Limnology and Fishery of Vottigedda Reservoir in Andhra Pradesh. J Ecobiol, 2: 81-88.

"Ramsar Convention". (1971): The Convention on Wetlands, Ramsar, Iran.

Rodhe, W., Hobbie, J.E. and Wright, R.T. (1966): Phototrophy and Heterotrophy in High Mountain Lakes. Verh Int Ver Limnol, 16: 302-313.

Saijo, Y., Mitamura, O., Hino, K., Ikusima, I., Matsumura, T. and Silva, V.P. (1997): Physicochemical Features of Rivers and Lakes in Pantanal Wetland. Jap J Limnol, 58: 69-82.

Sarwar, S.G. and Wazir, M.A. (1991): Physico-chemical Characteristics of a Freshwater Pond of Srinagar (Kashmir). Poll Res, 10: 223- 227.

Sedamkar, E. and Angadi, S.B. (2003): Physicochemical Parameters of Two Fresh Waterbodies of Gulbarga- India, With Special Reference to Phytoplankton. Poll Res, 22: 411-422.

Sharma, L.L. and Gupta, M.C. (1994): Some Aspects of Limnology of Amarchand Reservoir, District Rajsamad, Rajasthan: Physical Parameters. Poll Res, 13: 169-179.

Sinha, M.P. (1988): Effect of Waste Disposal on Water Quality of River Damodar in Bihar. Physico-chemical Characteristics. In Ecology and Pollution of Indian Rivers. Ashish Publishing House, New Delhi, India: 219-249.

Sinha, M.P. (1986): Limnobiotic Study on Tropic Status of a Polluted Fresh Water Reservoir of Coal Field Area. Poll Res, 5: 13-17.

Sreenivasan, A. (1964): Limnological Studies and Fish Yield in Three Upland Lakes of Madras State, India. Limnol Oceanogr, 9: 564-575.

Sreenivasan, A. (1970): Limnology of Tropical Impoundments: A Comparative Study of the Major Reservoirs in Madras State (India). Hydrobiology, 36: 443-469.

Stickney, R.R. (2000): Encyclopedia of Aquaculture. John Wiley and Sons, New York.

Subho Rao, D. and Govind, B.V. (1964): Hydrology of Tungabhadra Reservoir. Ind J Fish, 11: 321-344.

Timms, B.V. (1970): Chemical and Zooplankton Studies of Lentic Habitats in North Eastern New South Wales. Aust J Mar Wat Res, 21: 11-33.

Trivedi, R.K. and Goel, P.K. (1986): Chemical and Biological Method for Water Pollution Studies. 2nd Eds. Environmental Publication. Karad, India.

Thresh, J.C., Suckling, E.V. and Beale, J.F. (1994): In Taylor, E.W. (eds.), The Examination of Water Supplies.

U.S. Fish and Wildlife Service. (1989): Federal Manual for Identifying and Delineating Jurisdictional Wetlands, Washington, D.C., Cooperative technical publication: pp. 76.

Vaithiyanathan, P., Jha, P. K. and Subramanian, V. (1993): Phosphorus Distribution in the Sediments of the Hooghly (Ganges) Estuary, India. Estuar Coast Shelf Sci, 37: 603-614.

Vollenweider, R. A. (1968): Scientific Fundamentals of the Eutrophication of Lakes and Flowing Waters with Special Reference to Nitrogen and Phosphorus as Factors in Eutrophication. OECD, France 27: pp. 182.

Welch, P.S. (1952): Limnology (2nd Edition). Mc.Graw - Hill Book Co., New York.

Pages: 31-48

WATER RESOURCES MANAGEMENT: *MONITORING AND ASSESSMENT*

Edited by: Dr. Sandeep Gupta; Dr. Pawan Kumar 'Bharti'

ISBN: 978-93-5056-799-9

Edition: 2016

Published by: Discovery Publishing House Pvt. Ltd., New Delhi (India)

3

Trophic Status, Management and Restoration of Lakes in Mandya District, Karnataka, India

T.M. Devaraju

ABSTRACT

Large scale urbanization, industrialization and agricultural practices made the pollution a global phenomenon. The natural aquatic environment has been affected severely by man's activities. All over the world water bodies are polluted by both point source and non-point source pollutants. This problem creates several detrimental health hazards. Water pollution has adversely affected the aquatic flora and fauna in rivers, lakes, streams and ponds. Mandya district possesses a large number of freshwater ponds and lakes. Less work has been done on trophic status analysis of these lakes. Many lakes in Mandya district are free from industrial effluents since the district is predominantly agriculture based. But runoff from the surrounding agricultural fields and domestic waste reaches the lakes. Carlson's Trophic State Index (CTSI) was studied for selected fifteen Lakes. These lakes represent were selected from different parts of Mandya District. All fifteen lakes are classified as mesotrophic and are moderately polluted.

Keywords: Lake, Mandya, trophic state index, mesotrpohic, industry.

Department of Zoology, Govt. Science College, Nrupathunga Road, Bangalore - 560 001, (India)

INTRODUCTION

Water is one of the most important physical or abiotic factor that acts as a substratum for many of the organisms. It is the solvent for all chemical reactions occurs in living beings. It is also essential for turgidity maintenance of cells and functioning of protoplasm. It is one of the constituents of the protoplasm and is also essential for carrying out vital life processes.

Water is needed for daily use by human beings for irrigation, domestic use, industrial use, navigation and electricity production. Of the total water resources of the earth, 97.3% is salt water and the rest freshwater. This 2.7% amounts is about 1.4 billion km^3 of water. Of this, about 77.2% is permanently frozen, 22.4% occurs as ground water and soil moisture, 0.35% is found in lakes and wetlands and 0.01% in rivers and streams. Water bodies normally flowing through populated areas are often subjected for industrialization and urbanization pressures. Change in precipitation quality is one of the documented evidence for industrialization and urbanization pressures on water bodies (Ramalingaiah, 1985). Green revolution has led to uncontrolled use of various pesticides, herbicides, insecticides and chemical fertilizers which ultimately reach the nearby water bodies in the form of agricultural runoff, which in turn leads to undesirable changes in the receiving water bodies.

Nutrients which are present in fertilizers as well as domestic and industrial waste water have been identified as main cause for changing the trophic status of water bodies from oligotrophic to mesotrophic to eutrophic. It is of interest to note that most of the world's surface water bodies have been identified as mesotrophic. The process of increase in the nutrients of water and the resultant spurt in algal productivity is called eutrophication.

Large scale urbanization, industrialization and agricultural practices made the pollution a global phenomenon. The natural aquatic environment has been affected severely by man's activities. All over the world water bodies are polluted by both point source and non-point source pollutants. This problem creates several detrimental health hazards. Water pollution has adversely affected the aquatic flora and fauna in rivers, lakes, streams and ponds. A highly degraded water body represents a typical urban wetland polluted by direct entry of domestic sewage. In India it is estimated that 50 to 70 % of the pollutant load of rivers, lakes and streams is from domestic sewage. Lakes which are ideally suitable for recreational, domestic and irrigation purposes have to be preserved with utmost care as in western countries. Third world countries has become a dumping place due to lack of processing mechanism for sewage, garbage and other hazardous wastes.

In India there are numerous natural and artificial ponds, reservoirs and lakes (Rao, 1975). During recent years lakes are becoming the victim of the cultural eutrophication. Highly increased consumerism, agricultural wastes and fertilizers thus affecting the quality of water. Zutshi and Khan (1988) and Pandit (1996 ; 1999) have reported that disposal of sewage, soil erosion and encroachment for housing, road construction, development of floating gardens for agricultural purposes are all greatly responsible not only for deterioration of lakes environment but also the shrinking of their size.

In India, population explosion, advancement in technology and expansion of human activities has created wide spread and severe anthropogenic disturbances to freshwater bodies. Rural and urban areas encounter two contrast situations. In rural areas, a water body is normally used for all kinds of human requirements, such as bathing, washing, swimming, waste disposal, irrigation and often for drinking purpose too. Whereas, in urban areas the situation is still worse, where the water body is subjected to much greater pressure including direct discharge of sewage and industrial effluents.

Till the starting of the 80th decade these freshwater bodies were remained in a clean state. Industrialization, urbanization and use of modern technique in agriculture led to increase in water requirement. Eutrophication has become a major factor of anthropogenic disturbance to aquatic ecosystems. Nutrients are the major cause for eutrophication, particularly phosphorus (P). Use of phosphorus containing fertilizers, detergents and erosion of phosphorus containing earth sediments are the important causes for eutrophication. An undesirable consequence of eutrophication is the development of cyanobacteria that tend to form dense surface blooms, excreting organic compounds that impart bad odour and taste, creating serious problems in drinking waters (Ramachandra and Ahalya, 2001). Encroachment of lakes, introduction of exotic flora and fauna, domestic, agriculture and industrial runoff created a greater stress on natural wetlands leading to eutrophication, silt formation and decrease in water holding capacity. Increasing deforestration, intensification of agriculture and aquaculture have caused negative impacts on many lakes (Campos *et al*. 1983; 2001; Campos, 1984).

Most of the major lakes in India are facing acute pollution problem. Silt deposits and excessive algal growth limiting the life and use of lakes. Water temperature, physicochemical and biological factors of lakes change according to seasons. Temperature change alters the density. Usually upper layer water is heated up by radiations, whereas the bottom layer may remain cool. This develops the convection water currents and the result of this is mixing of lake water. During winter this mixing is prominent. But during summer, higher density checks the mixing of water, which results in thermal stratification. The thermal stratification, movement of oxygen and nutrients influence the abundance, distribution and diversity of life in lakes. Usually, floating plants, phytoplanktons and zooplanktons distribute throughout the lake, when large in quantity give a green colour to the water.

Freshwater bodies differ from each other in size, shape, aquatic vegetation, phyto - and zooplanktons, degree of pollution and physicochemical nature. Small freshwater bodies are gaining much significance as the large water bodies are too scattered to fulfill the needs of the present day. Better management strategies for these small water bodies help to maintain ecological integrity intact. These water bodies can be used to provide maximum service to the mankind. Such optimum strategies can be developed by studying hydrology of water bodies and their watersheds. Therefore, physical, chemical, biological water quality, human and industrial activities assessment in and around the water bodies are important.

A number of researchers in the last century published data on water ecology. A freshwater body plays a significant role in ecology and exhibits relationship with organisms that live in and use it. Many people have tried to ascertain facts of ecology and published reports on freshwater biota. Many workers have studied the physico-chemical conditions operating in a particular waterbody, distribution of unicellular and colonial organisms, influence of phytoplanktons and the growth of zooplanktons, the occurrence and importance of algal blooms in waterodies and causes of pollution and their relation to the growth of algae.

The present work was undertaken with the objective of assessing the trophic status of important lakes and to know the management and restoration of these lakes. The detailed work carried out (May, 2013 to April, 2015) has been presented under various headings.

MATERIAL AND METHODS

General Topography and Climate of Mandya District

Mandya district is situated in the southern part of Deccan peninsula and in southern plains of Karnataka. Mandya city is the district headquarter. The name Mandya is derived from the original term, 'Mandaya' means a sacred land of the saint 'Mandavya'. Before independence the Mandya district was part of erstwhile Mysore kingdom of Wodeyar dynasty. It is carved out of Mysore district in 1934 to form a new district. Mandya district has several international fame tourist places, historical importance and pilgrimage centers. Important of them are Krishna Raja Sagar, Shimsha (Bluf) power generation center, Gagana chukki and Bhara chukki water falls, Rangana thittu bird sanctuary, Kokre Bellur bird sanctuary, Tippu Sultan's capital Srirangapatna, Shivapura Sathyagraha Sowdha, Ramanuja's Melukote and other important places.

Mandya district consists seven taluks namely Krishnarajapet, Maddur, Malavally, Mandya, Nagamangala, Pandavapura and Srirangapatna. The total area of the district is 4958 square kilometers. The district is mainly drained by east flowing Cauvery river. Hemavathi, Lokapavani, Shimsha and

Veeravaishnavi are small rivers flow in the district and are tributaries of Cauvery river. Irrigation by canals and tanks are characteristic feature of the district.

The district is popularly known as "sugar bowl" of Karnataka. It is very famous for sugar cane and paddy cultivation. The climate of the district is congenial for the cultivation of food and commercial crops. The livestock wealth of the district is in considerable status and progress has been made in the development of dairy industry, poultry rearing, sheep rearing, piggery, sericulture and inland fisheries.

Location

Mandya district lies between $12^{\circ} 25^{1}$ and $13^{\circ} 35^{1}$ north latitude and $74^{\circ} 04^{1}$ and $77^{\circ} 84^{1}$ east longitude. The altitude of the district varies between 609.60 to 807.72 meters MSL. Mandya district is bounded on the north side by Tumkur and Bangalore Rural districts; on the south by Chamarajanagar and Mysore districts; on the east by Ramanagara district and on west side by Hassan and Mysore districts. Physiographically, the Mandya district situated completely in plain land. Only on the South – eastern part of the district, broken patches of Western ghats forests are present.

Soil

The soil of the district mainly consists red laterite, red fine loam and clay types.

Climate and Rainfall

Climate of Mandya district is moderate throughout the year. It may be divided broadly into three seasons. The summer season from March to about the end of June is followed by south - west monsoon season lasting upto the end of October. The period from November to February is the winter season. Mango showers usually occur in the month of May. November and December may be termed as retreating monsoon period. Though winter starts during November, but its severity is observed during January.

Mandya district receives the major portions of its rainfall from southwest monsoon. The normal rainfall is spread over a period of about seven months from May to November. The average rainfall in the district is about 635.00 mm according to IMD (Indian Meteorological Department) data available. October is considered as the wettest month.

Temperature and Humidity

Mandya district experience moderate temperature for the entire year. Summer months are moderately warmer and winters are cold. The period from March to May is on the continuous rise in temperature. April is usually the hottest month. The day temperature is appreciably low throughout the southwest monsoon period. The weather is cool and pleasant during this period. January is the coldest month. The relative humidity is generally high during southwest monsoon. It is dry during summer.

Cloudiness

The sky during southwest monsoon period is heavily clouded or overcast. For rest of the year the sky is almost clear. During summer there is some increase in cloudiness in the afternoon.

Wind

Winds are generally moderate for the entire year. During May and June southwest winds blow heavily indicating the onset of monsoon. It continues till October. Retreating monsoon winds blow from northeast side and are predominant during November and December.

Number of Lakes

Mandya district possesses a large number of freshwater ponds and lakes. Totally 891 lakes of varied size are recorded in the district. Out of these, as many as 173 tanks come under the control of fishery department, 6 under the forest department and 688 minor tanks are controlled by the gram panchayath.

Methods

Samples for the analysis of Chlorophyll-a and total phosphorous were collected during summer months at the maximum depth location. Seechi depth (SD) was determined at the study site by an 8″ diameter disc. The maximum depth at which the secchi disc can be seen when immersed into the water was noted.

Total Chlorophyll-a (CA) was estimated by acetone method and measured by using a spectrometer absorbance at 630 & 660 nm (APHA 2005). List of lakes studied from May 2013 to April 2015 are presented in Table 3.2.

Total phosphorous was determined by stannous chloride method and measured by using a spectrometer at 690nm (APHA 2005). The Trophic state index [TSI] of Carlson (1977) was determined using the following formula.

(a) TSI for Chlorophyll- a (CA) = 9.81 in chlorophyll- a +30.6

(b) TSI for seechi depth (meters) (SD) = 60-14.41 In seechi depth

(c) TSI for Total phosphorus (TP) = 14.42 in total phosphorus +4.15

Where TSI is Trophic state index In as natural logarithm,

$$\text{Carlson's Trophic state Index(CTSI)} = \frac{[\text{TSI(TP)} + \text{TSI(CA)} + \text{TSI(SD)}]}{3}$$

Where - TP & CA in micrograms/Liter

SD Transparency in meters.

A value of CTSI between 30 and 40 represent oligotrophic with low productivity, index values between 40 and 50 represent mesotrophic status (moderate productivity), index values of 50-60 associated with eutrophic (high productivity). The range of the trophic state index values between 70 and 100 + indicate hypertrophic status and presence of severe algal blooms.

RESULTS AND DISCUSSION

Trophic index in any water bodies generally may be used to assess its biological condition. Carlson's index is very commonly used trophic indices. Algal biomass is used as an objective classifier of a lake in Carlson trophic status index assessment. Generally, the Carlson Index is to be used with lakes where relatively few rooted plants and non-algal turbidity sources are present. Nitrogen and phosphorus quantities and other nutrients which are biologically useful are the primary determinants of trophic state index of a water body. Nitrogen and phosphorus tend to be limiting resources in lentic water bodies. Increased concentrations of these result in increased plant growth and subsequently trophic level of the water body. Trophic index of a water body may sometimes be used to assess its biological condition. Chlorophyll pigment, total phosphorus and secchi depth are three independent variables used to calculate the Carlson Index. Of all these three chlorophyll probably gives more accurate values, since its most accurate predictor of biomass. Though secchi depth is least accurate, but less expensive and easily affordable method.

The trophic status index values, corresponding trophic status and their attributes are presented in Table 3.1 and Figure 3.1. As per the indices all the 15 lakes studied in Mandya district from May 2013 to April 2015 were classified as Mesotrophic. All these lakes had trophic status index (TSI) within mesotrophic range from 40.87 to 49.61 (Table 3.5). Lowest value of TSI (40.87) was estimated in Hosaholalu lake in Krishnarajapet Taluk and highest 49.61 was determined in Sulekere lake in Maddur Taluk. The main parameter involved in the trophic state alteration is phosphorus content. Changes in the quantity of phosphorus in a fresh water ecosystem can alter the trophic status. Carvalho and Kirika (2003) reported that decrease in phosphorous quantity is due to reduction in external nutrient loading which in turn reduces Phytoplankton biomass. Monitoring eutrophication is an important part of assessing and managing lake ecosystems. Phosphorus is commonly the growth limiting nutrient for algae (Horne & Goldman 1994). Nutrients can enter the lake through agricultural runoff, increase the concentration of plant nutrients , primarily phosphorous (Haper 1972). This produces direct and indirect biological changes to lakes leading to the production of algal blooms. Indirectly eutrophication may cause depletion in the concentration of dissolved oxygen as s result of bacterial respiration during break down of dead algal biomass.

Table 3.1: Carlson's Trophic State Index Values and Classification of Lakes

TSI Values	Trophic Status	Attributes
30-40	Oligotrophic	Clear water, low primary productivity, low algal production, high drinking-water quality. lakes support fish growth, oxygen throughout the year in the hypolimnion
40-50	Mesotrophic	Intermediate level of productivity, clear water with submerged aquatic plants, medium levels of nutrients, increasing probability of anoxia during the summer
50-70	Eutrophic	High biological productivity, excessive nutrients, mainly nitrogen and phosphorus, support plenty of aquatic plants. dominated by aquatic plants or algae, decreased transparency, warm-water fisheries only.
70-100+	Hypertrophic	very nutrient-rich. severe algal blooms, low transparency, visibility depth of less than 3 feet, total chlorophyll is > 40 micrograms/litre and phosphorus is greater than 100 micrograms/liter, does not support fish growth

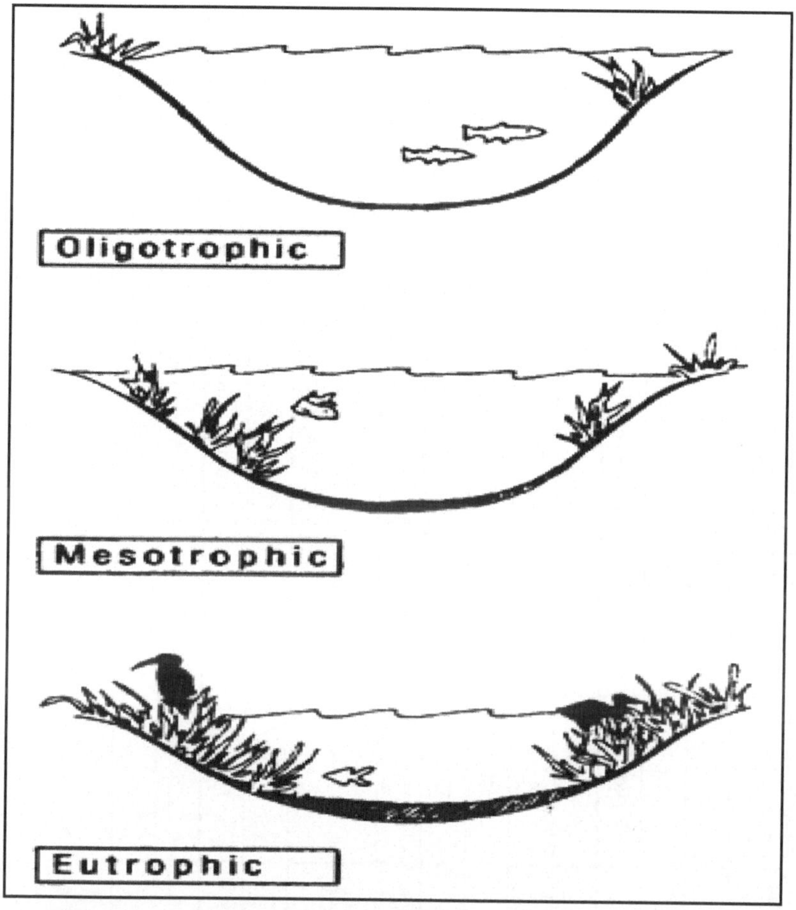

Fig. 3.1: Diagrammatic Representation of Oligotrophic, Mesotrophic and Eutrophic Lakes

Source: Hamlin Lake Improvement Board

Studies for two years revealed that Carlson trophic status index (CTSI) values are higher during summer season, moderate during winter and lesser during rainy season. Highest value (52.44) of CTSI is recorded in the month of June 2013 in Sulekere lake in Maddur Taluk (Table 3.3). Likewise lowest value of CTSI was recorded in Keelara lake in Mandya Taluk in the months of November 2013, January 2014, December 2014 and January 2015 (Tables 3.3 & 3.4). Minimum value of CTSI (39.00) also was recorded in Hosaholalu lake in Krishnarajpet Taluk during December 2013. Sulekere lake, Maddur lake, Malavalli lake, Marehalli lake, Thylur lake, Hosakere lake, Dudda lake, Thandekere lake and Ammanikere lake were in the upper range of mesotrophic status during summer. On the other hand during study period Keelara lake, Thonnur lake, Hosaholalu lake, Kirugavalu lake, Mangala lake and Halguru lake exhibited less values in CTSI index during summer.

Table 3.2: List of Lakes Studied and their Important Features

Sl. No.	Name of the Lake	Location	Area in Acres	Depth in mts.	Water Source	Usage
1.	Maddur lake	Maddur Taluk	320	7.0	Canal & Rain fed	Fishing & Irrigation
2.	Malavalli lake	Malavalli Taluk	273	5.9	Canal & Rain fed	Fishing & Irrigation
3.	Marehalli lake	-do-	218	6.3	Canal & Rain fed	Fishing & Irrigation
4.	Thylur lake	Maddur Taluk	280	4.6	Canal & Rain fed	Fishing & Irrigation
5.	Sulekere lake	-do-	436	7.8	Canal	Fishing & Irrigation
6.	Ammanikere lake	Nagamangala Taluk	193	4.9	Rain fed	Irrigation
7.	Keelara lake	Mandya Taluk	240	6.5	Canal & Rain fed	Fishing & Irrigation
8.	Thonnur lake	Pandavapura Taluk	453	8.6	Canal & Rain fed	Fishing, Boating & Irrigation
9.	Hosaholalu lake	Krishna Rajapet Taluk	220	5.7	Rain fed	Fishing & Irrigation
10.	Hosakere lake	Maddur Taluk	165	6.4	Canal & Rain fed	Fishing & Irrigation
11.	Kirugaavalu lake	Malavalli Taluk	294	6.8	Canal & Rain fed	Fishing & Irrigation
12.	Dudda lake	Mandya Taluk	208	6.4	Canal & Rain fed	Fishing & Irrigation
13.	Mangala lake	-do-	192	6.9	Canal & Rain fed	Fishing & Irrigation
14.	Halaguru lake	Malavalli Taluk	153	3.7	Rain fed	Irrigation
15.	Thandekere lake	Krishna Rajapet Taluk	195	5.2	Rain fed	Irrigation

Table 3.3: Carlson Trophic State Index (TSI) of Different Lakes of Mandya District during 2013-14

Sl. No.	Name of the Lake	May	June	July	August	September	October	November	December	January	February	March	April	Average
1.	Maddur lake	52.05	48.00	45.64	42.04	42.00	42.00	40.40	41.00	41.02	43.68	45.86	49.66	44.44
2.	Malavalli lake	47.12	47.00	47.00	44.08	43.68	41.08	40.00	40.30	40.24	42.00	45.34	47.84	43.80
3.	Marehalli lake	47.16	46.08	46.84	42.88	43.00	43.06	41.10	41.00	40.60	42.36	43.22	47.00	43.69
4.	Thylur lake	50.31	49.98	47.00	43.84	42.88	43.00	41.80	41.00	41.00	43.34	46.40	48.96	44.96
5.	Sulekere lake	52.00	52.44	50.06	49.54	49.00	49.00	48.24	48.10	48.32	48.16	49.00	50.68	49.54
6.	Ammanikere lake	45.00	44.64	44.00	41.00	41.06	41.54	41.00	41.40	42.00	42.00	44.58	46.20	42.87
7.	Keelara lake	43.65	43.00	43.08	39.08	39.84	39.44	39.00	39.22	39.00	40.06	43.26	44.82	41.12
8.	Thonnur lake	42.54	43.00	43.06	39.46	40.00	40.04	40.00	40.46	40.20	40.00	42.00	45.28	41.33
9.	Hosaholalu lake	40.04	42.00	42.00	40.06	40.08	38.98	39.62	39.00	39.88	41.46	43.64	45.00	40.98
10.	Hosakere lake	46.94	45.88	46.00	42.64	42.04	40.06	40.00	40.04	40.00	40.80	41.76	46.06	42.68
11.	Kirugaavalu lake	43.08	45.36	45.24	41.82	42.00	41.04	40.24	40.24	40.02	40.40	43.46	45.00	42.32
12.	Dudda lake	46.66	47.00	45.44	43.00	42.88	40.68	39.86	40.00	40.06	40.10	44.64	46.00	43.02
13.	Mangala lake	45.06	44.64	42.06	39.88	40.34	40.00	40.04	40.00	40.20	41.22	42.88	45.00	41.77
14.	Halaguru lake	46.00	47.68	45.00	42.40	42.10	41.64	41.00	41.04	41.00	41.46	44.00	44.80	43.17
15.	Thandekere lake	47.84	47.40	46.74	42.80	42.00	40.58	39.68	40.00	40.00	40.08	45.62	45.88	43.21

Table 3.4: Carlson Trophic State Index (TSI) of Different Lakes of Mandya District during 2014-15

Sl.No.	Name of the Lake	May	June	July	August	September	October	November	December	January	February	March	April	Average
1.	Maddur lake	50.00	51.04	48.86	46.40	44.70	42.64	41.24	41.00	40.06	41.00	43.36	47.42	44.81
2.	Malavalli lake	48.68	48.00	46.70	43.54	42.82	40.42	41.00	41.26	40.32	43.10	46.20	47.00	44.08
3.	Marehalli lake	47.84	47.28	45.48	43.42	41.30	41.00	41.20	40.64	40.28	41.28	44.46	46.32	43.37
4.	Thylur lake	49.00	49.22	46.48	44.46	41.40	40.72	41.00	40.36	40.42	45.00	46.98	48.00	44.42
5.	Sulekere lake	50.28	51.64	51.28	50.26	50.00	48.32	48.06	48.00	48.64	49.02	50.42	50.30	49.69
6.	Ammanikere lake	46.10	45.84	43.60	42.00	41.58	41.00	41.00	41.10	41.84	43.00	44.62	46.00	43.14
7.	Keelara lake	43.00	43.50	43.80	41.32	40.80	39.68	39.68	39.00	39.00	41.26	44.00	44.38	41.62
8.	Thonnur lake	43.22	44.30	43.00	38.72	40.20	41.00	40.60	40.32	40.00	39.30	40.00	42.14	41.06
9.	Hosaholalu lake	41.24	41.00	41.62	40.28	40.00	39.18	39.22	39.62	39.62	41.04	42.58	43.62	40.75
10.	Hosakere lake	47.28	46.78	46.46	42.66	42.14	40.00	40.24	40.56	40.06	41.00	41.92	44.86	42.83
11.	Kirugaavalu lake	44.00	45.28	45.00	43.16	42.72	42.04	40.38	40.38	40.00	41.00	42.94	46.30	42.77
12.	Dudda lake	47.02	47.10	46.00	43.50	42.90	41.00	39.46	39.30	40.00	40.70	43.92	45.70	43.05
13.	Mangala lake	44.00	44.00	43.08	42.46	40.00	40.00	40.72	39.42	40.00	40.00	43.68	45.90	41.93
14.	Halaguru lake	45.46	47.00	46.30	43.90	41.60	40.82	41.00	40.20	40.62	42.00	43.22	44.00	43.01
15.	Thandekere lake	48.00	47.26	46.00	43.46	42.86	41.50	40.20	40.32	40.16	40.00	43.88	46.24	43.32

This variation may be attributed to variation in the quantity of nutrients that flow from agricultural fields. Since these lakes have more area of agriculture covered.

Table 3.5: Average Values of Carlson Trophic State Index (TSI) of Different Lakes of Mandya District during 2013-15

Sl. No.	Name of the Lake	CTSI Value
1.	Maddur lake	44.62
2.	Malavalli lake	43.94
3.	Marehalli lake	43.53
4.	Thylur lake	44.69
5.	Sulekere lake	49.61
6.	Ammanikere lake	43.00
7.	Keelara lake	41.37
8.	Thonnur lake	41.19
9.	Hosaholalu lake	40.87
10.	Hosakere lake	42.76
11.	Kirugaavalu lake	42.54
12.	Dudda lake	43.03
13.	Mangala lake	41.85
14.	Halaguru lake	43.09
15.	Thandekere lake	43.26

Increase in the value of total phosphorus (TP) during summers is due to evaporation of water, accumulation of nutrients over rainy season associated with Kharif crops and depletion of more organic contents in the water bodies. During rainy and winter seasons volume of water stored in lakes and also that flow out is enormous. This carry away the nutrients and reduce CTSI index values.

LAKES MANAGEMENT AND RESTORATION

Present Scenario

Streams, rivers, ponds, lakes and wetlands like freshwater systems are important components of landscapes. Both anthropogenic activities and natural phenomenon influence trophic status of a lake. Any alteration in these activities either increase or decrease water bodies trophic index. A water body present in nutrient rich area with high net primary productivity obviously exhibit more values of CTSI and tend to be eutrophic. Nutrients added into water bodies from point and nonpoint source all increase the algal biomass and can easily turn an oligotrophic lake into a hypereutrophic lake. Major sources of point and non point nutrients are:

Point Sources

- Wastewater effluent from municipal and industrial sectors
- Runoff and leach ate from waste disposal systems
- Runoff and infiltration from animal fields
- Runoff from mines, oil fields and industrial sites
- Overflows of combined storm and sanitary sewers
- Runoff from construction sites.
- Untreated sewage

Nonpoint Sources

- Runoff from agriculture/irrigation
- Runoff from pasture and range
- Urban runoff from unsewered areas
- Runoff from abandoned mines
- Atmospheric deposition over a water surface

Desired trophic index differs among different groups of stakeholders. Fishermen and residents often want a lake to be oligotrophic, on the other hand duck rearing people may want it to be eutrophic. Natural Resource agencies are generally responsible for reconciling these conflicting uses and determining what a water body's trophic index should be.

The water-spread area of wetlands in Karnataka in the pre-monsoon period is 204053.74 ha whereas in the post monsoon period it is 246643.00 ha (Ramachandra T.V. and Ahalya N). Inland wetlands exhibit seasonal variations in the water-spread area.

Threats to lakes: common reasons for losses of lakes include:

- Agricultural Conversion
- Deforestation in wetlands
- Alteration of upper watersheds
- Degradation of water quality
- Ground water depletion
- Introduced species and extinction of native biota

Increased growth of aquatic vegetation affects normal functioning of the ecosystem, causing a variety of problems such as lack of oxygen for fish survive. The water becomes cloudy and coloured. Eutrophication also decreases the value of rivers, lakes and aesthetic enjoyment. Recreational activities such as fishing, swimming, kayaking, and canoeing give great aesthetic pleasure to many.

MANAGEMENT AND RESTORATION

Wetlands such as lakes, ponds, steams etc., are defined as 'lands transitional between terrestrial and aquatic eco-systems where the water table is usually at or near the surface or the land is covered by shallow water (Mitsch & Gosselink., 1986). The value of the world's wetlands are increasingly receiving due attention as they contribute to a healthy environment in many ways.

Aquatic ecosystems (lakes, rivers, etc.) in India support a large biodiversity and represent almost all taxonomic groups. Studies have shown that habitat losses have threatened the diversity of these ecosystems. Exotic species like *Eichornia crassipes* (water hyacinth), *Salvinia molesta* (salvinia) have invaded the wetlands and threatened native species. About 6% of global land account for wetland ecosystems. These are the most threatened of all the natural type resources. Agricultural expansion, industries, hydro-power projects, residential projects, pollution, deforestation, depletion in water level etc., are the significant reasons for the disappearance of wetlands.

The progression of lakes from oligotrophy to eutrophic condition is a natural process. Without human interference it occurs slowly. Cultural eutrophication can alter the rate of the natural process and shorten period required for this change. This can be avoided by adopting suitable conservation measures. Lakes and other natural water sources need to be protected for the benefit of present and future generations. Indian society is on a course of rapid change, transforming itself from rural to urban habitat. In this process, the most affected part of the region are the lakes of the region. This threatened the ecology, environment and water security of the region. Resoration efforts include immediate action to remove encroachments from lake area and also the Raja Kaluves (canals interconnecting lakes). This can be done by conducting a survey of all lakes and canal areas. This will be helpful in protecting the entire watershed area.

Lakes which have high biodiversity of migratory waterfowl, has to be notified for conservation under the Wetland Conservation and Management Rules- 2010. Supporting the involvement of local communities like dhobis (washer people), fisher community and other traditional users in preservation and restoration is considered as an important step. Constitution of local management committees with holistic approach can be a good measure in preserving water bodies.

GOVERNMENT INITIATIVES IN WETLAND PROTECTION

Since Indian Fisheries Act – 1857 several laws and acts are in force to enact the management, maintenance and restoration of lakes in particular and wetlands in large. Wetlands in India are indirectly protected by many laws given below (Parikh. J and Parikh K., 1999):

- The Indian Fisheries Act - 1857
- The Indian Forest Act - 1927
- Wildlife (Protection) Act - 1972

- Water (Prevention and Control of Pollution) Act - 1974
- Territorial Water, Continental Shelf, Exclusive Economic Zone and other Marine Zones Act - 1976
- Water (Prevention and Control of Pollution) Act - 1977
- Maritime Zone of India (Regulation and fishing by foreign vessels) Act - 1980
- Forest (Conservation act) - 1980
- Environmental (Protection) Act - 1986
- Coastal Zone Regulation Notification - 1991
- Wildlife (Protection) Amendment Act - 1991
- National Conservation Strategy and Policy Statement on Environment and Development - 1992

Restoration is an adapted method to improve the quality of water and its catchment conditions in order to make the wetland resources suitable for sustainable use. It is restoration of an ecosystem to its original condition. Restoration activity include several aspects of the ecosystems such as habitat restoration, reducing phosphorus imports, elimination of exotic species, limited harvests of fish and retaining native species. All these to be done with holistic approach at larger outlook , rather than manipulation of isolated elements. In achieving these goals management should emphasize long term sustenance of historical, natural and functional values.

Proper planning, execution and maintenance are the three steps in restoring lakes for long-term sustenance. These include:

- Control of pollution
- Draining the water
- Desiltation
- Removing exotic species and macrophytes

Point and non-point sources of pollution must be identified and steps to be taken to avoid their discharge into lakes. periodical cleaning or draining of water helps in maintenance of trophic status. Removal of the sediments or ooze in the lake improve soil permeability, volume of water and ground water level. Removal of exotic species is to be manually or mechanically or chemically or biologically.

The other restoration method include Aeration of lake water, Aeration of sediment and reduction in the external loading.

Watershed management practices are needful for proper land use, water conservation for farm use, flood management and silt reduction. This is helpful in increasing land productivity. Some of the methods for best management practices are as follows:

- Pollution controlling practices through source reduction, waste minimization and process control.
- Afforestation with local species in an around wetland to reduce the entry of silt and other unwanted things.
- Creating public awareness regarding proper use and maintenance of lakes.

Restoration attempts through Best Management Practices (BMPs) helps in managing point and non-point pollution sources. Regulations and planning for wildlife habitat also adds to maintain water quality and reducing the rate of wetland loss. Financial resources, active involvement of governmental and non-governmental organisations, research organisations, media, community centers, educational institutions etc. all play important role in restoration.

In Mandya district most of these lakes are managed by Zilla Panchayath. A separate department called minor irrigation department maintains and manage all these lakes. Out of total 891 lakes of varied size, as many as 173 tanks come under the control of fishery department, 6 under the forest department and 688 minor tanks are controlled by the gram panchayath. Zilla Panchayath initiated several programmes to restore the originality of these lakes. Most of these lakes are filled with ooze and mud. This has drastically reduced their water holding capacity. Neglected agricultural practices, turning away of youths from agriculture in rural areas, migration towards towns and cities, invasion of exotic weeds all added to depletion in the status of water bodies.

CONCLUSION

Mesotrophic lakes are intermediate between oligotrophic and eutrophic conditions. All the fifteen lakes studied were mesotrophic in nature. But some of them are on the verge of becoming eutrophic. Supporting organic farming practices , reduce the dependency on chemical fertilizers and suitable treatment of domestic sewage are the desired and essential measures to manage and restore the lakes. Creating awareness about significance of fresh water bodies among the stake holders is the needed step to be taken by concerned authorities.

REFERENCES

Campos, H. (1984): Limnological Studies of Araucanian Lakes, Chile. *Internationale Vereinigungtur Limnologi,* (22): 1319-1327.

Campos, H., Hamilton, D.P., Villalobos, L., Imberger, J. and Jaram, A. (2001): A Modeling Assessment of Potential for Eutrophication of Lake Rihinue. *Archiv fur Hydrobiologie,* (151): 101-125.

Campos, H., Steffen, W., Roman, C., and Aguero, G. (1983): Limnological Studies in Lake Villarica; Morphometrical, Physical, Chemical, Planktonical Factors and Primary Productivity. *Archiv fur Hydrobiologie,* (5): 371-406.

Carvalho L and Kirka. (2003): Changes in Shallao Lake Functioning Response to Climate Changes and Nutrient Load and Lake Water Chemistry in Lake Rings Join Southern Sweden from 1966-1996 Hydrobiologia, (400): 9-18.

Haper, D. (1972): Eutrophication of Fresh Water Chapman & Hill, London.

Horne. A.J. and Goldman C.R. (1994): Limnology 2nd edition MC Graw Hill New York.

Mitsch WJ, and Gosselink JG, 1986. Wetlands. Van Nostrand Reinhold, New York.

Pandit, A.K. (1996): Lakes in Kashmir Himalaya.(eds.): Khan, A.H. and Pandit, A.K., *Ecology Environment and Energy*. University of Kashmir, Srinagar. J & K, pp. 1-40.

Pandit, A.K. (1999): Trophic Structure of Plankton Community in Some Typical Wetlands of Kashmir, India. In Mishra, S.R. (ed.) *Limnological Research in India*, Daya Publishing House, New Delhi - 110 035, India. pp. 190-224.

Parikh. J and Parikh K., (1999): Sustainable Wetland. J Environ Res Dev, 7(1A): 576-583.

Ramachandra, T.V. and Ahalya, N. (2001): Monograph. *Essentials in Limnology and Geographic Information System* (GIS). pp. 38-39.

Ramachandra, T.V. and Ahalya, N.(2001): Conservation and Management of Wetland Ecosystems in Karnataka. Centre for Ecological Sciences, Indian Institute of Science, Bangalore.

Ramalingaiah, (1985): Monitoring of Water Quality Changes Between the Protected Chain Lakes and Unprotected Chocolate Lake. Halifax, Nova Scotia, Canada. pp: 127-134.

Rao, V.S. (1975): An Ecological Study of Three Freshwater Ponds of Hyderabad, India III. The Phytoplankton. *Hydrobiologia*, 47: 319-337.

Zutshi and Khan, A.K. (1988): Eutrophic Gradient in the Dal Lake, Kashmir. *Indian J. Env. Health*, 30: 348-354.

Pages: 49-60

WATER RESOURCES MANAGEMENT: *MONITORING AND ASSESSMENT*

Edited by: Dr. Sandeep Gupta; Dr. Pawan Kumar 'Bharti'

ISBN: 978-93-5056-799-9

Edition: 2016

Published by: Discovery Publishing House Pvt. Ltd., New Delhi (India)

4

Assessment of Water Quality of the Tail Race of the Dikhow River, Assam, Through Appropriate Biotic Indices

Bristi Dutta

ABSTRACT

The present study has been conducted in the tail race of Dikhow River which is a southern tributary of River Brahmaputra, Assam, India. The study has been conducted for one year (from January, 2013 to December, 2013). The aim of the study was to portray a vivid picture of the river ecosystem by considering an important biotic community (macro invertebrate) as a tool. Appropriate Biotic indices were used to assess the water quality. 13 species (*Rhyncobdella sp, thiarea tuberculata, margaritifera margaritifera, Gammarus sp, Fenneropeneaus indicus, Isotomurus sp, caenius sp, Gomphus sp, Lithoserous sp, Hydrophylus sp, Chaoborus sp, Chironomus sp)* of macroinvertebrates belonging to 13 families, (Hirudinidae, Thiaridae, Margaritiferidae, Gamaridae, Paenidae, Isotomidae, Caenidae, Gomphidae, Belostometidae, Nepidae, Hydrophilidae, Chaoboridae, Chironomidae), 11 orders (Gnathobdelida, Mesogastropoda, Unionida, Amphi[poda, Decapoda, Collembolla, Ephomeroptera, Odonata, Hemiptera, Coleoptera, Diptera), 5 classess (Hirudinea, Gastropoda, Bivalvia, Ceustacea and Insecta) and 3 phyla (Annelida, Mollusca, Arthropoda) have been recorded from the tail race of Dikhow river (Table 4.2)

Department of Zoology, S.P.P. College, Namti, Sivsagar, Assam - 786 004, (India) during the study period. The highest population of macroinvertebrates is contributed by Thiaridae family of class Gastropoda of Phylum Mollusca. Macro invertebrate species diversity was subjected to diversity analysis using different indices like Shannon – Weiner index (H); Simpson index of diversity (1-D); Pielou Evenness Index ; Family Biotic Index. Shannon diversity index and family biotic index showed poor water quality and degradation of habitat structure.

Keywords: Dikhow River, diversity index, water quality, macro-invertebrates.

INTRODUCTION

Benthic macroinvertebrates are differentially sensitive to many biotic and abiotic factors in their environment. Consequently, macroinvertebrate community structure has commonly been used as an indicator of the condition of an aquatic system [1], [17], [18]. Biotic index systems have been developed which give numerical scores to specific "indicator" organisms at a particular taxonomic level [1], [17], [18]. Such organisms have specific requirements in terms of physical and chemical conditions. Changes in presence/absence, numbers, morphology, physiology or behaviour of these organisms can indicate that the physical and/or chemical conditions are outside their preferred limits [18]. Presence of numerous families of highly tolerant organisms usually indicates poor water quality [13].

Diversity index is a statistical method which is planned to evaluate the variety of a data group consisting of different types of components. Features of a population such as number of existing species (richness), distribution of individuals equally (evenness) and total number of existing individuals underlie the basis of diversity indices. Thus, any changes in any of these three features will affect the whole population, so that the diversity indices depending upon these features are used effectively to determine the changes in a population [14].

Keeping all these views in mind, a comprehensive study was done to portray a vivid picture of the river ecosystem by considering an important biotic community (macro invertebrate) as a tool.

METHODOLOGY

Demarcation of the Study Area

The selected study area is the tailrace of Dikhow river of 65 km stretch which has been demarcated into five sectors as follows:

Table 4.1: Details of the Sampling Sites

Sampling Site	Name	Lacality	GPS Position
I	Silghat	Nazira	(N-26°54′51.6″ and E-94°44′14.6″)
II	Kujibali	Hanhsora	(N-26°57′2.3″ and E- 94°42′30.2″)
III	Dikhow Bridge	Sivasagar	(N-26°58′35.1″ and E-94°37′49.2″)
IV	Baliaghat	Gaurisagar	(N-26°57′48.9″ and E- 94°30′49.4″)
V	Dikhowmukh	Dikhowmukh	(N- 26°59′58.5″ and E-94°28′ 03.9″

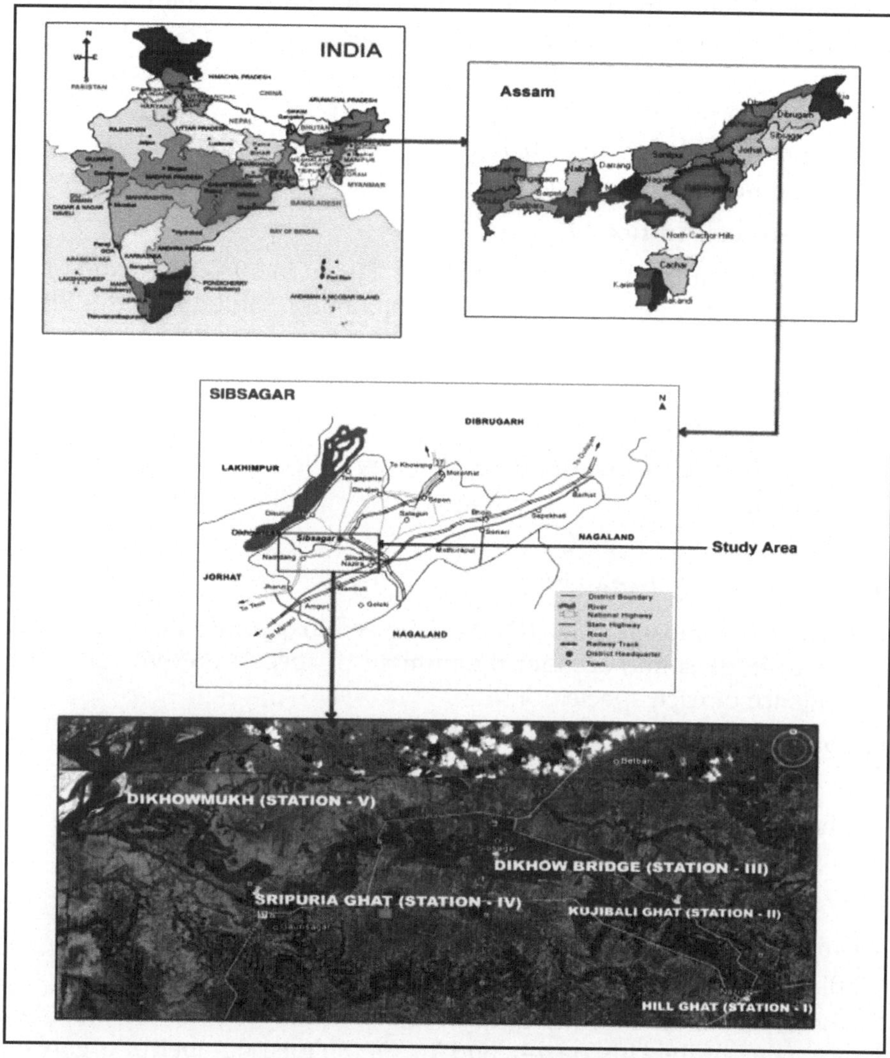

Fig. 4.1: Location Map of the Study Area

Macroinvertebrate assessment: Benthic macroinvertebrates were collected from each sampling sectors using drag nets and preserved on sites in 70% ethyl alcohol and identified as suggested by Edmondson (1993)

Statistical Analysis

Macro invertebrate species diversity was subjected to diversity analysis using different indices like Shannon – Weiner index (H); Simpson index of diversity (1-D); Pielou Evenness Index; Family Biotic Index.

Shannon-Weiner Diversity Index "H"

Shannon-Weiner index is the most preferred index among the diversity indices used in biological science. It is calculated as follows $H = -\Sigma[(ni/N) \times (\ln ni/N)]$

H: Shannon Diversity Index

ni: Number of individuals belonging to i species

N: Total number of individuals

Pielou Evenness Index "J"

It was derived from Shannon index by Pielou in 1966. The ratio of the observed value of Shannon index to the maximum value gives the Pielou Evenness Index result. It is expressed as:

J = H/Hmax

J: Pielou evenness index

H: The observed value of Shannon index

Hmax : lnS

S: Total number of species

Simpson Diversity Index "D"

In ecology, Simpson index (D) is often used to quantify the biodiversity of a habitat. It takes into account the number of species present, as well as the abundance of each species.

Simpson's Index of Diversity

$$D = 1 - \Sigma ni\ (ni-1)/N\ (N-1)$$

Where, ni = the total number of individuals of a particular species. N = the total number of individuals of all species.

Family Biotic Index (FBI)

Family Biotic Index (FBI) can be calculated as:

$$FBI = (\Sigma\ x_i\ t_i/n)$$

where "xi" is the number of individuals in the "ith" taxon, "ti" is the tolerance value of the "ith" taxon, and "n" is the total number of organisms in the sample. The FBI was then used to evaluate the water quality of the ecosystem.

RESULT

Table 4.2: List of Macroinvertebrates with their Tolerance Level as Recorded from Dikhow River during the Study Period

Taxa	Tolerance	Reference
ANNELIDA Hirudenea Rhynchobdelida Hirudinideae *Rhynchobdella sp*	10	Barbour *et al*, 1999
MOLLUSCA Gastropoda Mesogastropoda Thiaridae *Thiaria tuberculata*	8	Bode *et al*. 1996
MOLLUSCA Bivalvia Unionida Margaritiferideae *Margaritifera margaritifera*	8	Barbour *et al*, 1999
ARTHROPODA Crustacea Amphipoda Gammarideae *Gammarus sp.*	6	Bode *et al*, 1996
ARTHROPODA Crustacea Decapoda Pennideae *Fenneropenaeus indicus*	8	Barbour *et al*, 1999
ARTHROPODA Insecta Colembola Isotomidea Isotomurus sp	5	Bode *et al*, 1996
ARTHROPODA Insecta Ephomeroptera Caenidae *Caenius sp.*	7	Hauer & Lamberti, 1996
ARTHROPODA Insecta Odonata Gomphidae *Gomphus sp.*	5	Bode *et al*, 1996

(Table Contd...)

Taxa	Tolerance	Reference
ARTHROPODA Insecta Hemiptera Belostometidae *Lethocerus sp.*	5	Barbour *et al*, 1999
ARTHROPODA Insecta Hemiptera Nepidae —	–	–
ARTHROPODA Insecta Coleoptera Hydrophilidae *Hydrophyllus sp.*	5	Bode *et al*, 2002
ARTHROPODA Insecta Diptera Chaoboridae *Chaoborus sp.*	8	Bode *et al*, 1996
ARTHROPODA Insecta Diptera Chironomidae *Chironomus sp.*	8	Hauer & Lamberti, 1996

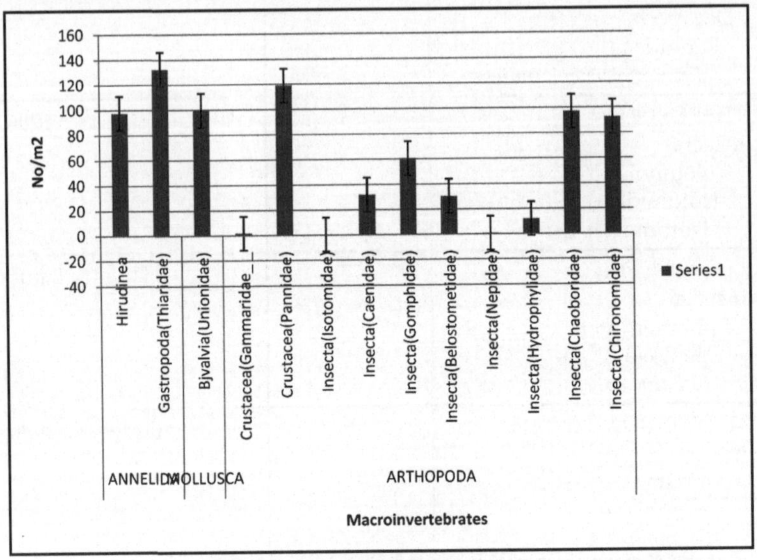

Fig. 4.2: Population Density of Macrinvertebrates in Dikhow River during the Study Period

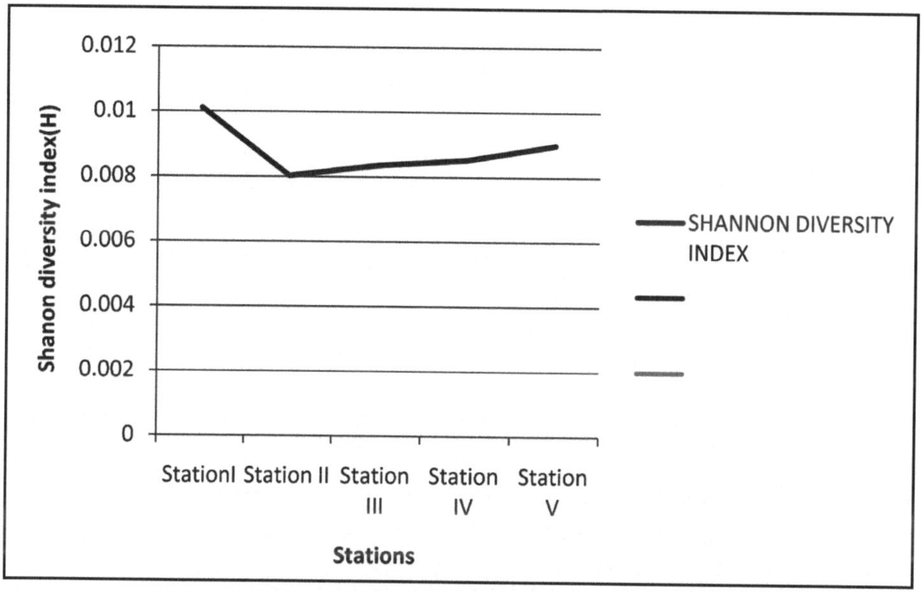

Fig. 4.3: Shanon Diversity Index Value of Five Stations

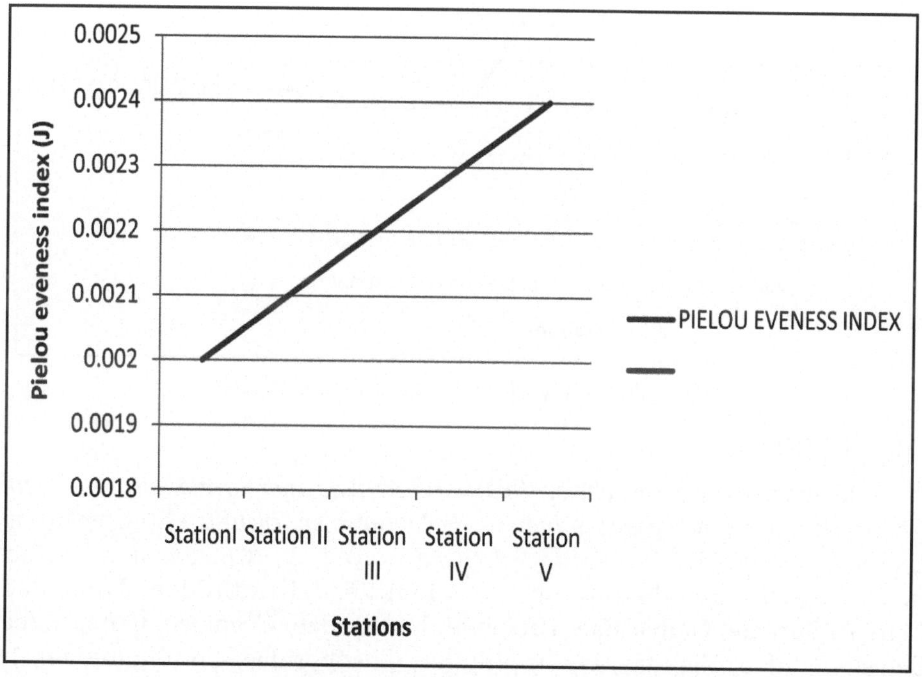

Fig. 4.4: Pielou Eveness Index of Five Stations

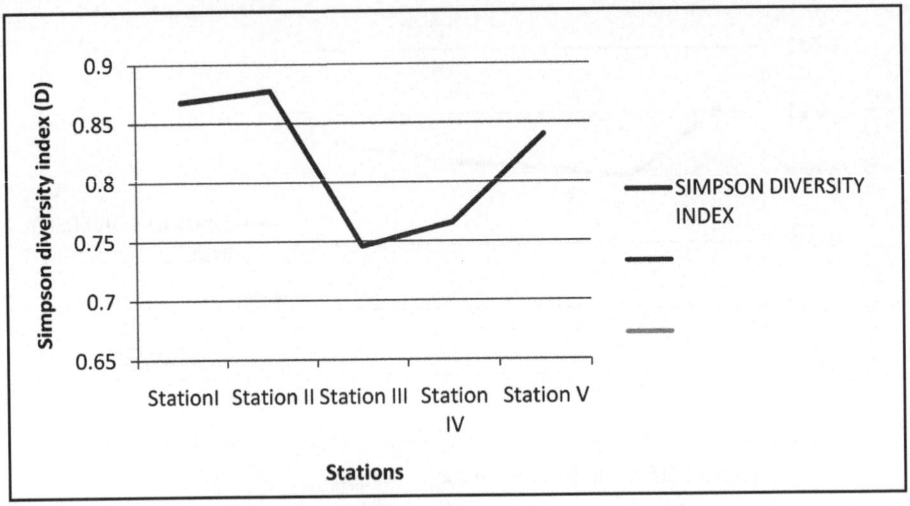

Fig. 4.5: Simpson Diversity Index of Five Stations

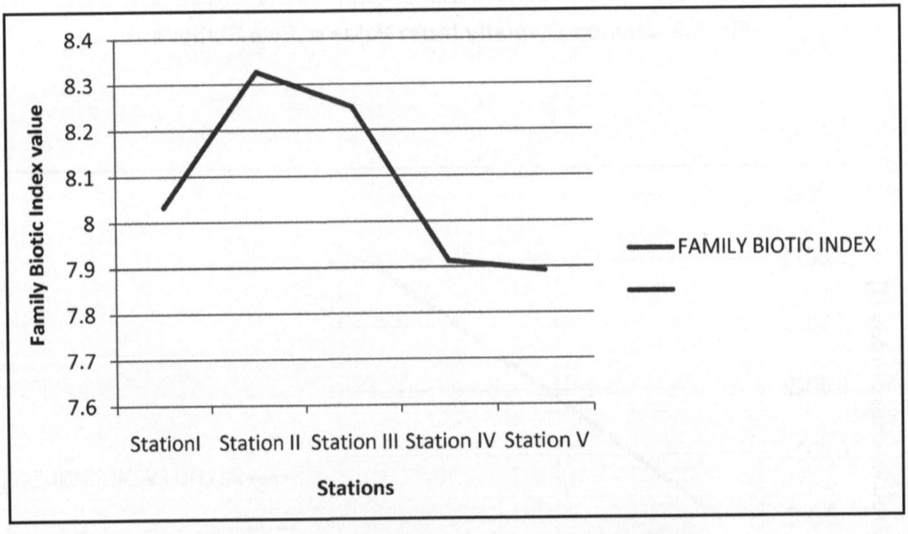

Fig. 4.6: Family Biotic Index of Five Stations

DISCUSSION

13 species (*Rhyncobdella sp, thiarea tuberculata, margaritifera margaritifera, Gammarus sp, Fenneropeneaus indicus, Isotomurus sp, caenius sp, Gomphus sp, Lithoserous sp, Hydrophylus sp, Chaoborus sp, Chironomus sp)* of macroinvertebrates belonging to 13 families,(Hirudinidae, Thiaridae, Margaritiferidae, Gamaridae, Paenidae, Isotomidae, Caenidae, Gomphidae, Belostometidae, Nepidae, Hydrophilidae, Chaoboridae, Chironomidae), 11 orders (Gnathobdelida, Mesogastropoda, Unionida, Amphi[poda, Decapoda,

Collembolla, Ephomeroptera, Odonata, Hemiptera, Coleoptera, Diptera), 5 classess (Hirudinea, Gastropoda, Bivalvia, Ceustacea and Insecta) and 3 phyla (Annelida, Mollusca, Arthropoda) have been recorded from the tail race of Dikhow river (Table 4.2) during the study period.

The highest population of macroinvertebrates is contributed by Thiaridae family of class Gastropoda of Phylum Mollusca (Fig. 4.2), followed by family Pannidae of class Crustacea. Pannidae is followed by family Unionidae (Fig. 4.2) of class Bivalvia , followed by population of family Hirudinidae of class Hirudinea. (Fig. 4.2). Family Chaoboridae of class Insecta followed Hirudinidae. Chaoboridae is followed by family Chironomidae of class Insecta (Fig. 4.2). Family Gomphidae, Belostometidae and Caennidae of class insect contributed with very low population compared to above mentioned families. FamilyGammaridae of class Crustacea, Nepidae and Isotomidae of class Insecta showed lowest population during the study period. (Fig. 4.2). Family Thiaridae and Unionidae of classBivalvia belonging to phylum Mollusca showed comparatively higher population in station: 5(S5) during the study period (Table 4.2).

Tolerance is a listing of tolerance values for each taxon used in the calculation of the Hilsenhoff species-level Biotic Index and the Family Biotic Index. Tolerance values range from 0 for organisms very intolerant of organic wastes to 10 for organisms very tolerant of organic wastes. Most of these values were taken from Hilsenhoff, Bode *et al*, Barbour *et al* and Hauer & Lamberti [2], [4],[5], [8], [10] While compared the tolerance level of the macroinvertebrate texa recorded from the Dikhow river, it has been noticed that, *Chironomus sp* and *Chaoborus sp* belonging to class insecta of phylum arthropoda with tolerance level 8 (Table 4.2, Fig. 4.2), *Fenneropenaeus indicus,*belonging to insecta of Arthropoda, with tolerance level 8 (Table 4.2, Fig. 4.2), *Margaretifera margaretifera* under class Bivalvia and *Thiaria tuberculata* under class Gastropoda belonging to phylum Mollusca with tolerance level 8 (Fig. 4.1) and *Rhyncobdella sp.* Belonging to class Hirudinea of phylum Annelida with tolerance level 10 (Table 4.2, Fig. 4.2) recorded with maximum no. from the stations during the study period. Among them Bivalvia was found to be highest in No. particularly in station: V (Fig. 4.2) during the study period. But, compared to them other classes with tolerance level 5 and 6 recorded to be less in no. from the stations (Fig. 4.2). It indicates the water quality of Dikhow River likely to be polluted or introduction of organic pollutants (Bode *et al.*, 1991, 1996, 2002).

Shannon – Weiner index "H" which depends on both the number of species present and the abundance of each species. The index values are between 0.0-5.0. The values above 3.0 indicate that the structure of habitat is stable and balanced; the values under 1.0 indicate that there are pollution and degradation of habitat structure. The value of Shannon Diversity Index in all the sectors was found to be between 0.008985 to 0. 010114 (Fig. 4.3); i,e the value was below 1 which indicate there is pollution and degradtation of habitat structure. Sector wise Shannon diversity index of macroinvertebrate was highest in Sector I (0. 010114) and lowest in sector II (0.008024). Pielou Eveness Index value was between 0.002 to 0.0024 and values was approximately similar in all stations (Fig. 4.4). The values are between 0 – 1.When the value is getting closer to 1, it means that the individuals are distributed equally. Simpson diversity index was derived by Simpson in 1949. Simpson index values (D) are between 0-1. But while calculating, final result is subtracted from 1 to correct the inverse proportion. Simpson's diversity index is a measure of diversity. Simpson Diversity index value ranged between 0.745 to 0. 877 (Fig. 4.5). Simpson Diversity Index was highest in sector II (0.877) and lowest in sector III (0.745). Thus the diversity index values in all the sectors indicate introduction of organic pollutants to the river. The sectors are mainly human populated areas. Sector I and III are industrial areas. Disposal of organic pollutants must be reduced. Organic pollutants originate from domestic sewage (raw or treated), urban run-off, industrial (trade) effluents and farm wastes. Unplanned and unusual fishing must be stopped. River should be protected from fish poachers. Unplanned construction of hatcheries should be avoided. Catching of fish during their breeding season must be stopped.

ROLES TO BE PLAYED TO PREVENT FURTHER POLLUTION

Effluents must be treated to acceptable levels and standardize before discharging them in river. Details of all effluents generated each industry or urban runoff must be mainained as database in the State water resource Information System, The State Pollution Control Board and local administration and nust be made available to local people. scientific fishing should be practiced. Important information on scientific procedures for fishing must be published n local Assamese newspapers and magazines. Government or any other appropriate agencies must take initiatives in this.

Above all, we must not forget to play our individual roles starting from our own homes to save this diminishing commodity, our precious water. There are many easy ways to save water from wastage. Never let used water to go down the drain when there may be another use for it such as recycling it by watering the plants or washing the cars. Verify that your home is leak-free, because many homes have hidden water leaks. Read your water meter before and after a two-hour period when no water is being used. If the meter does not read exactly the same, there is a leak. Avoid flushing the toilet unnecessarily. Dispose tissues, insects and other such wastes in the trash rather than the toilets. Take shorter showers. Replace your showerhead with an ultra-low-flow version.

REFERANCES

1. Armitage, P.D., D. Moss, J.F. Wright, and M.T. Furse. 1983. The Performance of a New Biological Water Quality Score System Based on Macroinvertebrates Over a Wide Range of Unpolluted Running-Water Sites. Water Res. 17: 333-47.
2. Barbour, M.T., Gerritsen, J., Snyder, B.D., Stribling, J.B. 1999. Rapid Bioassessment Protocols for Use in Streams and Wadeable Rivers: Periphyton, Benthic Macroinvertebrates, and Fish. Second Edition. EPA 841-B-99-002. U.S. Environmental Protection Agency; Office of Water; Washington, D.C. xiv, 11 chapters, 4 appendices.
3. Bode, R.W., Novak, M.A., and Abele, L.E. 1991. Methods for Rapid Biological Assessment of Streams. NYS Department of Environmental Conservation, Albany, NY. 57p.
4. Bode, R.W., Novak, M.A., and Abele, L.E. 1996. Quality Assurance Work Plan for Biological Stream Monitoring in New York State. NYS Department of Environmental Conservation, Albany, NY. 89p
5. Bode, R.W., Novak, M.A., and Abele, L.E. 2002: Quality Assurance Work Plan for Biological Stream Monitoring in New York State. NYS Department of Environmental Conservation, Albany, NY.
6. David, S.M., Somers, K.M., Reid, R.A., Hall, R.J., and Girard, R.E. 1998. Sampling Protocols for the Rapid Bioassessment of Streams and Lakes Using Benthic Macroinvertebrates. Second Edition, Ontario Ministry of the Environment. ISBN 0-7778-7378-8.29 p., Appendices 1-6.
7. Edmondson, W.T. (1967). *Fresh Water Biology*, 2nd Edn. John Wiley and Sons, New York Friberg, N., Sandin, L. and Pedersen, M.L., 2009. Assessing the Effects Hydromorphological Degradation on Macroinvertebrate Indicators in Rivers: Examples, Constraints, and Outlook. Integrated Environmental Assessment and Management, 5(1): 86-96.
8. Hauer, F.R., and Lamberti, G.A. (eds.) 1996. Methods in Stream Ecology. Academic Press. ISBN: 0-12-332906-X. 696 pp.
9. Hellawell, J.M., 1978. Biological Surveillance of Rivers, a Biological Monitoring Handbook. Water Research Centre, Medmenham and Stevenage, UK, 331 pp.
10. Hilsenhoff, W.L. 1987. An Improved Biotic Index of Organic Stream Pollution. Great Lakes Entomol. 20: 31-39.
11. Hilsenhoff, W.L. 1988. Rapid Field Assessment of Organic Pollution with a Family-level Biotic Index. J. N. Am. Benthol. Soc. 7(1): 65-68.
12. Hutchinson, G.E. 1993. A Treatise on Limnology. Vol. IV, The Zoobenthos. Ed. Y.H.Edmondson. John Wiley & Sons, Inc. Xx, 944 pp.
13. Hynes, K.E. 1998. Benthic Macroinvertebrate Diversity and Biotic Indices for Monitoring of 5 Urban and Urbanizing Lakes within the Halifax Regional Municipality (HRM), Nova Scotia, Canada. Soil & Water Conservation Society of Metro Halifax. xiv, 114p.
14. Mandaville, S.M. 1999. Bioassessment of Freshwaters Using Benthic Macroinvertebrates-A Primer. First Ed. Project E-1, Soil & Water Conservation Society of Metro Halifax. viii, Chapters I-XXVII, Appendices A-D. 244p.
15. Mandaville, S.M. 2000a. Limnology- Eutrophication and Chemistry, Carrying Capacities, Loadings, Benthic Ecology, and Comparative Data. Project F-1, Soil & Water Conservation Society of Metro Halifax. Synopses 1, 2, 3, 13, and 14. 210p.

16. Mandaville, S.M. 2000b. Limnology in Nova Scotia: Lake Data and Predictive Phosphorus Models - Archives in Electronic Format. First Ed. Project F-2, Soil & Water Conservation Society of Metro Halifax. xii, 74p, a-d. 90p., & CD media (*and its latest updates*).
17. Ohio Department of Natural Resources, Division of Natural Areas and Preserves, Scenic Rivers Programme. Stream Quality Monitoring. Unpublished Report.
18. Rosenberg, D.M. and Resh, V.H. (eds.) 1993. Freshwater Biomonitoring and Benthic Macroinvertebrates. Chapman & Hall, New York. ISBN: 0-412-02251-6. x, 488pp.
19. Simpson, K.W. and R.W. Bode. 1980. Common Larvae of Chironomidae (Diptera) from New York State Streams and Rivers, with Particular Reference to the Fauna of Artificial Substrates. N.Y.S. Museum Bull. No. 439. p. 105.

Pages: 61-74

WATER RESOURCES MANAGEMENT: *MONITORING AND ASSESSMENT*

Edited by: Dr. Sandeep Gupta; Dr. Pawan Kumar 'Bharti'

ISBN: 978-93-5056-799-9

Edition: 2016

Published by: Discovery Publishing House Pvt. Ltd., New Delhi (India)

5

Fluoride and Fluorosis a Major Problem in India

Y.S. Narwaria*; **R.B. Dinkar**[1] and **D.N. Saksena**[2]

INTRODUCTION

Fluoride is a key aspect of water quality in rural water supply system, which potentially affects the sustainability of water if it exceeds its prescribed limits. First time in 1937, the excessive fluoride in groundwater was reported in India in the State of Andhra Pradesh. More than 200 million people from all over the world suffer from dental fluorosis caused mainly by excessive fluoride in drinking water (Chandrajith *et al.*, 2007). India is amongst the 23 nations around the globe, where health problem have been reported due to excessive fluoride in drinking water. In India occurrence of fluoride in ground water has been detected in 19 states. The problem of fluorosis has been reported in various states of India, affecting more than 150,000 villages seriously (Teotia and Teotia, 1991). It has been establishment that about 45% of drinking water source in India are contaminated by fluoride (Teotia and Teotia, 1984). Approximately 62 million people including 6 million children

Ministry of Rural Development, Department of Land Resources, CGO Complex, Lodhi Road, New Delhi - 110 003, (India)

1 VRG, Post Graduate, College, Gwalior - 474 005, Madhya Pradesh, (India)

2 Aquatic Biology Laboratory, School of Studies in Zoology, Jiwaji University Gwalior - 474 011, Madhya Pradesh, (India)

suffer from fluorosis because of consumption of water with high fluoride concentrations (Susheela, 1999). The amount of fluoride occurring naturally in groundwater is governed by climate, composition of the rock, and hydrogeology (Gupta *et al.*, 2006). Fluoride is the most electronegative of all chemical elements and is therefore, never encountered in nature in the elemental form. It is seventeenth in the order of frequency of occurrence of the elements, and represents about 0.06 to 0.09% of the earth's crust (Wedephol, 1974). Fluoride is an essential ion for all living beings from the health point of view. It helps in the normal mineralization of bones and formation of dental enamel. Fluoride when consumed in inadequate quantities (less than 0.5ppm) causes health problems like dental caries, lack of formation of dental enamel and deficiency of mineralization of bones, especially among the children (WHO, 1996). On the contrary, if fluoride is consumed or used up in excess (more than 1.0ppm), it can cause different kinds of health problems which equally affect both young and old (WHO, 1996;Mascarenhas and Burt, 1998; Vani and Reddy, 2000).

The fluoride concentration in groundwater depends on the geological, chemical and physical characteristics of the soil and rocks. Fluorine is highly reactive and is found naturally as fluoride. Fluoride is of mild character in areas with drinking water containing fluoride levels up to 1.5-2.0 mgL-1 naturally but there is 100% prevalence of skeletal fluorosis in consuming water with 5.2 mgL-1 fluoride concentration in drinking water. Wide-spread incidences of mottled teeth were also observed even when fluoride is within the range of 0.7-1.5 mgL-1. Fluorosis in all forms is considered untreatable but reversal of dental fluorosis is possible. There is an urgent need to reduce fluoride intake through water as much as possible. In nut shell, a multidisciplinary approach involving health aspects, quality water supply and nutritional aspects and in depth research particularly on effects of fluoride on human health through epidemiological studies in various areas will have to be adopted. However, there appears to be straight correlation between content of fluoride in drinking water and severity of fluorosis.

FLUORIDE

In India, the problem of high fluoride concentration in groundwater resources has now become one of the most important public health, toxicological and geo-environmental issue. India is also confronting the problem of fluoride and around a million people in villages are consuming water having high fluoride (Agrawal *et al.*, 1997, Choubisa, 1998; Susheela, 1999). The fluoride concentrations from traces to maximum of 44 mgL^{-1} fluoride has been observed in Indian ground water. High fluoride in ground water ranges from 0.3 to 20 mgL^{-1} in Andhra Pradesh (Ramesam and Rajagopalan, 1985; Ramesam, 1987; Rao *et al.*, 1993 Kumar *et al.*, 1993; Srikanth *et al.*, 1994; Rao and Prasad, 1997; Reddy *et al.*,1999), from 0.4 to 20.6 mgL^{-1} in

Karbi Anglong in Assam (Handa, 1975; Gupta, 1999; Chakraborti *et al.*, 2000), from 2.5 mgL^{-1} in Bihar (Handa, 1975; Ray *et al.*, 2000), from 0.2 to 32.5 mgL^{-1} in Delhi (Susheela *et al.*, 1996), from 0.1 to 40.0 mgL^{-1} in Gujrat (Sahu and Karim, 1989; chinoy *et al.*, 1992, Gupta and Sarma, 1995), form 0.4 to 7.4 mgL^{-1} in Karnataka (Wodeyar and Sreenivasan, 1996; Latha *et al.*, 1999), 0.1 mgL^{-1} in Kerala (Handa, 1975), from 0.1 to 16.4 mgL^{-1} in Orissa (Handa, 1975; Das *et al.*, 2000), from 0.1 to 16.5 mgL^{-1} in Punjab (Singh *et al.*, 1965), from 0.51 to 4.0 mgL^{-1} in Tamil Nadu (Handa, 1975; Aparao and Karthikeyan, 1986), from 0.1 to 17.5 mgL^{-1} in Uttar Pradesh (Singh *et al.*, 1987; Gupta *et al.*, 1994a, b, 1999a), from 0.1 to 2.2 mgL^{-1} in West Bengal (Handa, 1975), from 0.1 to 44.0 mgL^{-1} in Rajasthan (Bhargava *et al.*, 1978; Gupta, 1981; Gupta, 1991; Ozhe et al., 1993; Gupta *et al.*, 1993; Choubisa *et al.*, 1995, 1996 (a & b); Maithani *et al.*, 1998; Gupta and Varshney, 1999; Datta *et al*, 1999; Patra *et al.*, 2000) from 0.2 to 3.91 mgL^{-1} in Madhya Pradesh (Chandrawanshi and Patel, 1999; Nawlakhe *et al.*, 1995 and Narwaria and Saksena, 2012 have been reported.

The major availability and solubility of the parent fluoride minerals with which the waters are in contact (WHO, 1970). Other factors affecting the dissolution of fluoride in water are pH, alkaline and metallic ions in water. High pH of water favours the dissolution of fluoride in water. However, at acidic pH, fluoride tends to form complexes with the metals present in water. Aluminum is found to be very active in formation of complex with fluoride at acidic pH. Solubility of fluoride in water also increases alkalinity of water. It is also present in most of our everyday needs, viz., toothpastes, drugs, cosmetics, chewing gums, mouthwashes, etc. Though, a small amount of it is beneficial for human health for preventing dental carries, it becomes very harmful when present in excess of 1mg/L.World Health Organisation (WHO, 1984) and Indian standards have (IS: 10500) recommended that the fluoride content in drinking water should be in the range of 1-1.5 mg/L.

FLUOROSIS IN HUMAN POPULATION

High fluoride level in groundwater leads to health threat among millions of people around the world. An inventory of fluoride concentration in drinking ground water is important to curb spread of the disease of fluorosis. Although initial entry of fluorine into the hard tissues is beneficial for the health of teeth and bones, entry of more fluorine results in dental and skeletal fluorosis. Once fluorine levels in the hard tissues reach physiological saturation (0.02 to 0.83%), further ingestion of fluoride leads to flooding of fluoride in the soft tissues leading to skin, urinary, gastric, muscular and brain causing neurological problems, besides death due to some inter-current infection. The prevailing social customs make most men in the fluorosis villages to remain at the same place right from birth using locally available high-fluoride water for both drinking and cooking. They develop progressively severe symptoms of fluorosis till death.

Lithology and Fluoride Concentration in the Ground Water in Different States of India

Sample Location	Geological Information	Fluoride (mg/L^{-1})	Reference
Guntur, Andhra Pradesh	Archean granite and gneissic complex	0.6-2.5	Rao, 2003
Anantpur, Andhra Pradesh	Archean granite and gneissic complex	0.56-5.8	Rao *et al*., 2003
Hyderabad, Andhra Pradesh	Archean granite and gneissic complex	0.38-4.0	Sreedevi *et al*., 2006
Ranga Reddy, Andhra Pradesh	Archean granite and gneissic complex	0.4-4.8	Sujatha 2003
Karbi Anglong Assam	Cretaceous sandstone	0.4-20.6	Chakraborti *et al*., 2000
Bihar	Archean gneissic complex	0.1-2.5	Ray *et al*., 2000
Delhi	Amphibolites and quartzite's	0.2-32.5	Susheela *et al*., 1996
Gujarat	Basalth and quaternary sediments	0.1-40	Chinoy *et al*., 1992
Bellary Karnataka	Archean granite and gneissic complex	0.33-7.8	Woodeyar *et al*., 1996
Karnataka	Archean granite and gneissic complex	1-7.4	Sumalatha *et al*., 1999
Kerala	Archean granite and gneissic complex	0.2-5.75	Shaji *et al*., 2007
Chandrapur Maharastra	Archean granite and gneissic complex	–	Deshmukh *et al*., 1995
Orissa	Archean granite and gneissic complex	0.3-10.1	Kundu *et al*., 2001
Orssa	Archean granite and gneissic complex	0.1-16.4	Das *et al*., 2000
Churu Rajasthan	Granite and micaceous sands	0.1-14	Muraldharan *et al*., 2002
Dungarpur Rajasthan	Archean granite and gneissic complex	0.1-10	Choubisa *et al*., 1996
Tamil Nadu	Gneissic complex	0.51-4.0	Handa, 1975
Tamil Nadu	Charnokite and gneissic complex	0.5-40	Apparao *et al*., 1986
Varanasi Uttar Pradesh	Quaternary –Upper Tertiary deposits	0.2-2.1	Ray *et al*., 1983
Unnao, Uttar Pradesh	Archean granite and gneissic complex	–	Chadha *et al*., 1999
Agra Uttar Pradesh	Archean granite and gneissic complex	0.1-17.5	Gupta *et al*., 1999
Mathura, Uttar Pradesh	Archean granite and gneissic complex	0.6-2.5	Mishra *et al*., 2006
Sonbhadra, Uttar Pradesh	Archean granite and gneissic complex	0.49-6.7	Janardhan *et al*., 2009
Chandidongri, Madhya Pradesh	Archean granite and gneissic complex	1.5-4	Chatterjee *et al*., 1998
Shivpuri, Madhya Pradesh	Archean granite and gneissic complex	0.2-6.4	Nawlakhe *et al*., 1995
Shivpuri, Madhya Pradesh	Archean granite and gneissic complex	1.65-3.91	Narwaria and Saksena, 2012

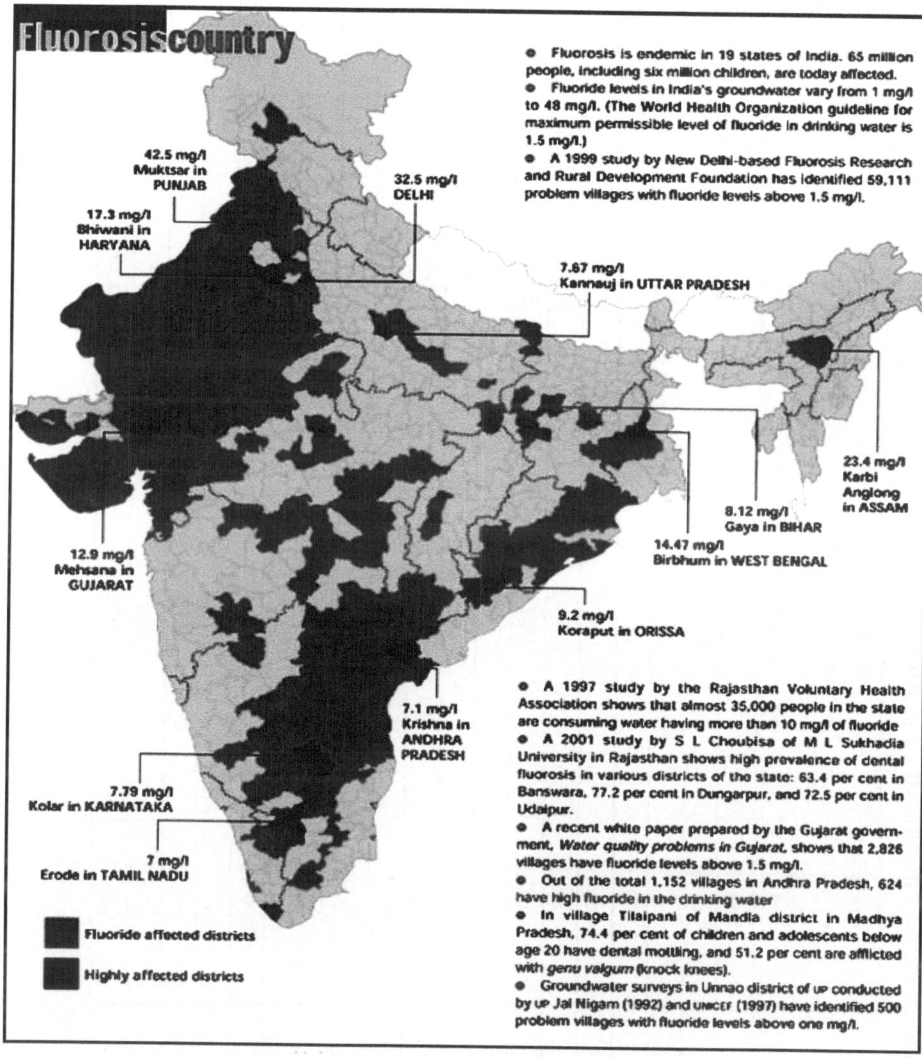

Fig. 5.1: Distribution of Fluorosis in India

Source: Choubisa *et al.* (2001)

Table 5.1: State-wise Population Influenced by Fluoride (F) Content in Groundwater

State	Population (Millions)	Population Influenced by $F<1.0 mg/L^{1}$ (Millions)	Population Influenced by $F=1.0\text{-}1.5\ mg/L^{-1}$ (Millions)	Population Influenced by $F>1.5\ mg/L^{-1}$ (Millions)
Uttar Pradesh	139.11	110.28	17.18	11.63
Andhra Pradesh	66.50	63.62	1.60	1.27
Rajasthan	44.00	22.70	6.42	14.83
Maharashtra	78.93	76.41	-	2.44
Madhya Pradesh	66.18	61.48	3.04	1.52
Karnataka	44.97	36.88	5.26	2.78
Punjab	20.28	14.15	2.79	3.28
Haryana	16.46	7.19	2.57	6.67
Delhi	9.42	7.68	0.99	0.73
Orissa	31.66	26.31	1.90	3..41
Bihar	86.37	84.99	1.29	2.68
Tamil Nadu	55.85	47.87	6.36	1.56
Gujarat	41.31	38.83	1.03	1.40
Wes Bengal	67.98	67.98	–	–
Kerala	29.09	28.74	0.11	0.14
Jammu and Kashmir	7.71	7.71	–	–
Himachal Pradesh	5.17	4.71	0.25	00.6
North Eastern State	31.55	31.55	–	–
Total	**842.54**	**739.08**	**50.79**	**54.39**

Source: CGWB Report, 1999.

DENTAL FLUOROSIS

Table 5.2: Criteria for Dean's Fluorosis Index [20] Score Criteria

Source	Criteria
Normal	The enamel represents the usual translucent semivitri form type of structure. The surface is smooth, glossy, and usually of a pale creamy white colour.
Questionable	The enamel discloses slight aberrations from the translucency of normal enamel, ranging from a few white flecks to occasional white spots. This classification is utilized in those instances where a definite diagnosis of the mildest form of fluorosis is not warranted and a classification of "normal" is not justified.
Very Mild	Small opaque, paper white areas scattered irregularly over the tooth but not involving as much as 25% of the tooth surface. Frequently included in this classification are teeth showing no more than about 1-2 mm of white opacity at the tip of the summit of the cusps of the bicuspids or second molars.
Mild	The white opaque areas in the enamel of the teeth are more extensive but do not involve as much as 50% of the tooth.
Moderate	All enamel surfaces of the teeth are affected, and the surfaces subject to attrition show wear. Brown stain is frequently a disfiguring feature.
Severe	Includes teeth formerly classified as "moderately severe and severe." All enamel surfaces are affected and hypoplasia is so marked that the general form of the tooth may be affected. The major diagnostic sign of this classification is discrete or confluent pitting. Brown stains are widespread and teeth often present a corroded-like appearance.

DENTAL FLUOROSIS IN CHILDREN

Table 5.3: Prevalence of Dental Fluorosis Among School going Children Study in Different States of India

Effected Area	Objectionable Dental Fluorosis (%)	Fluoride (ppm)	Reference
Cuddalore district, Tamil Nadu	31.4%	2.1	Saravanan, *et al.* 2008
Anna district. Tamil Nadu	30%	3.8-8.0	Karthikeyan *et al.*, 1996
Kanyakumari district, Tamil Nadu	15.8%	1.5-1.7	Jagan *et al.*, 2008
Shivdaspur, Vanasthali, Rajasthan	82.5%	4.5	Gupta, *et al.*, 1993
Jaipur Rajasthan	61.7%	0.4-6.4	Sohu *et al.*, 2007
Jodhpur Rajashtan	44.5-55.4%	0.7-1.2	Solanki *et al.*, 2011
Banswara,Udaipur Rajasthan	77.1%	1.5-4.0	Choubisa, 2001
Gurgaon district, Haryana	89.2%	1.90-5.20	Garg, and Singh, 2007

(Table Contd...)

Effected Area	Objectionable Dental Fluorosis (%)	Fluoride (ppm)	Reference
Jhajjar district, Haryana	30-80%	1.86-2.49	Yadav *et al.*, 2009
Gurgaon, Hisar Haryana	54.4%	0.34-8.25	Mary *et al.*, 2010
Alappuzha district, Kerala	35%	1.17-2.92	Gopala Krishnan, *et al.*, 1999
Barabanki district, Uttar Pradesh	78.35%	1.2	Singh, *et al.*, 2011
Karnataka, India	89%	0.6-13.4	Shivashankara, *et al.*, 2000
Karnataka, India	75.54%	1.8-2.0	Veersh, *et al.*, 2010
Assam India	31.3%	5.23	Kotoky, *et al.*, 2008
Raipur Chhattigarh	55-66.2%	1.64-3.12	Pandey, 2010
Mandla, Madhya Pradesh	56%	0.14-11	Dubey, 2004
Mandla, Madhya Pradesh	74.4%	9.22-13	Chakma, *et al.*, 1997
Shivpuri, Madhya Pradesh	45.46%	1.65-3.91	Narwaria and Saksena, 2013

DENTAL FLUOROSIS IN MAN

Table 5.4: Prevalence of Dental Fluorosis Human Population Study in Different States of India

Effected Area	Objectionable Dental Fluorosis (%)	Reference
Vadodara, Gujrat	39.2-59.3	Kotecha, *et al.*, 1999
Birbhum, West Bengal	61-66.7	Majumdar, *et al.*, 2011
Durg, Chattisgardh	8.2	Pandey, 2010
Dungarpur, Rajasthan	39.2-72.1	Choubisa, *et al.*, 2010
Assam	31.3	Chakraborti, *et. al.*, 2000
Uttar Pradesh	28.0	Shrivastave, *et.al.*, 2011
Shivpuri, Madhya Pradesh	86.8	Saksena and Narwaria, 2012
Nalgonda, Andhra Pradesh	30.6	Nirguda, *et al.*, 2010

SKELETAL FLUOROSIS

It was started in 1993 that crippling skeletal fluorosis might occur in people who have ingested 10 to 20 mg fluoride per day for over 10 to 20 year (NRC, 1993). The symptoms include mild rheumatic/arthritic pain in the joints and muscles to severe pain the cervical spine region along with stiffness and rigidity of the joints. The disease may be present in an individual at sub clinical, chronic or acute levels of manifestation (Teotia and Teotia, 1988).

Table 5.5: Prevalence of Skeletal Fluorosis Human Population Study in Different States of India

Effected Area	Objectionable Skeletal Fluorosis (%)	Reference
Nalgonda, Andhra Pradesh	24.9	Nirguda, *et al.*, 2010
Durg, Chattisgarh	38.1	Pandey, 2010
Dungarpur, Rajasthan	27.6	Choubisa, *et al.*, 2010
Bihar	20	Khandare, *et al.*, 2005
Assam	1.74	Chakraborti, *et al.*, 2000
Jhankhand	47.4	Srikanth, *et al.*, 2008
Uttar Pradesh	14.2	Shrivastave, *et al.*, 2011
Shivpuri, Madhya Pradesh	39.2	Saksena and Narwaria, 2012

FLUOROSIS IN CATTEL POPULATION

High-fluoride drinking water in the fluorosis affected villages causes skeletal fluorosis not only in human beings but also in cattle. Despite that, the cases of livestock showing severe symptoms of dental fluorosis in the fluorosis villages are almost absent. Once livestock develop symptoms of dental fluorosis, impairing of health usefulness, they are disposed off to non-fluorosis villages on economic grounds. Once they move to non-fluorosis villages, they become once again healthy and fit to take up productive work. This facility available to cattle is however not available to human beings.

Many of the problems of pollution emanating from livestock system have mostly remained confined to the developed nations. In severely contaminated areas, it has been observed that livestock can survive only for 2-3 years, thereby limiting the reproduction and reducing drastically the success of animal husbandry (Wang, *et al.*, 1992; Wang, *et al.*, 1995). Chronic exposure of fluoridated ground water cause a health problem not only in human beings, but also in domestic animals in the form of fluorosis (Dong, *et al.*, 1992; Wang, *et al.*,1994; Choubisa, 2001; Swarup and Dwivedi, 2002; Yur, *et al.*,2003). Intake or ingestion of high amount of fluoride by humans and animals over a prolonged period is known to cause dental and skeletal fluorosis (WHO, 1970). Chronic fluoride toxicity in the form of dental, skeletal and non-skeletal fluorosis has been studied in cattle (*Bos taurus*), buffaloes (*Bubalus bubalis*) (Choubisa, 2008). Ameliorative salt, aluminum sulphate-$Al_2(SO_4)_3$), has been found to be useful in restoring hematological values except clotting time produced due to sub-acute exposure of sodium fluoride in goats (Vinaykant, 2009).

Table 5.6: Prevalence of Dental Fluorosis in Domestic Animal Fluoride Endemic Area of Shivpuri District

Effected Area	Objectionable Skeletal Fluorosis (%)	Reference
Dungarpur, Rajasthan	18.09-20	Chaubisa, 2010
Bikaner, Rajasthan	37.3-41.7	Chaubisa, *et al.*, 2012
Shivpuri, Madhya Pradesh	38.67	Narwaria and Saksena, 2012
Shivpuri, Madhya Pradesh	45	Narwaria and Saksena, 2013

RECOMMENDATIONS

The remedial measure such as rainwater harvesting, supply of drinking water and food supplements for the places where fluoride is present, are needed. Environmental awareness programme for the health implications due to fluoride should be emphasized through public education and rural community participation. Rural people and cattle owners need to be made aware of the plants that are easily available in the surrounding and rich calcium and vitamin C. It should be emphasized that these plants can be cultivated easily without any large investment, and their water demand is also less. These plants and their leaves, fruit and flower are available to the goats all round the year. A list of calcium and vitamin C rich plants available in this area has been given in Table 5.7.

Table 5.7: Calcium and Vitamin Content (mg/100 % dry wt) in Edible Parts* of Common Plants in Studies Area

Sl. No.	Name of Plant	Common Name (% Dry wt)	Calcium (mg/100g)	Vitamin C	Reference
1.	*Acacia nilotica*	Babool	F-0.64%L-2.53%	–	Carter, 1980
2.	*Zizphusjujube*	Ber	F-106.3-117.5 L-3612.7-4961.3%	F-309.3-364	San *et al.*, 2009
3.	*Zizphus nummularia*	Jungli/Jar ber		F-85	Goyal & Sharma, 2009
4.	*Temarindus Indica*	Imali	S-248.56 Pu-35-17 Fl-35.5	Pu-0.7-3.0 Fl-13.8 L-3.0	Pugalenthi, *et al.*, 2004
5.	*Emblica officinals*	Amala	F-0.05%	F-6000	Khan, 2009
6.	*Cordia dichotoma*	Indian Cherry	F-55	–	Rathor, 2009
7.	*Ficus bengalensis*	Bargad	F-1.8	–	Roby, 2000

* L-Leaves, Pu- Pulp, Fl-Flower, F= Fruits, S=Seeds.

REFERENCES

1. Agarwal, V., Vaish, A.K. and Vaish, P. (1997). Ground Water Quality: Focus on Fluoride and Fluorosis in Rajasthan. *Cur. Sci.*, 73 (99): 743-746.
2. Apparao, B.V. and Karthikeyan, G. (1986). Permissible Limits of Fluoride Ion in Drinking Water in Indian Rural Environment. *Indian J. Environ. Protection*, 6: 172-175.
3. Bhargava, R.K., Saxena, S.C. and Thergaonkar, V.P. (1978). Ground Water Quality in Ajmer District. *Indian J. Environ. Hlth.*, 20: 290-299.
4. Carter, J.O. (1980). Acacia Nilotica: A Tree Legume Out of Control in: Gutteridge R.C. Shelton H.M. Editors. Forage Tree Legumes in Tropical Agriculture. St. Lucia, Queensland, Australia: The Tropical Grassland Society of Australia; Chapter 7.2: 279-290.
5. Chakraborti, D., Chanda, C.R., Samanta, G., Chowdhury, U.K., Mukherjee, S.C., Pal, A.B.,Sharma, B., Mahanta, K.J., Ahmed, H.A., Singh, B. (2000). Fluorosis in Assam, India. *Curr. Sci.*, 78: 1421-1423.
6. Chandrajith, R., Abeypal, U. Dissanyaka, C.B. and Tobschall H.J (2007). Fluoride in Ceylon Tea and its Implications to Dental Health. Environ Geoch and Health 29(5): 429-434.
7. Chandrawanshi, C.K., and Patel, K.S. (1999). Fluoride Deposition in Cental India. *Environ. Mon. Assess.*, 55: 251-265.
8. Chinoy, N.J., Narayana, M.V., Sequeira, E., Joshi, S. M., Barot, J.M., Purohit, R.M., Parikh, D.J. and Ghodasara, N.B. (1992). Studies on Effects of Fluoride in 36 Villages of Mehsana District, Norht Gujarat. *Fluoride*, 25: 101-110.
9. Choubisa, S. L., Sompura, K., Bhatt, S.K., Choubisa, D.K., Pandya, H., Joshi, S.C. and Choubisa, L. (1996a). Prevalence of Fluorosis in Some Villages of Dungarpur District of Rajasthan. *Indian J. Environ. Hlth.*, 38: 119-126.
10. Choubisa, S.L., Sompura, K., Choubisa, D.K. and Sharma, O.P. (1996b). Fluoride in Drinking Water Sources of Udaipur District of Rajasthan. *Indian J. Environ. Hlth.*, 38: 286-291.
11. Choubisa, S.L., Sompura, K., Choubisa, D.K., Pandya, H., Bhatt, S.K., Sharma, O.P. and Parmer, L. (1995). Fluoride Content in Domestic Water Sources of Dungarpur District of Rajasthan. *Indian J. Environ. Hlth.*, 37: 154-160.
12. Choubisa, S.L. (1998). Fluorosis in Some Tribal Villages of Udaipur District (Rajasthan). *J. Environ. Bio.*, 19: 341-352.
13. Choubisa, S.L. (2001). Endemic Fluorosis in Southern Rajasthan, India. Fluoride 34(1): 61-70.
14. Choubisa, S.L. (2008). Dental Fluorosis in Domestic Animals. Curr. Sci.95(12): 1674-1675.
15. Das, S., Mehta, B.C., Samanta, S.K., Das, P.K., Srivastava, S.K. (2000). Fluoride Hazards in Groundwater of Orissa, India. *Indian J. Environ. Hlth.*, 42: 40-46.
16. Datta, P.S., Tyagi, S.K., Mookerjee, P., Bhattacharya, S.K., Gupta, N. and Bhatnagar, P.D. (1999). Groundwater NO3 and F Contamination Processes in Puskar Valley, Rajasthan as Reflected from 18O Isotopic Signature and 3H Recharge Studies. *Environ. Monit. Asses.*, 56: 209-219.
17. Dong, B.S., G.Y. Zhao and Q.X. Li (1992). Studies on the Goat Tooth of Industrial Fluorosis Areas, Inner Monglian. J. Animal Sci. Prod.47(2): 1-4.

18. Goyal, M and S.K. Sharma (2009). Traditional Wisdom and Value Edition Prospects of Arid Foods of Desert Region of North West India. Indian J. Trad. Know.8(4): 581-585.
19. Gupta S.S., Banerjee, R. Saha J.K. Datta and Mondal N.(2006). Fluoride Geochemistry of Groundwater in Birbhum, West Bengal, India Fluoride, 39: 318-320.
20. Gupta, A. (1999). Assam.s Karbi Anglong District is Hit by Crippling Fluoride Contamination. Sunday, *ABP Publishers*, Calcutta, 26: p. 52.
21. Gupta, M.K., Singh, V. and Dass, S. (1994a). Ground Water Quality of Block Bichpuri, Agra (India) with Special Reference to Fluoride. *Fluoride*, 27: 89-92.
22. Gupta, M.K., Singh, V., Rajwanshi, P., Agarwal, M., Rai, K., Srivastava, S., Srivastav, R., and Dass, S. (1999a). Groundwater Quality Assessment of Tehsil Kheragarh, Agra, (India) with Special Reference to Fluoride. *Environ. Monit. Asses.*, 59: 275-285.
23. Gupta, S.C. (1991). Chemical Character of Groundwater in Nagur District, Rajasthan. *Indian J.Environ. Hlth.*, 33: 341-349.
24. Gupta, S.C., 1981. Evaluation of Well Waters in Udaipur. *Indian J. Environ. Hlth.*, 23: 195-202.
25. Gupta, S.C., Rathore, G.S., and Doshi, C.S. (1993). Fluoride Distribution in Groundwaters of Southeastern Rajasthan. *Indian J. Environ. Hlth.*, 35: 97-109.
26. Gupta, S.K. and Sharma, P. (1995). An Approach to Tackling Fluoride Problem in Drinking Water. *Curr. Sci.*, 68: 774.
27. Gupta, S.C., and Varshney, C.P. (1999). Iodide Concentration in Groundwaters of Western Rajasthan, *Indian J. Environ. Hlth.* 41: 59-64.
28. Handa, B.K. (1975). Geochemistry and Genesis of Fluoride Containing Ground Waters in India. *Groundwater*, 13: 275-281.
29. Khan, K.H. (2009). Roles of Emblica Officinalis in Medicine: A Review. Bot. Res. Inernt.2 (4): 218-228.
30. Kumar, V.V., Sai, C.S.T., Swami, M.S.R. and Rao, P.L.K.M. (1993). Nitrates in Groundwater Sources in Medchal Block of Andra Pradesh. *Indian J. Environ. Hlth.*, 35: 40-46.
31. Latha, S.S., Ambika, S.R. and Prasad, S.J. (1999). Fluoride Contamination Status of Groundwater in Karnataka. *Curr. Sci.*, 76: 730-734.
32. Mascarenhas, A.K and Burt, B.A. (1998). Fluorosis Risk from Early Exposure to Fluoride Toothpaste. Commun. Dentist. Oral Epidem., 26: 241-248.
33. Maithani, P.B., Gurjar, R., Banerjee, R., Balaji, B.K., Ramachandran, S. and Singh, R. (1998). Anomalous Fluoride in Groundwater from Westen Part of Sirohi District, Rajasthan and its Crippling Effects on Human Health. *Curr. Sci.*, 74: 773-777.
34. Narwaria, Y.S and D.N. Saksena (2012). Incidence of Dental Fluorosis in Domestic Animals of Shivpuri, Madhya Pradesh, India. J. Environ. Res. Devlop.7(1A): 426-430.
35. Narwaria, Y.S. and Saksena, D.N. (2013). Prevalence of Dental Fluorosis in Goats (Copra Hircus) in Some Villages of Karera Block in Shivpuri District, Madhya Pradesh, Int. J. cur. Tren. Res., 2 (1): 22-26.
36. Narwaria, Y.S. and Saksena, D.N. (2013). Prevalence of Dental Fluorosis Among Primary School Children in Rural Areas of Karera Block of Shivpuri District, Madhya Pradesh, India, Indian J. pedi., 80 (9): 718-720.
37. National Research Council. Health Effects of Ingested Fluoride, National Academy Press. Washington DC 1993.
38. Nawlakhe, W.G., Lutade, S.L., Patni, P.M. and Deshpande, L.S. (1995). Groundwater Quality in Shivpuri District in Madhya Pradesh. *Indian J. Environ. Hlth.*, 37: 278-284.

39. Ozha, D.D., Varshney, C.P. and Bohra, J.L. (1993). Nitrate in Groundwater of Some Districts of Rajasthan. *Indian J. Envriron. Hlth.*, 35: 15-19.

40. Patra, R.C., Dwivedi, S.K., Bhardwaj, B., Swarup, D., (2000). Industrial Fluorosis in Cattle and Buffalo Around Udaipur, *India, Sci. Total Environ.*, 253: 145-150.

41. Pugalenthi, M.,V. Vadivel, P. Gurumoorthi and K. Janardhana (2004). Comparative Nutritional Evaluation of Little Known Legume, Tamarindus Indica, Erathyrina Indica and Sesban Bispinosa. Trop. Subtrop. Agro Ecosyst. 4: 107-123.

42. Ramesam, V and Rajagopalan, K. (1985). Fluoride Ingestion into the Natural Waters of Hard-rock Areas, Peninsular India. *J. Geol. Soc. India,* 26: 125-132.

43. Ramesam, V. (1987). Hydrogeochemistry of Fluoride in the Drought-prone Hard-rock Regions of Peninsular India. *Fluoride,* 20: 4-10.

44. Rao, N.S. and Prasad, P.R. (1997). Phosphate Pollution in the Groundwater of Lower Vamsadhara River Basin, India. *Environ. Geol.*, 31: 117-122.

45. Rao, N.V.R., Rao, N., Rao, K.S.P. and Schuiling, R.D. (1993). Fluorine Distribution in Waters of Nalgonda District, Andra Pradesh, India. *Environ. Geol.*, 21: 84-89.

46. Rathor, M. (2009). Nutritional Content of Important Fruit Trees from Arid Zone of Rajasthan. J. Hortic. Forest 1(7): 103-108.

47. Ray, D., Rao, R.R., Bhoi, A.V., Biswas, A.K., Ganguly, A.K. Sanyal, P.I., (2000). Physico-chemical Quality of Drinking Water in Rohtas District of Bihar, *Environ. Monit. Asses.*, 61: 387-398.

48. Reddy, K.S., Prasad, K.S.S. and Raju, A.N. (1999). A Bigeochemical Study of the Podili and Tirupati Area of Andhra Pradesh, India. *Environ. Geol.*, 37: 313-316.

49. Roby, J., T. Nathan, J. Balasingh, T.H. Kunz (2000). Chemical Composition of Leaves Eaten by Shot Note Fruit Bat Cynopterus sphinx. J. Chem. Eco. 26: 2825-2841.

50. Saksena, D.N. and Narwaria, Y.S. (2012). Incidence of Fluoride in Groundwater and its Potential Health Effects in Ten Villages of Karera Block in Shivpuri District, Madhya Pradesh, India Int. J. Environ. Sc., 3(3): 1141-1149.

51. Sahu, N.K. and Karim, M.A. (1989). Fluoride Incidence in Natural Waters in Amreli District, Gujarat. *Jour. Geol. Soc. India,* 33: 450-456.

52. San, B., A.N. Yildirim, M. Polat and F. Yildirim (2009). Mineral Composition of Leaves and Fruits of Some Promising Jujube (Zizyphus Jujube Milller) Genotypes. Asian J.Chem. 21: 2898-2902.

53. Singh, A., Malkotra, K.C., Singh, B.M. and Mathur, O.C. and Khosla, H.M. (1965). Endemic Fluorosis: Chemical Constituents of Water. *Ind. J.. Med. Res.*, 53: 866-870.

54. Singh, V. Narain, R. and Prakash, C. (1987). Fluoride in Irrigation Waters of Agra District, Uttar Pradesh. *Wat. Res.*, 21: 889-890.

55. Srikanth, R., Khanam, A. and Rao, A. M.M. (1994). Fluoride in Borehole Water in Selected Villages of Medak Districk, Andra Pradesh, India. *Fluoride,* 27: 93-96.

56. Susheela, A.K., Bhatnagar, M. and Kumar, A. (1996). Status of Drinking Water in the Mega City Delhi. Proceedings of the 22nd WEDC (Water, Environment and Management Conference), New Delhi, India: 1-3.

57. Susheela, A.K. (1999). Fluoride Management Programme in India. Curr. Sci 77(10) 1250-1256.

58. Swarup, D and S.K. Dwivedi (2002). Environmental Pollution and Effects of Lead and Fluoride on Animal's Health New Delhi. Indian Coun. Agri. Res.

59. Teotia SPS, Teotia M. Endemic Skeletal Fluorosis: Clinical and Radiological Variants. Fluoride1988; 21: 39-4.

60. Teotia, S.P.S and Teotia M. (1991). Endemic Fluoride: Bone and Teeth Update. Indian. J. Environ Toxicol. 1:1-6.

61. Teotia, S.P.S and Teotia M. (1994). Endemic Fluorosis in India: A Challenging National Health Problem. J. Assoc. Phys., 1984; 32:347-352.

62. Vani, M.L. and Reddy, K.P. (2000). Effects of Fluoride Accumulation on Some Enzymes of Brain and Gastrocneminus Muscle of Mice. Fluoride, 33: 17-26.

63. Vinaykant, A. Srivastava, P.K. Verma, R. Raina, K.P. Nrip and R.S. Pura (2009). Negligible Ameliorative Effect of Alluminium Sulphate on Oxidative Stress Parameters in Goats during sub Acute Fluoride Intoxication. Fluoride 42(2): 117-120.

64. Wang, J.D., C.W. Zhan, Y.F. Chen, J.X. Li, W.F. Wang and J.P. Cai (1992). A Study of Damage of Hard Tissues of Goats due to Industrial Fluoride Pollution. Fluoride 25(3): 123-130.

65. Wang, J.D., J.H. Hong, J.X Li and J.P. Cai (1994). The Rffect of Nutrition Supplementation during the Annual Dry Grass Season on Tooth Wear in Industry- Fluorosed Goats. Fluoride 27 (3): 136-140.

66. Wang, J.D., J.P. Hong and J.X. Li (1995). Studies on Alleviation of Industrial Fluorosis in Baotou Goats. Fluoride 28(3): 131-134.

67. Wedepohl (1974). Hand Book of Geochemistry. Springer-Verlage Berlin. Heidelberg. Newyork. 2(4): 9K-1 pp.

68. Wodeyar, B.K. and Sreenivasan, G. (1996). Occurrence of Fluoride in the Groundwaters and its Impact in Peddavankahalla Basin, Bellary District, Karnataka - A Preliminary Study. *Curr. Sci.*, 70: 71-73.

69. World Health Organisation (1970). Fluoride and Human Health Monograph Series No. 59, WHO, Geneva.

70. World Health Organisation (1984). Guideline for Drinking Water Quality (Vol. II) Health Criteria and Supporting Information. World Health Organisation, Geneva, Switzerland.

Pages: 75-86

WATER RESOURCES MANAGEMENT: ***MONITORING AND ASSESSMENT***

Edited by: Dr. Sandeep Gupta; Dr. Pawan Kumar 'Bharti'

ISBN: 978-93-5056-799-9

Edition: **2016**

Published by: **Discovery Publishing House Pvt. Ltd., New Delhi (India)**

6

Environmental Assessment of Harvested Rain Water from Bodo Community in Rivers State, Nigeria

Osu, Charles I; Ikhioya Peace E., Obuzor, G.U.

ABSTRACT

This study was carried out to determine the quality of rainwater from three different roofing materials (asbestos, aluminum and zinc) in Bodo Community of Rivers State, Nigeria. Samples were taken to the laboratory and analyzed using standard analytical procedures. The average result obtained ranged from 6.0-7.0, 40-66 µsi/cm, 18-48 mg/l, 32.52-86.67 mg/L, 0.06-3.18 mg/L, 5.02-13.76 mg/L, 2.79-5.02 mg/L, 0.16-0.77 mg/L, 0.27-5.79 mg/L, 0.24-0.62 mg/L and 0.03-4.08 mg/L for pH, conductivity, chloride, salinity, nitrate, sulphate, sodium, magnesium, calcium, iron and zinc respectively. Of interest were rainwater samples from asbestos roofing sheets which gave high calcium and magnesium content. Also, zinc roofing sheet gave high zinc and iron content compared to other roofing sheets. Physico-chemical properties and metal content of the harvested water from the roofing sheets were considerably different from those of control samples (water collected directly from raindrop). This could mean that the impinging of rain drop on the roof gradually erodes the roof material or could be as a result of anthropogenic inputs (deposits of pollutants in contact

Department of Pure and Industrial Chemistry, University of Port Harcourt, P.M.B 5323 Choba, Port Harcourt, Rivers State, Nigeria with roofing sheet) or geographical location. Considering the result of the analysis the harvested water could be put to other domestic use, as they cannot be consumed directly.

Keywords: rainwater, roof materials, water quality

INTRODUCTION

The issue of rainwater harvesting is now a widely used technique for the provision and supply of both portable and non-portable supply of water especially in developing Worlds where the main water are insufficient to meet the growing needs of the society due to rapid industrialization and development as well as population growth (Olaoye and Olaniyan, 2012). In many areas of the world today, it can either be the only source of water for the household or more commonly a supplementary supply to ease the burden of water collection from other sources (Vikaskumar *et al.*, 2007). Of all the rainwater harvesting methods, the rainwater runoff from household roofs is the most common form of rainwater harvesting.

Apart from being cost effective and the ease of maintenance for effective long term system operation, the roof top runoff also has less contamination of rainwater runoff as compared with ground catchment system. Furthermore, roof catchment provides water supply at the point of consumption (Gould and Nissen-Peterson, 1999). The harvest is relevant in areas having significant rainfall but lacking conventional water supply system. The effective roof area and material used in construction influence the efficiency of collection, water quality and quantity. Despite having some clear advantages over other sources, rainwater use has frequently been rejected on the ground of its limited capacity or due to water quality concerns. This is unfortunate as in many cases some simple upgrading and the integrated use of rainwater collection with other technologies is all that is required to obtain a cost effective and reliable water supply solution (Ragab, *et al.*, 2003). Roofs provide an ideal catchment surface for harvesting rainwater, provided they are clean. However, Chang *et al.*, 2004 reported that roofs can be a serious source of nonpoint source pollution as well. Contamination by chemical pollutants may arise from a variety of materials with which the rainwater comes into contact; starting from the atmosphere. Rainwater could dissolve gases and wash off chemicals from contacting dust particles and roof materials (Quek and Forster, 1993).

Several studies have looked at the effect of roofing material on harvested rainwater quality but common roofing materials and coating will vary across the country and the world (Olaoye and Olaniyan, 2012). It therefore becomes important to assess the quality of rainwater from different roof material within the case study area.

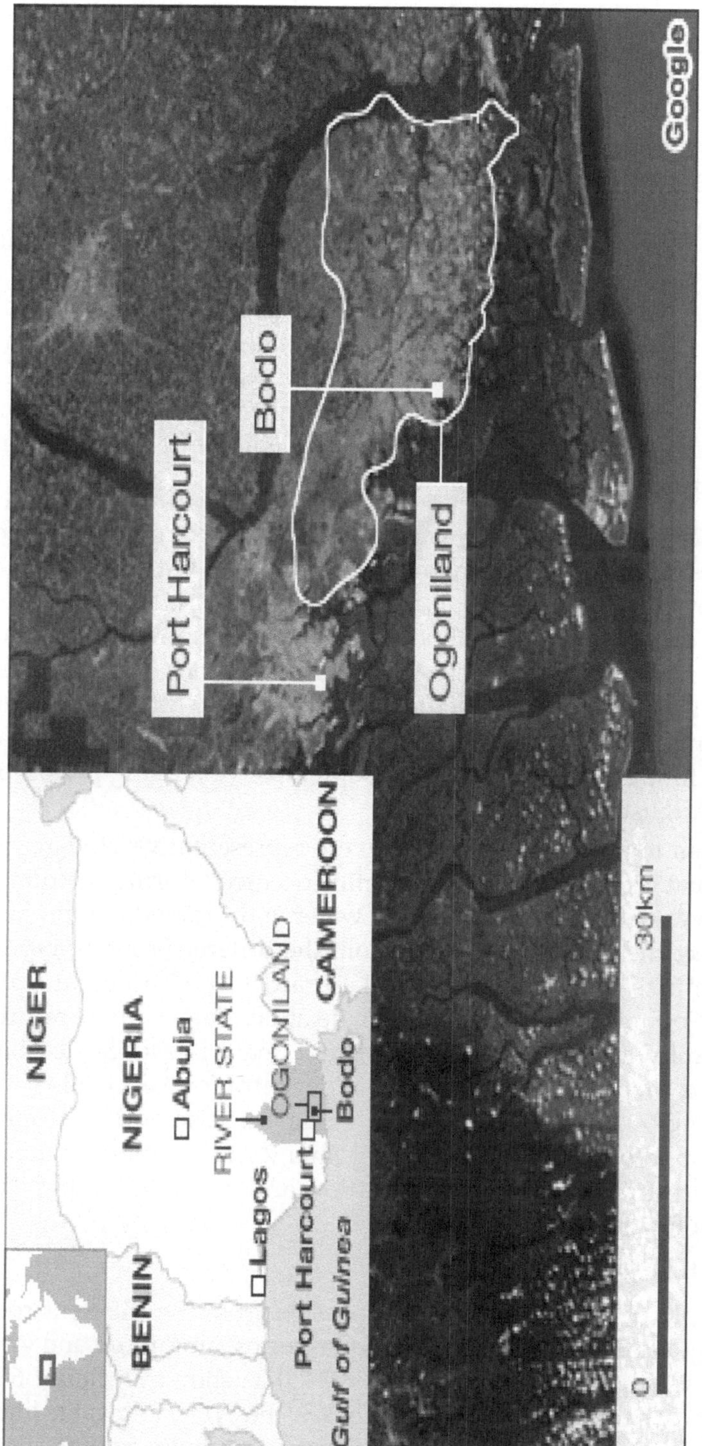

Fig. 6.1: Map showing the position of Bodo

This chapter investigates the physical and chemical properties of rainwater harvested from different types of roofing sheets.

Study Area

Bodo is an Ogoni community located in Gokana Local Government Area of Rivers State. It has an estimated population of 69,000 people. It is located at an elevation of 399 meters above sea level. It is made up of 35 villages. The vast community is Ogoni but other ethnic groups are represented including Ibibio, Igbo and Hausa. This study area was chosen because of non-availability of public or private water mains in the area, the major source of water for domestic use are from rain, hand dug well and borehole. Unfortunately, the majority of the wells dry up during the dry season when the rain ceases while the borehole water is sold. The community relies extensively on available rainwater because it is cheap and accessible in the raining season.

MATERIALS AND METHODS

A random sampling technique was employed in selecting the sampled household. Harvested rainwater samples were collected via roof-top run off. Three selected roofing sheet materials were analyzed for physico-chemical and metal content using standard method for the examination of water. The roofing materials include asbestos (A), Aluminum (B), Zinc(C) and control samples (D) which was collected directly without contact with any roofing material. Water samples were collected in the months of May (at the onset of rainfall), July (the first peak of rainfall) and September (the rising period of rainfall after the August break).

Care was taken to ensure that samples were representative of water to be examined and that no accidental contamination occurred during sampling. Sample containers were rinsed with distilled water and drained before they were used to collect the rainwater sample from the different roofing types. The collected samples were taken to the laboratory for immediate pH determination. All pH measurements were made at laboratory temperature. Samples and control were treated in triplicate and analysis was carried out following standard methods (APHA, 1998). Concentration of metals (Na, Mg, Ca, Fe, Pb and Zn) were determined using Buck scientific atomic absorption spectrophotometer (AAS), GBC Avanta 2.02. Samples for metal determination were first subjected to digestion and aspirated using the appropriate lamps for the metals.

RESULT AND DISCUSSION

The average pH of rainwater samples collected from the different roof types ranged from 6.0-6.2, 6.6-6.8 and 6.2-6.4 for asbestos, aluminum and zinc roofs respectively while control ranged from 6.7-7.0 as shown in figure 6.2. The pHvalues of most samples analyzed were below the WHO allowable limit for portable water (6.5-8.5) except water samples from aluminum roofing sheet that fell within WHO allowable limit. The pH values obtained in this study agreed with the result of Yaziz, *et al.,* (1989) and Simmons *et al.,* (2001) with reported pH of 5.2 to 11.4 for harvested rainwater.

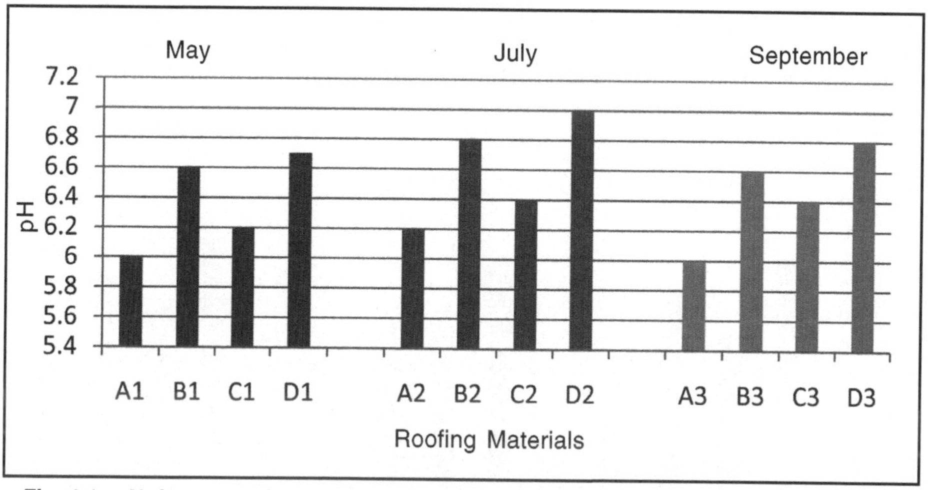

Fig. 6.2: pH Concentration of Rainwater Harvested from Different Roofing Materials
A = Asbestos, B = Aluminum, C = Zinc, D = Control

The conductivity values obtained ranged from 57-66µsi/cm, 45-48µsi/cm, 47-52µsi/cm for asbestos, aluminum and zinc respectively while control ranged from 40-42µsi/cm. This is in accordance with Mendez *et al.,* (2010) that reported a range from 18 to 61µsi/cm. It was observed that conductivity was highest in the water collected from rooftop with asbestos roofing sheet irrespective of the period of collection as shown in Figure 6.3. This was followed by zinc roofing sheet and then aluminum roofing sheet. However, all the values were less than 900µsi/cm which is the WHO drinking water quality standard.

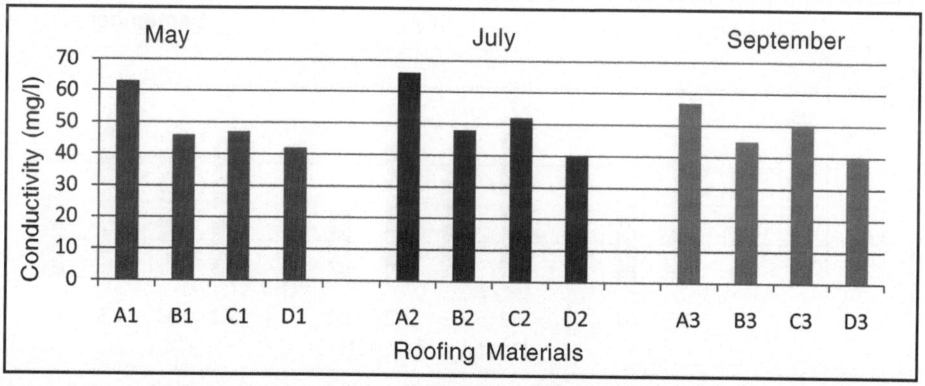

Fig. 6.3: Conductivity Concentration of Rainwater Harvested from Different Roofing Materials
A = Asbestos, B = Aluminum, C = Zinc, D = Control

The average salinity values ranged from 75.84-86.67 mg/l, 52.38-61.40 mg/l, 63.21-72.23 mg/l for asbestos, aluminum and zinc roofing sheets respectively while control ranged from 32.52-45.16 mg/l. It was observed from Figure 6.4 that salinity was highest in water samples obtained from asbestos roofing sheet irrespective of the period of collection. However, all the values were less than the WHO maximum allowable limit for drinking water standard (500mg/l).

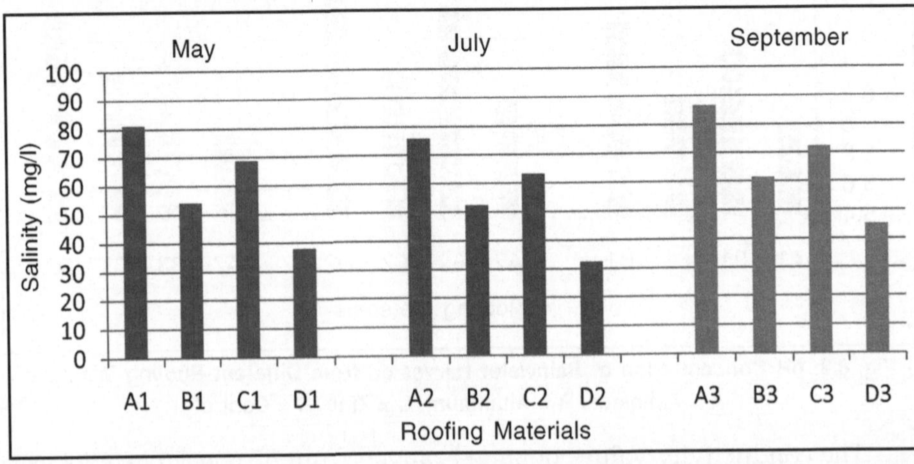

Fig. 6.4: Salinity Concentration of Rainwater Harvested from Different Roofing Materials
A = Asbestos, B = Aluminum, C = Zinc, D = Control

Figure 6.5 shows chloride concentrations from the different roofing materials. The chloride concentration in all analyzed samples ranged from 42-48 mg/l, 29-34mg/l, 35-40 mg/land 18-25 mg/l for asbestos, aluminum, zinc and control respectively. The chloride values agreed with Eruola *et al.*, (2010) that ranged from 20 to 35mg/l.

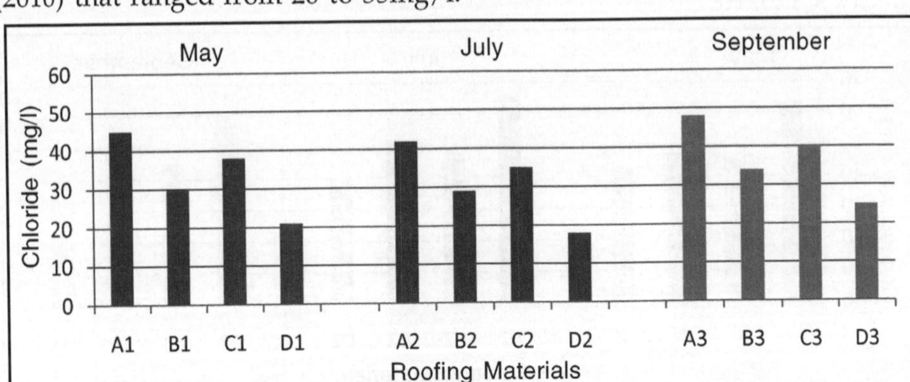

Fig. 6.5: Chloride Concentration of Rainwater Harvested from Different Roofing Materials
A = Asbestos, B = Aluminum, C = Zinc, D = Control

Nitrate values obtained from all the water samples analyzed fell below the WHO standard (50mg/l), ranging from 2.44-3.18 mg/l for asbestos roofing sheet, 0.16-1.12mg/l for aluminum roofing sheet, 1.15-1.56 mg/l for zinc and 0.06-0.12 mg/l for water collected directly from raindrop (Figure 6.6). Sulphate values obtained ranged from 11.23-13.76 mg/l for asbestos roofing sheet, 8.46-10.34 mg/l for aluminum roofing sheet and 10.81-12.38 mg/l for zinc roofing sheet while control ranged from 5.02-7.22 mg/l. The WHO limit for sulphate is 250mg/l.

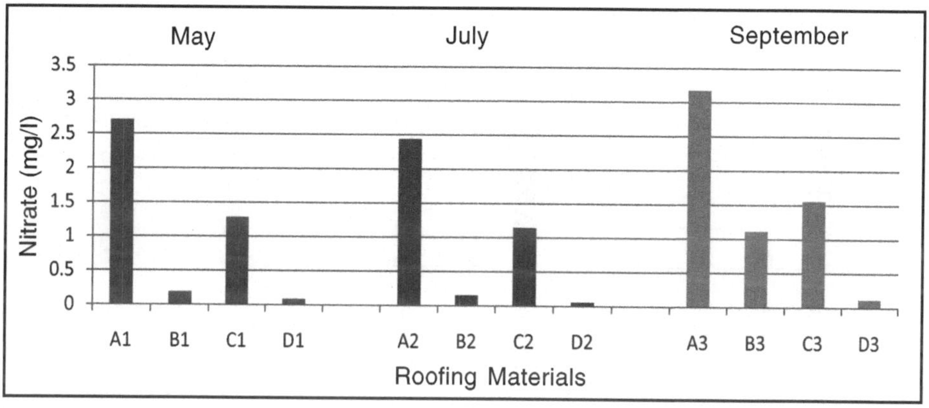

Fig. 6.6: Nitrate Concentration of Rainwater Harvested from Different Roofing Materials
A = Asbestos, B = Aluminum, C = Zinc, D = Control

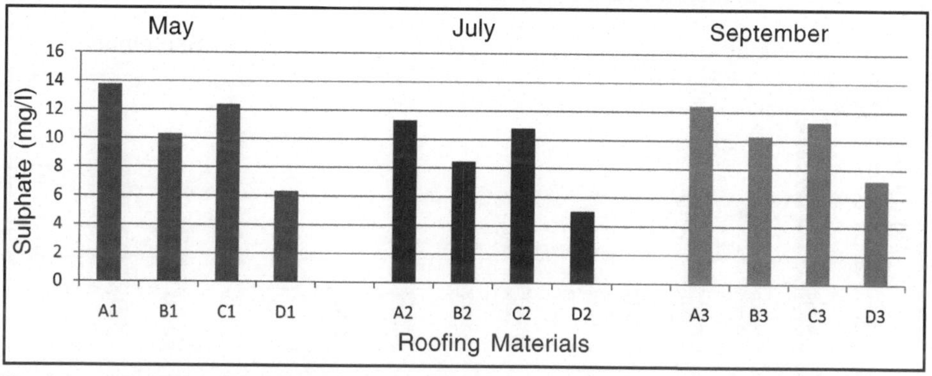

Fig. 6.7: Sulphate Concentration of Rainwater Harvested from Different Roofing materials
A = Asbestos, B = Aluminum, C = Zinc, D = Control

Figure 6.8 and Figure 6.9 shows calcium and magnesium concentration of the different roofing materials during the various rainfall periods in the study area. The calcium values ranged from 4.26-5.79 mg/l, 1.08-1.28 mg/l, 2.04-3.01 mg/l and 0.27-0.81 mg/l for asbestos, aluminum, zinc roofs and control samples respectively. The magnesium values ranged from 0.50-0.77 mg/l, 0.31-0.49 mg/l, 0.45-0.63 mg/l and 0.16-0.23 mg/l for asbestos, aluminum, zinc roofs and control samples respectively. Calcium and Magnesium in water gives rise to hardness of water. It was observed from Fig. 6.7 and Fig. 8 that water samples collected from asbestos roofing sheet gave the highest calcium and magnesium concentrations irrespective of the period of collection. This could be traceable to the level of magnesium and calcium carbonate content that can be leached from the roofing material.

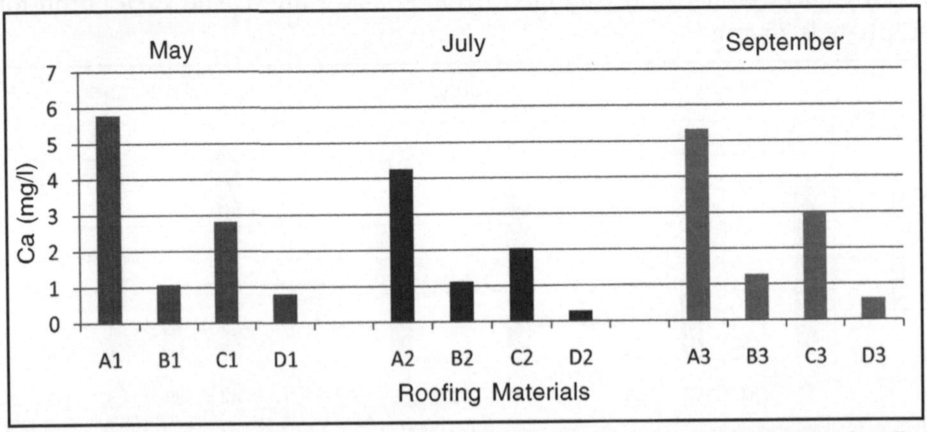

Fig. 6.8: Calcium Concentration of Rainwater Harvested from Different Roofing Materials
A = Asbestos, B = Aluminum, C = Zinc, D = Control

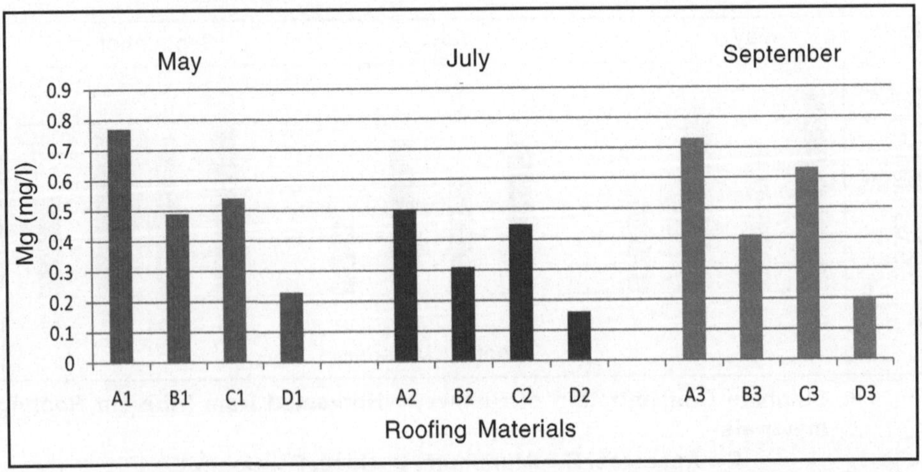

Fig. 6.9: Magnesium Concentration of Rainwater Harvested from Different Roofing Materials
A = Asbestos, B = Aluminum, C = Zinc, D = Control

The value of sodium for all water samples analyzed from the roofing sheets ranged from 3.15-3.41 mg/l, 3.04-3.90 mg/l, 3.94-5.02 mg/l and 2.79-3.01 mg/l for asbestos roof, aluminum roof, zinc roof and control respectively. Water sample from zinc roof had the highest value of sodium (Figure 6.10).

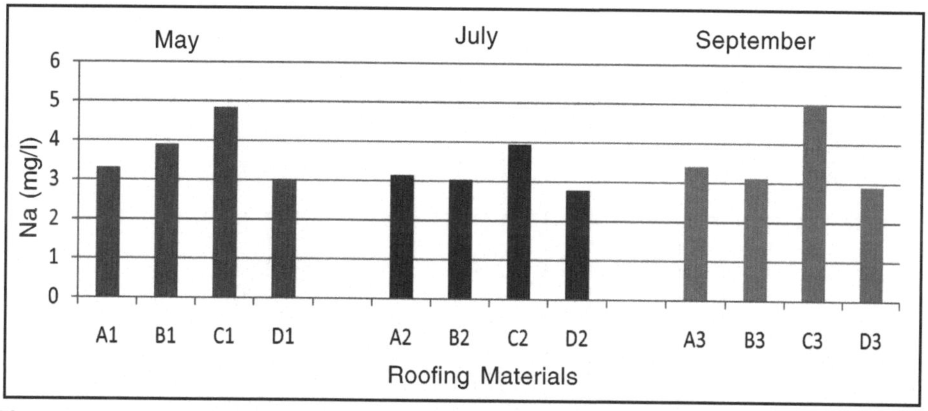

Fig. 6.10: Sodium Concentration of Rainwater Harvested from Different Roofing Materials
A = Asbestos, B = Aluminum, C = Zinc, D = Control

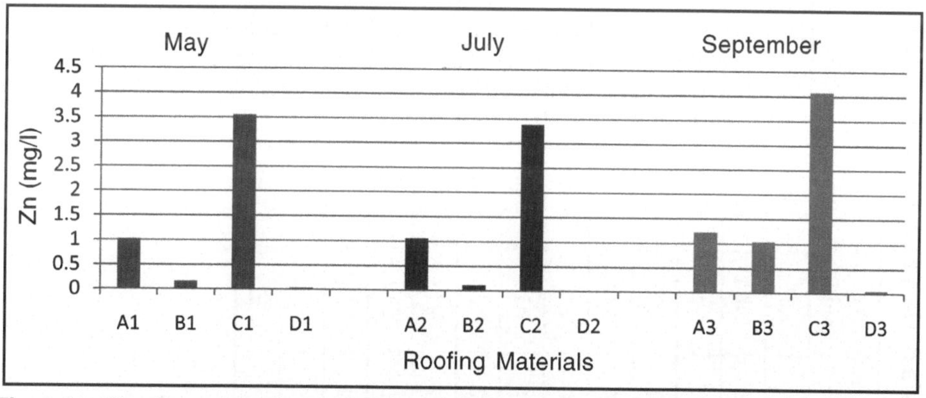

Fig. 6.11: Zinc Concentration of Rainwater Harvested from Different Roofing Materials
A = Asbestos, B = Aluminum, C = Zinc, D = Control

It was observed from Figure 6.11 that samples from zinc roofing sheet had the highest value of zinc as compared to other roofing sheets and the control. The values of zinc concentration from all the samples ranged from 1.02-1.23 mg/l, 0.11-1.04 mg/l, 3.39-4.08 mg/l and 0.01-0.05 mg/l for asbestos, aluminum, zinc roofs and control water samples respectively. This reflects a general contamination of the runoff from the zinc roofing sheet by the metal, which could be as a result of corrosion. Lead was not detected in any of the water samples analyzed. This may be due to the fact there are no industries and heavy traffic in the study area in which the samples were collected. According to Eletta and Oyeyipo, 2008 lead was also not detected from most of the rainwater samples harvested from roof runoff. However, all analyzed samples for metals fell within the WHO allowable limits for metals in drinking water except for Iron which had a value of 0.37mg/l and 0.62 mg/l in water sample collected from zinc roofing sheet (Table 6.1).

Table 6.1: Physicochemical and Metal Analysis of Harvested Roof Top Water Sample

Sample	pH	EC (µsi/cm)	Cl^- (mg/l)	Salinity (mg/l)	NO_3^{2-} (mg/l)	SO_4^{2-} (mg/l)	Na (mg/l)	Mg (mg/l)	Ca (mg/l)	Fe (mg/l)	Pb (mg/l)	Zn (mg/l)
A1	6.0	63	45	81.26	2.71	13.76	3.31	0.77	5.79	Nil	Nil	1.02
B1	6.6	46	30	54.18	0.19	10.32	3.90	0.49	1.08	Nil	Nil	0.16
C1	6.2	47	38	68.62	1.28	12.38	4.84	0.54	2.82	0.37	Nil	3.55
D1	6.7	42	21	37.94	0.09	6.33	3.01	0.23	0.81	Nil	Nil	0.03
A2	6.2	66	42	75.84	2.44	11.23	3.15	0.50	4.26	Nil	Nil	1.06
B2	6.8	48	29	52.38	0.16	8.46	3.04	0.31	1.12	Nil	Nil	0.11
C2	6.4	52	35	63.21	1.15	10.81	3.94	0.45	2.04	0.24	Nil	3.39
D2	7.0	40	18	32.52	0.06	5.02	2.79	0.16	0.27	Nil	Nil	0.01
A3	6.0	57	48	86.67	3.18	12.43	3.41	0.73	5.33	Nil	Nil	1.23
B3	6.6	45	34	61.40	1.12	10.34	3.12	0.41	1.28	Nil	Nil	1.04
C3	6.4	50	40	72.23	1.56	11.32	5.01	0.63	3.01	0.62	Nil	4.08
D3	6.8	40	25	45.16	0.12	7.22	2.91	0.20	0.60	Nil	Nil	0.05
WHO LIMIT	6.5 -8.5	900	250	500	50	250	200	20	75	0.3	0.01	5

CONCLUSION

Rooftop runoff quality is dependent on both the roof type and the environmental conditions (not only the local climate but also the atmosphere pollution). From the results presented in this research, it is observed that though quality of water harvested from the selected roofing materials at different rainfall periods fall within the WHO standard limit, some level of contamination was prominent. The water samples from asbestos roofing sheet relatively had the highest level of contamination, followed by zinc roofing sheet and then aluminum roofing sheet had the least contamination.

The result also indicated that that the concentrations of the physicochemical parameters as well as the metals from the roofing sheets were considerably higher than those of control samples. This could mean that the impinging of rain drop on the roof gradually erodes the material used in the making of the roof. However, the variations in the concentration could be as a result of anthropogenic inputs (deposit pollutants in contact with roofing sheets). Also, geographical location could have affected the level of contamination. Rainwater from aluminum roofing sheet proved to be most suitable. None the less, to ensure rainwater satisfies health requirement for consumption, all rainwater should be given some level of treatment. However, all rainwater samples are quite safe for all other domestic uses such as laundry, bathing, toilet flushing and other cleaning works.

REFERENCES

APHA, (1998). Standard Method for the Examination of Water and Waste Water, 20th ed., American Public Health Association, Washinton, DC, p. 1220.

Chang, M; McBroom, W and Beasley, R. (2004). Roofing as a Source of Non-point Water Pollution. *Journal of Environmental Management*. 73(4): 307-315.

Eletta, O.A and Oyeyipo, J.O. (2008). Rainwater Harvesting: Effect of Age of Roof on Water Quality. *International Journal of Applied Chemistry*. 4(2): 157-162.

Eruola, A.O; Ufoegbune, G.C; Awomeso, J.A; Adeofun, C.O; Idowu, O.A; and Sowunmi, A. (2010). Qualitative and Quantitative Assessment of Rainwater Harvesting from Rooftop Catchments: Case Study of Oke-Lantoro Community in Abeokuta, Southwest Nigeria. *European Water* 32: 47-56.

Gould, J. and Nissen-peterson, E. (1999). Rainwater Catchment Systems for Domestic Rain: Design Construction and Implementation Intermediate Technology Publication London. p. 335.

Mendez, B.C; Brigit, R.A; Kerry K; Micheal, E.B and Mary, K.(2010). Effect of Roof Material on Water Quality for Rainwater Harvesting Systems. Texas Water Development Board Report, p. 2.

Olaoye, R.A and Olaniyan, O.S (2012). Quality of Rain Water from Different Roof Materials: *International Journal of Engineering and Technology 2(8): 1413-1414.*

Quek, U. and Forster, J. (1993). Trace Metalsin Roof Runoff. *Water Air and Soil Poll* 68 (3-4): 373-89.

Ragab, R; Bromey, J; Roser, P; Cooper, J.D and Cash, H.C. (2003). "Experimental Study of Water Fluxes in a Residential Area: Rainfall, Roof Runoff and Evaporation, the Effect of Slope and aspect" *Journal of Hydrological Process,* 17(12): 2409-2422.

Simmons, G; Hope, V; Lewis, G; Whitmore, J. and Gao, W. (2001). Contamination of Potable Roof-collected Rainwater in Auckland, New Zealand. *Water Res.* 35(6): 1518-1524.

Vikaskumar, G.S; Hugh, D; Phillip, M.G; Peter, C; Timothy, K.R and Tony, R. (2007). Comparison of Water Quality Parameters from Diverse Catchments during Dry Periods and Following Rain Events. *Water Research 41(16): 3655-3666.*

Yaziz, M; Gunting, H; Sapari, N; and Ghazali, A. (1989). Variations in Rainwater Quality from Roof Catchments, *Water Resource* 23(6): 761-765.

Pages: 87-107

WATER RESOURCES MANAGEMENT: ***MONITORING AND ASSESSMENT***

Edited by: Dr. Sandeep Gupta; Dr. Pawan Kumar 'Bharti'

ISBN: 978-93-5056-799-9

Edition: 2016

Published by: Discovery Publishing House Pvt. Ltd., New Delhi (India)

7

Hydro-meteorological Hazards and Indian Agriculture

Alok Kumar Patra[1] and **Pulak Kumar Patra**[2]

ABSTRACT

The decline in share of the agricultural sector to gross domestic product over the years has not affected the importance of the sector in the Indian economy. However, food security in India is severely challenged by hydro-meteorological hazards such as floods, cyclones and drought. Over 60 per cent of the rural households depend on agriculture as their principal means of livelihood. Agriculture is also a major supplier of raw materials for industry. Although it is not possible to completely avoid the hydro-meteorological hazards, their effects can be minimised by taking some known long and short term structural and non-structural mitigation measures such as developing proper early warning systems, creating awareness at all levels in the concerned communities, coastal afforestation, construction of shelters, embankments, dykes, coastal roads, bridges, canals, *etc.* through better preparedness, mitigation measures and improved response mechanisms. By issuing accurate forecasts and warnings in

1 Associate Professor (Agronomy), All India Coordinated Research Project on Integrated Farming Systems, Orissa University of Agriculture and Technology, Bhubaneswar- 751003, (Odisha), (India)

2 Associate Professor, Department of Environmental Studies, Institute of Science, Visva-Bharati, Santiniketan - 731235, (West Bengal), (India)

a form that is readily understood and by educating people about how to prepare against such hazards, before they become disasters, lives and property can be protected. Timely release and dissemination of agroadvisories based on short, medium and long range weather forecast can save the crops and farm animals from the hydro-meteorological hazards.

INTRODUCTION

Meteorological hazards are severe and extreme weather and climate events that occur in all parts of the world, although some regions are more vulnerable to certain hazards than others. These are related to atmospheric weather patterns or conditions. These hazards are generally caused by factors related to precipitation, temperature, wind speed, humidity, or other, more complex factors. Meteorological hazards include cyclones, droughts, floods, hurricanes, hailstorms, heat waves, and tornadoes. The hazard is distinguished from an extreme event and a disaster. An extreme event is simply an unusual event; it does not necessarily cause harm. A disaster is an event that does cause harm in significant amounts. Meteorological hazards are often called as natural hazards. The natural hazards become natural disasters when people's lives and livelihoods are destroyed. Hydrologic hazards are the result of either excess or a severe lack of water, *i.e.*, flood or drought. Hydro-meteorological hazard is a process or phenomenon of atmospheric, hydrological or oceanographic nature that may cause loss of life, injury or other health impacts, property damage, loss of livelihoods and services, social and economic disruption, or environmental damage. Global analysis of records reveals that nearly 90% of loss of life due to natural disasters was caused by weather and water-related hazards (Gupta *et al.*, 2009). Human and material losses caused by natural disasters are a major obstacle to sustainable development. By issuing accurate forecasts and warnings in a form that is readily understood and by educating people about how to prepare against such hazards, before they become disasters, lives and property can be protected.

India is highly disaster prone country and much of the nation's land mass falls in high risk zones. It is estimated that over 44 million people are affected by natural disasters every year in India. More than 70% of the population occupy 80% of its geographical area that is vulnerable to cyclones, floods, landslides, drought, earthquakes as well as other localized hazards (Gupta and Nair, 2012). Rapid changes in climate has already resulted in glacial retreat, global sea level rise, changes in temperature and rainfall patterns and also affecting the natural resources productivity and quality, and also lead to increase in the frequency and intensity of hydro-meteorological disasters like drought, floods, heat and cold waves, desertification and coastal hazards like cyclone, coastal and sea erosion, storm surges and flooding (Gupta *et al.*, 2009).

The contribution of agriculture to gross domestic product has declined from 51.9% in 1950-51 to 16.1% during 2014-15 (at 2011-12 prices) due to growth in other sectors of the economy. The decline in share of the agricultural sector, however, has not affected the importance of the sector in the Indian economy. Over 60 per cent of the rural households depend on agriculture as their principal means of livelihood. Agriculture is also a major supplier of raw materials for industry. About 50% of the income generated in the manufacturing sector in India is attributed directly or indirectly to agricultural production. For a country that has about 70% of its population relying on agriculture directly or indirectly, the impact of extreme weather events is critical for its food security. Food security in India is severely challenged by natural hazards such as floods, cyclones and drought. India is prone to flood in about 49.8 million hectares which accounts for 12.3% of the geographical area. Out of the total geographical area of India, about one-sixth area with 12% of the population is found to be susceptible to drought and 8% of the total area of India is cyclone prone. India is quite susceptible to cyclones and floods due to its geographical location surrounded by water on three sides. West Bengal, Odisha, Andhra Pradesh, Tamil Nadu, Kerala and Gujarat come under most severely cyclone and flood affected areas of India (Kumar *et. al.*, 2014). In the last few decades India has been repeatedly battered by successive hydro-meteorological hazards. For example, for the last 100 years in the state of Odisha, 49 years have experienced floods, 30 have had droughts, and 11 faced cyclones. These extreme weather events are not mutually exclusive. It is not unusual for a year to have a combination of drought, cyclones (Gupta *et al.*, 2009).

DROUGHT

Drought is a relative term used with reference to deficiency of rainfall when compared to normal rainfall of a given location. It is an extended period when a region experiences a deficiency in its water supply, whether atmospheric, surface or ground water. However, drought cannot be defined in terms of amount of rainfall or number of days without rain. Since ancient times droughts have had far-reaching effects on humankind by causing the failure of crops, decreasing natural vegetation, and depleting water supplies. Drought is different from other hazards, in that it develops slowly. It is a hazard that requires many months to emerge and that may persist for many months or years thereafter. This type of hazard is known as a 'creeping' hazard. Generally, this occurs when a region receives consistently below average precipitation.

Classification of Drought

Drought results from a long continued dry weather and/or insufficient rain, which causes loss of soil moisture, depletion of underground water supply and reduction of stream flow (NDMA, 2010). Drought is frequently defined according to disciplinary perspective, where droughts are related to precipitation (meteorological), streamflow (hydrological), soil moisture (agricultural) or any combination of the three (Dracup, *et al.*, 1980). It can also be classified based on duration and nature of users. However, in both the types of classification, demarcation between any two types is not well defined and at times there is overlapping of the cause and the effect of one on the other.

The National Commission on Agriculture in India defines three types of droughts; meteorological, hydrological and agricultural depending upon the degree of deficiency of rainfall or soil moisture. A drought is said to be meteorological if the rainfall deficiency is more than 25% of the normal rainfall over an area. When deficiency is between 25 to 50%, it is called moderate drought and the term severe drought is used for rainfall deficiency of more than 50%. However, most locations around the world have their own definition of meteorological drought based on the climate normals in the area. The country as a whole may have a normal monsoon, but different meteorological districts or subdivisions can have below normal rainfall. The rainfall categories for smaller areas are defined by their deviation from normal rainfall of a meteorological area. Meteorological drought usually precedes the other kinds of drought.

A prolonged meteorological drought can result in hydrological drought with marked depletion of surface water and consequent drying up of reservoirs, lakes, rivers and fall in the ground water table. Hydrological drought tends to show up more slowly because it involves stored water that is used but not replenished. Hydrological drought may occur even when the rainfall is normal, if there has been a substantial reduction in surface water holding capacity.

Agricultural drought occurs when soil moisture and rainfall are inadequate during the growing season to support healthy crop growth. This condition can also arise independently from any change in precipitation levels when soil conditions and erosion triggered by poorly planned agricultural endeavours cause a shortfall in water available to the crops. There are three different types of agricultural drought; permanent, seasonal and contingent. Permanent drought occurs in arid areas where there is not enough precipitation to satisfy the water needs of plants. Such droughts are noticed in western Rajasthan and Gujarat and agriculture is impossible without irrigation throughout the crop season. In most parts of tropics, seasonal drought is noticed with well defined wet and dry seasons. Drought can be expected every year owing to seasonal variations in atmospheric circulation patterns. Contingent drought is the characteristic of the humid and sub-humid areas and occurs over a period of time when the rains fail. It is the serious hazard to agriculture in India because of the unpredictability of the monsoon rain. Depending on the arrival and behaviour of the monsoon during the crop season, contingent drought can further be divided into early, mid and late season droughts. In India, crops are selected across the country to fit the normal rainfall conditions. If there is any deviation in normal rainfall towards deficit, it adversely affects the crop's growth, development and production under rainfed conditions. The delay in monsoon (early season drought) adversely affects sowing area of different crops across the country reducing the cropped area. Mid and late season droughts also affect the food grain production. The late season drought is known as terminal drought.

Agricultural drought can also be categorised into three types; atmospheric, soil and physiological droughts. Low humidity with hot and dry desiccating winds cause atmospheric drought even under conditions of adequate moisture in the soil. Wilting of crops occur due to an underdeveloped root system or the physical inability of roots to draw water to compensate the water loss from the leaves during the stress period. But wilting due to atmospheric drought is always reversible. Soil drought occurs when soil moisture content lags behind evapotranspiration at times of greatest need of water by plants, such as during grand growth period. Physiological drought occurs when plant root systems fail to absorb water from the soil due to increased concentration of soluble salts in soil solution. Presence of soluble salts in soil water in high concentration reduces the availability of water to the plants, although sufficient water is in the soil. Presence of certain chemicals in soil solution may also restrict absorption of water by the root system.

The India Meteorological Department (IMD) defined drought on the basis of rainfall received and the area affected due to drought during the monsoon season. If the rainfall over the country is less by 10% of the long period average and 20% of the cropped area is affected due to drought, it is known as an all-India drought. As per IMD, there are 27 such recorded drought years since 1875; 1877, 1891, 1899, 1901, 1904, 1906, 1907, 1911, 1913, 1916, 1918, 1920, 1926, 1930, 1941, 1951, 1965, 1966, 1968, 1972, 1974, 1979, 1982, 1986, 1987, 2002 and 2009. The worst drought year was 1918 when nearly 70% of the country was affected by drought.

Causes of Drought

Drought can be caused by a number of factors. The most important one though relates to the amount of water vapour in the atmosphere as it creates precipitation. Generally, rainfall depends on the amount of water vapour carried by regional atmosphere, combined with the upward forcing of the air mass containing that water vapour. If these combined factors do not support precipitation volumes sufficient to reach the surface, the result is a drought. More rain occurs where there are moist, low pressure air systems. If there are dry, high pressure air systems, less moisture is available to produce precipitation. This results in a deficit of water for the areas over which they move.

Human activities like over farming, excessive irrigation, deforestation, and soil erosion can also directly trigger droughts. Widespread cutting down of trees for fuel or for clearing forests for agriculture reduce the soil's ability to hold water that causes desertification leading to drought. Constructing a dam on a large river may help provide electricity and water to irrigate farmland near the reservoir. However, it may also cause drought downstream by severely reducing the flow of water.

Common causes of drought in India include inadequate monsoon rainfall, high temperature coupled with high wind speed causing higher evapotranspiration, inadequate water availability due to high water loss in storage, distribution and utilities, shift in agricultural practices (from low to moderate and to high water demanding crops), high rate of increase in human and animal population in a specific location, and over exploitation of surface and ground water.

Impacts of Drought

A drought is caused for an extended period of months or years when a region notes a deficiency in its water supply. Although droughts can persist for several years, even a short, intense drought can cause significant damage and harm the local economy. One of the sectors where the immediate impact of drought is felt is agriculture. The impact of water deficit is also felt in ground water recharge, non-availability of quality seeds, land degradation and reduced power supply.

The impact of a drought may be either direct or indirect and varies in nature as well as intensity. The extent and intensity of drought impact is determined by prevailing economic conditions, the structure of the agricultural sector, management of water resources, food grain reserves, *etc*. The direct impact of drought is generally classified under four categories, *viz*. physical, economic, social and environmental. The relative and absolute magnitudes of each impact will however, depend on specific regional characteristics. Droughts cause a loss of assets in form of crops, livestock, fisheries and productive capital as these are immediate consequences of water shortage (NDMA, 2010). Many of these losses are then passed on to consumers in the form of higher commodity pricing. The social impacts include increased chance of conflict over commodities, fertile land, and water resources. Other social impacts include abandonment of cultural traditions, loss of homelands, changes in lifestyle, and increased chance of health risks due to poverty and hygiene issues. The environmental impacts of drought include loss in species biodiversity, migration changes, reduced air quality, and increased soil erosion.

Influence of Drought on Crop Plants

Water stress due to drought has a tremendous adverse effect on crop plants. The physiological and morphological characters of a plant are influenced by the water balance in the plant system. The crop plants vary in critical growth periods with respect to water requirement, and water stress during these critical stages would drastically reduce the biomass production. During flowering stage, a little stress of moisture by virtue of drought substantially reduces the size of inflorescence thereby affecting the final yield. Water shortage at fertilisation and grain filling also influence the final yield of any crop.

Water constitutes about more than 80% of the fresh weight of the herbaceous plants and 50% of the woody plants. Cell division and enlargement are very sensitive to drought stress. Water content in the protoplasm below a certain level results in stunted growth or even kills the plant. Drought also affects nutrient absorption, carbohydrate and protein metabolism and translocation of ions and metabolites. Protein breakdown injures the drought stressed plant due to the accumulation of toxic products of protein breakdown such as ammonia. Abscission of leaves, fruits and seeds are induced by plant water deficit during droughts.

Drought Preparedness and Mitigation

Drought preparedness, coupled with appropriate mitigation actions and programmes, can reduce and, in some cases, eliminate many of the impacts associated with drought. Drought planning process has three components; monitoring and early warning, risk assessment, and mitigation. The monitoring and early warning component of a drought plan essentially provides the foundation on which timely decision can be made by decision makers at all levels, from farmers to national policy makers. Given drought's creeping characteristics, monitoring the hydrological system can detect drought's early onset and its potential impacts. There should be interdisciplinary approach to reduce and mitigate the impacts of drought. The meteorological and hydrological observations should be systematically collected and processed to support and strengthen the scientific networks for the enhancement of technical capacities in meteorology, hydrology and other related fields.

Conservation practices minimise the disruption of the soil's structure, composition and natural biodiversity, thereby reducing erosion and soil degradation, surface runoff, and water pollution. The established practices of soil and water conservation are crop rotation, contoured row cropping, terracing, minimum tillage practices, erosion control structures, water retention and detention structures, windbreaks and shelterbelts, litter management, and reclamation of salt-affected soil. Soil and water conservation can be approached through agronomic and engineering measures. Agronomic measures include contour farming, off-season tillage, deep tillage, mulching and providing vegetative barriers on the contour. These measures prevent soil erosion and increase soil moisture. Alternate land use system like agroforestry, *i.e.*, integrating tree crops with annual herbaceous crops, may be encouraged. Carefully planned crop rotation can help to minimise erosion and allow farmers to plant less water-dependent crops in drier years.

Engineering measures differ with location, slope of the land, soil type, and amount and intensity of rainfall. These include soil and water conservation through regulated runoff, collection of surplus rain water, checking evaporational and seepage loss of water and recycling of collected water for life saving irrigation. These can be achieved by making water harvesting structures, scooping the land, opening ridges and furrows, contouring across the slope, and compartmental bunding, *etc.* Contour bunds, trenches and stone walls can prevent soil erosion and obstruct the flow of runoff. The retained water increases soil moisture and recharges the groundwater. Check dams (check dams are temporary structures constructed with locally available materials) and other gully-plugging structures can be constructed to restrict the runoff and soil erosion. Percolation ponds can be constructed by excavating a depression to form a small reservoir, or by constructing an embankment in a natural ravine or gully to form an impoundment. These features store water for livestock and recharge the groundwater. Rainwater can be collected from roofs or other suitable catchments and stored for later use. The wastewater (sewage) can also be recycled by proper treatment and purification. Water-supply projects can also be implemented for drought mitigation, with a view to strengthen drought preparedness. Activities such as water-use planning, rain-water harvesting, runoff collection using surface and underground structures, improved management of channels and wells, exploration of additional water resources through drilling and dam construction, are implemented as a part of a drought-mitigation plan.

The physiological approaches include application of suitable chemicals in crops as antitranspirants, growth retardants, and radiation reflectants for reducing the transpiration rate, checking the shoot growth and encouraging the root growth, and reducing the radiation, respectively which ultimately may reduce the impact of drought on crops. Genetic approaches for reducing the adverse impacts of drought aimed at developing new plant types, known as 'ideo types' which possess wider adaptability, shorter growth duration, drought resistance and high genetic yield potentiality. Plant breeders have developed many short duration varieties for various crops. These varieties are characterised by effective and extensive deep root system, drought tolerance, resistance to diseases, effective photosynthetic behaviour, dwarf plant types with lesser number of erect leaves and high yield potentiality. Thus, the drought can be evaded or escaped by substituting the traditional long duration varieties with these ideo types.

FLOODS

A flood is an overflow of water that submerges land which is usually dry. Flooding may occur as an overflow of water from water bodies, such as a river or lake, in which the water overtops, resulting in some of that water escaping its usual boundaries. Floods are recurrent phenomena since time immemorial. Almost every year some parts of the world or the other are affected by the floods of varying magnitude. Even in the same country, while some parts are suffering from devastating floods, other parts experience severe drought. Flood is the single most frequent disaster faced not only in India but by various parts of the world.

Causes of Flood

The years in which actual rainfall exceeds the normal value by twice the standard deviation or more are defined as the years of flood. Most often floods are a secondary hazard resulting from other meteorological processes, such as prolonged rainfall, localized and intense thunderstorms, or onshore winds.

Inadequate capacity of the rivers to contain within their banks the high flows brought down from the upper catchment areas following heavy rainfall, leads to flooding. In coastal areas, floods are caused by cyclones and typhoons. Other causes include backing up of waters in tributaries at their outfalls into the main river often with synchronisation of floods in them, and landslides blocking stream courses resulting in the backwater overflowing river banks. However, the root cause of flood is excessive rainfall which occurs mainly in the monsoon months. Because of the varying rainfall distribution, many a times, areas which are not traditionally prone to floods also experience severe inundation. Areas with poor drainage facilities get flooded by accumulation of water from heavy rainfall. Flood may also occur due to an accumulation of rainwater on saturated grounds. Excess irrigation water applied to command areas and increase in ground water levels due to seepage from canals and irrigated fields also are factors that accentuate the problem of water logging. The problem is exacerbated by factors such as silting of the riverbeds, reduction in the carrying capacity of river channels, erosion of beds and banks leading to changes in river courses, obstructions to flow due to landslides, synchronisation of floods in the main and tributary rivers and retardation due to tidal effects (NDMA, 2008).

Flash Floods

Flash floods occur with little or no warning, and are the result of intense rainstorms within a brief period of time. These cause high damages because of their suddenness. Flash floods occur in hilly and sloping lands where heavy rainfall and thunderstorms or cloudbursts are common. The phenomenon of sudden unprecedented heavy rain due to some peculiar climatic conditions is known as cloudbursts. Depression and cyclonic storms in the coastal areas of Odisha, West Bengal, Andhra Pradesh, Karnataka, and Tamil Nadu also cause flash floods. The states of Arunachal Pradesh, Assam, Odisha, Himachal Pradesh, Uttarakhand, the Western Ghats in Maharashtra and Kerala are more vulnerable to flash floods caused by cloudbursts. Sudden release of waters from upstream reservoirs, breaches in landslide dams and embankments on the banks of the rivers leads to disastrous floods.

Effects of Floods

The primary effects of floods include loss of life, damage of crops and livestock, loss of properties, damage to buildings and other structures including bridges, roads and transport infrastructure, sewerage systems, roadways, canals, and disruption of power supply. Flood waters typically inundate farm land, making the land unworkable and preventing crops from being planted or harvested, which can lead to shortage of food both, for humans and farm animals. The pulses and oilseeds and vegetable crops are highly susceptible to flood and the flood may result in their complete crop loss. Entire harvests for a region may be lost in extreme flood circumstances. Some tree species may not survive prolonged flooding of their root systems. Floods are followed by epidemics. Supply of drinking water and restoration of sanitation are post flood challenges. Secondary effects of flooding include coastal erosion and soil erosion. Economic hardship due to a temporary decline in tourism, rebuilding costs, or food shortage leading to price increases is a common after-effect of severe flooding. The flood problem in India is mostly confined to the states located in the Indo-Gangetic plains, northeast India and occasionally in the rivers of central India.

Frequent or smaller floods may also bring many benefits, such as recharging ground water, making soil more fertile and increasing nutrients in some soils. Flood waters provide much needed water resources in arid and semiarid regions where precipitation are very unevenly distributed throughout the year. Flooding can spread nutrients to lakes and water reservoirs, which can lead to increased biomass and improved fisheries for a few years.

Flood Preparedness and Mitigation

Floods being the most common natural disaster, people have, out of experience, devised many ways of coping with them. However, encroachments into the floodplains over the years have aggravated the flood problem and a need to take effective and sustained flood management measures has been felt (NDMA, 2008).

Flood forecasting has been recognised the most important reliable and cost effective non-structural measure for flood mitigation. Forecasting of floods allows for precautions to be taken and people to be warned so that they can be prepared in advance for flooding conditions. A long time-series of historical data that relates stream flows to the measured past rainfall events can have fairly accurate flood forecasts. Coupling this historical information with real-time knowledge about volumetric capacity in catchment areas, such as spare capacity in reservoirs, groundwater levels, and the degree of saturation of area aquifers is also needed in order to make the most accurate flood forecasts. Radar estimates of rainfall and general weather forecasting techniques are also important components of good flood forecasting. The intensity and height of a flood can be predicted with plenty of lead time, if good quality data is available. In India, the Central Flood Board was set up in 1954. The India Meteorological Department (IMD) and Central Water Commission (CWC) are working in close co-ordination for issue of flood forecasts. IMD has 10 flood meteorological offices and CWC has 20 flood forecasting divisions located in different flood prone river basins in the country.

Various mitigation measures can be taken to reduce the adverse impact of floods. In order to achieve control over the flow and height of the water carried by the river, the channel, floodplain or watershed must undergo some physical alterations.

1. Dams, retention basins or reservoirs on mainstreams or tributaries can be constructed to store excessive water and release it gradually after the threat is over.
2. Levees or floodwalls can be constructed to confine flood waters to a floodway, thereby reducing flood damage.
3. Channel improvement works can be taken up to increase the efficiency of drainage system. These include straightening to remove undesirable bends, deepening and widening to increase size of waterways; clearing to remove trees and other obstructions; lining with concrete to increase efficiency.
4. Watershed treatment can also be employed to help the soil on slopes to become more absorbent of rainfall until flood height is receded. Watershed treatment involves crop rotation, construction of terrace, contour strip cropping; selective planting and reforestation.
5. Any type of construction or land filling should not be allowed on the lateral boundaries of the designated floodways. This is done to ensure that the flow of water is not obstructed.

Other mitigation measures include change in crop management practices, flood insurance, temporary evacuation of persons, livestock and property from the path of flood waters, etc.

1. The crops and varieties which can withstand water logging conditions for a fairly long period should be preferred in the flood prone areas.

At present varieties for various crops, particularly for rice many varieties are available which are tolerant to flood conditions. Awareness should be created among the farmers of flood prone areas and adequate seeds of these varieties should also be ascertained.

2. In areas of perennial waterlogging where even rice cultivation is difficult, aquatic crops with economic importance such as water chestnut can be introduced with fish farming. Colocasia can also be cultivated in flood prone waterlogged areas.
3. The contingent crop plans should be prepared for post flood areas. Short duration pulses and vegetable crops should be encouraged and package of practices for these crops should be standardised for difficult situations.
4. In lowlands under high rainfall region and flood prone areas, land modification such as raised and sunken bed technique can be practised. Trenches of 5-8 metre width and 1.2-1.5 metre depth with 10 metre or suitable length can be opened at a spacing of 10-15 metre in-between two trenches. The excavated soil is put on the space between two trenches to prepare raised beds. Vegetables and short duration fruit crops can be grown on the raised beds while trenches are utilized for fish farming. In dry season irrigation can be provided to the crops on the raised beds from the trenches.
5. In flood prone and waterlogged areas, the practice of bio-drainage using *Casuarina* and *Eucalyptus* plantations would act as a viable flood resilient system. Crops can be grown on the tree alleys. This increases land productivity.

TROPICAL CYCLONES

Major storms in the tropics are known as tropical cyclone. Depending on its location and strength, a tropical cyclone is referred to by names such as hurricane, typhoon, tropical storm, cyclonic storm, tropical depression, and simply cyclone. All forms of storm fall under the definition of tropical cyclone which is a synoptic scale cyclonic circulation with organised convection and surface wind circulation originating over tropical waters. In meteorology, a cyclone is an area of closed, circular fluid motion rotating in the same direction as the earth. This is usually characterised by inward spiralling winds that rotate anti-clockwise in the northern hemisphere and clockwise in the southern hemisphere of the earth. Tropical cyclones are characterised by large low pressure centres and numerous thunderstorms that produce strong winds and heavy rain. Tropical cyclones feed on heat released when moist air rises, resulting in condensation of water vapour contained in the moist air. While tropical cyclones can produce extremely powerful winds and torrential rain, they are also able to produce high waves and damaging storm surge as well as spawning tornadoes. They develop over large bodies of warm water, and lose their strength if they move over land. This is why coastal regions can receive significant damage from a tropical cyclone, while inland regions are relatively safe from receiving strong winds. Heavy rains, however, can produce significant inland flooding, and storm surges can produce extensive coastal flooding up to 40 kilometres from the coastline.

Tropical cyclones are classified based on intensity into three main groups; tropical depressions, tropical storms, and a third group of more intense storms, whose name depends on the region. For example, a tropical violent windstorm in the north-western Pacific referred to as a 'typhoon'; in the northeast Pacific or in the Atlantic, it is called a 'hurricane' and in the southern hemisphere or the Indian Ocean basins, storms of tropical nature are referred simply as 'cyclones'. A tropical depression is an organised system of clouds and thunderstorms with a defined, closed surface circulation and maximum sustained winds of less than 63 km/hour. A tropical storm is an organised system of strong thunderstorms with a defined surface circulation and maximum sustained winds between 63 and 117 km/hour. A hurricane or typhoon or tropical cyclone is a system of sustained winds with a speed of at least 119 km/hour. Storm surge is the abnormal rise of sea level which occurs when the cyclone moves from ocean to continent. It is a disastrous and destructive feature of cyclone, which could cause massive destruction in the coastal region and misery to the coastal human population and livestock. The intensity of tropical cyclones is expressed by using Saffir-Simpson scale as given in table 7.1.

Cyclones and Their Impact in India

Indian subcontinent is the worst affected region of the world, having a coast line of 7516 km; 5400 km along the mainland, 132 km in Lakshadweep and 1900 km in Andaman and Nicobar Islands. The states Andhra Pradesh, Odisha, Tamil Nadu, West Bengal and the union territory Puducherry on the east coast and Gujarat on the west coast are more vulnerable to cyclone disasters. Cyclones occur in the month of May-June and October-November, with primary peak in November and secondary peak in May. Although cyclones affect the entire coast of India the east coast is more prone compared to the west coast.

Cyclones are known to cause severe damage to infrastructure through high speed winds. Very strong winds accompanying a cyclonic storm damage trees, installations, residences, communication systems, *etc.*, which results in loss of life and property. Torrential rainfall (more than 30 cm/hour) associated with cyclones is another major cause of damages. Unabated rain gives rise to unprecedented floods. Heavy rainfall from a cyclone is usually spread over wide area and cause large scale soil erosion and weakening of embankments. A severe tropical cyclone causes storm surge; as a result of which sea water inundates low lying areas of coastal regions drowning human beings and livestock. This also erodes beaches and embankments, destroys vegetation and leads to reduction of soil fertility.

Table 7.1: Saffir-Simpson Scale to Express Intensity of Tropical Cyclones

Category	Intensity	Pressure (mb)	Wind speed (km/hour)	Storm Surge (m)	Damage
1.	Minimal	>980	119-154	1.0-1.7	Damage to shrubs and trees; no major damage to most building structures; flooding of low-lying coastal areas
2.	Moderate	965- 979	155-178	1.8-2.6	Considerable damage to shrubs and some trees being blown down; damage to door and windows of residences; flooding of coastal roads and low-lying areas
3.	Extensive	945-964	179-210	2.7-3.8	Large trees blown down; some structural damage to small buildings; flooding of sea-level coastland 10 km or more inland
4.	Extreme	920-944	211-250	3.9-5.6	Many shrubs, trees are blown out; severe damage to roofing structures, windows, and doors of buildings; flooding of low-lying areas as much as 13 km inland; major damage to structures near shore due to battering by waves
5.	Catastrophic	<920	>250	>5.6	All shrubs, trees blown out; complete failure of roofs on residences and industrial buildings; overturning/ sweeping away of small buildings; evacuation of all residential areas on low-lying ground within 16 km of shore

Source: https://www.nws.noaa.gov

The cyclone and its associated flood incidence cause severe damage to agriculture in several ways. The crops get affected both in terms of establishment and productivity. Recurring frequency of cyclones leads to drastic transformation in the pattern of coastal land use by turning fertile areas into saline wastelands due to marine incursions. In addition, standing crops are destroyed; salt deposits from saline water render farms unproductive and even barren. An entire cropping season is lost and areas affected by severe storm surge are sometimes not cultivable during subsequent seasons also. Very often harvested food crop stocks are also destroyed. Horticultural crops suffer heavy losses. Livestock including farm and dairy cattle, poultry, sheep and goats also suffer.

Although tropical cyclones are known for destruction they cause, they may be important factors in the precipitation regimes of places they affect, as they may bring much-needed precipitation to dry regions, relieving drought conditions. Tropical cyclones also help maintain the global heat balance by carrying warm, moist air from the tropics to the temperate latitudes and polar regions. This helps to maintain equilibrium in earth's troposphere and maintains relatively stable and warm temperature worldwide.

Cyclone Preparedness and Mitigation

Although it is not possible to completely avoid natural disasters, their effects can be minimised by taking some known long and short term structural and non-structural mitigation measures such as developing proper early warning systems, creating awareness at all levels in the concerned communities, coastal afforestation, construction of shelters, embankments, dykes, coastal roads, bridges, canals, *etc.* through better preparedness, mitigation measures and improved response mechanisms (NDMA, 2008).

The India Meteorological Department (IMD) has introduced a 4-stage warning system as described below to issue cyclone warnings to the disaster managers.

1. **Pre-cyclone watch:** The pre-cyclone watch is issued when a depression forms over the Bay of Bengal irrespective of its distance from the coast and is likely to affect Indian coast in future. It is issued at least 72 hours in advance of the commencement of adverse weather. It is issued at least once a day.
2. **Cyclone alert:** The cyclone alert is issued at least 48 hours before the commencement of the bad weather when the cyclone is located beyond 500 km from the coast. It is issued every three hours.
3. **Cyclone warning:** The cyclone warning is issued at least 24 hours before the commencement of the bad weather when the cyclone is located within 500 km from the coast. Information about time and place of landfall are indicated in the bulletin.

Table 7.2: Damage Potential of Cyclonic Disturbances

System (Intensity in km/hour)	Damage Expected	Action Suggested
Deep depression (52-61)	Minor damage to loose and unsecured structures	Fishermen advised not to venture into the seas
Cyclonic storm (62-87)	Damage to thatched huts; breaking of tree branches causing minor damage to power and communication lines	Total suspension of fishing operations
Severe cyclonic storm (88-117)	Extensive damage to thatched roofs and huts; minor damage to power and communication lines due to uprooting of large avenue trees; flooding of escape routes	Total suspension of fishing operations; coastal hutment dwellers to be moved to safer places; people in affected areas to remain indoors
Very severe cyclonic storm (118-167)	Extensive damage to *kutcha* houses; partial disruption of power and communication line; minor disruption of rail and road traffic; potential threat from flying debris; flooding of escape routes	Total suspension of fishing operations; mobilise evacuation from coastal areas; judicious regulation of rail and road traffic; people in affected areas to remain indoors
Very severe cyclonic storm (168- 221)	Extensive damage to *kutcha* houses; some damage to old buildings; large-scale disruption of power and communication lines; disruption of rail and road traffic due to extensive flooding; potential threat from flying debris	Total suspension of fishing operations; extensive evacuation from coastal areas; diversion or suspension of rail and road traffic; people in affected areas to remain indoors
Super cyclone (222 or more)	Extensive structural damage to residential and industrial buildings; total disruption of communication and power supply; extensive damage to bridges causing large scale disruption of rail and road traffic; large-scale flooding and inundation of sea water; air full of flying debris	Total suspension of fishing operations; large-scale evacuation of coastal population; total suspension of rail and road traffic in vulnerable areas; people in affected areas to remain indoors

Source: Attri and Tyagi, 2010

4. **Post landfall outlook:** The post landfall outlook is issued 12 hours before the cyclone landfall, when the cyclone is located within 200 km from the coast. More accurate and specific information about time and place of landfall and associated bad weather is indicated in the bulletin.

The sector that is most affected by tropical cyclones is agriculture and food security. The sharpest falls in agricultural production has been recorded during those years that have experienced the occurrence of severe cyclones in India. Various options have been conceptualised for protecting the crops (NDMA, 2008). The crop calendar for major crops should be adjusted to normal cyclone periods. The cultivation of high yielding varieties and hybrids of rice in the coastal areas, which can withstand surge waters, floods and cyclone winds without damaging the grain and straw quality, should be encouraged. Short height crops should be grown to avoid lodging in cyclone prone areas. The crops can be protected from floods caused by cyclonic rainfalls through improvement of drainage systems by strengthening of bunds all along canals and tanks; de-silting of water reservoirs, canals and drains; widening and deepening of drains and canals; keeping reservoirs and canals weed free; and diversion of existing drains and canals and alignment of new canals and drains keeping in view that water will be flowing out freely during disaster periods. The drains which are directly joining the sea should be maintained regularly.

The animals and birds should be shifted to a higher and safer place as soon as warnings for impeding cyclones are received. Cowsheds should be constructed in a way that they can withstand strong cyclone winds. Sufficient nutritious feed should be preserved for the bad weather periods. The animals and birds should be vaccinated beforehand against communicable diseases during emergency periods. The farmers should be advised to insure their crops and livestock. Contingent planning should be made sufficiently ahead. The farmers may be provided with the required inputs like seeds/seedlings and fertilisers timely to go for a contingent crop to compensate the crop loss due to cyclonic storms and storm surges.

HAILSTORMS

Any thunderstorm which produces hail that reaches the ground is known as a hailstorm. Hail is a form of solid precipitation. It consists of balls or irregular lumps of ice, each of which is called a hailstone. Hailstones consist mostly of water ice and measure between 5 millimetres and 15 centimetres in diameter. Hail is composed of transparent ice or alternating layers of transparent and translucent ice at least 1 millimetre thick, which are deposited upon the hailstone as it travels through the cloud, suspended aloft by air with strong upward motion until its weight overcomes the updraft and falls to the ground. Stones larger than 2 cm are usually considered large enough to cause damage.

Hail is possible within most thunderstorms as it is produced by cumulonimbus clouds. It is most common within continental interiors of the mid-latitudes, as hail formation is considerably more likely when the freezing level is below the altitude of 3400 m. Movement of dry air into strong thunderstorms over continents can increase the frequency of hail by promoting evaporational cooling which lowers the freezing level of thunderstorm clouds giving hail a larger volume to grow in. Hail is less common in the tropics despite a much higher frequency of thunderstorms than in the mid-latitudes because the atmosphere over the tropics tends to be warmer over a much greater altitude. In the tropics, hail formation tends to be confined mainly to higher elevations.

Agriculture is typically the most affected by hailstorms because it causes severe crop damage and even a minor storm with relatively small size hailstones can have a devastating effect on agriculture. Hailstorms cause fruit injury, canopy damage besides uprooting and breakage of plants in the horticultural crops like pomegranate, grapes, citrus, mango, banana, papaya, onion and vegetables. Though in some cases the losses are irreparable, in others where the damage is less the crop can be saved. The extent of losses varies from mild to high depending upon the force and size of hail that falls, and intensity, duration and time of occurrence of hailstorm during the growing season.

Various preventive measures can be taken to minimise the damage by hailstones. The formation of hailstones or their size can be reduced through cloud seeding. This may be done by injecting sufficient ice nuclei like silver iodide into the cloud environment so that the hailstones are prevented from being large enough to hit the crops with high force, or even they get melted before reaching the ground. However, the success of cloud seeding to prevent hailstorms depends upon the accuracy in forecasting of hailstorms with sufficient lead time for placement of seeding materials in the right quantity at the right place. Weather satellites and weather radar imagery are very useful tools to detect the presence of hail-producing thunderstorms. The radar data has to be complemented by a knowledge of current atmospheric conditions which can allow one to determine if the current atmosphere is conducive to hail development.

Fixing hail damage on plants is not always possible. The best approach is to clean up the debris and trim off broken stems and leaves. The hail damage to trees may require pruning away of the most affected branches. Injuries to minor trees will heal. But fungicide should be applied immediately to prevent rot in the injured branches. Open wounds on the growing shoots, branches and scaffolds present entry points for bacterial and fungal pathogens and also insects. Some plants may be too heavily affected and fixing hail damage is not possible. These plants should be removed and replaced. Short duration fruit crops like banana and papaya which suffer from more than

50% permanent damage to the plants should be replanted. Mango, pomegranate, grapes and citrus fruit crops do not have permanent loss. The remedial measures for these crops depend upon the vegetative and reproductive growth stage of crops and the extent of damage. Physical barriers such as hail nets or other protective screens can be used in the orchards of these high value fruit crops as a preventive measure.

HEAT WAVES

A heat wave is a prolonged period of excessively hot weather, which may be accompanied by high humidity. A heat wave is generally measured relative to the usual weather in the area and relative to normal temperature for the season. Temperature that is considered to be normal by people from a hotter climate area can be termed a heat wave in a cooler area if they are outside the normal climate pattern for that area. The definition of heat wave recommended by the World Meteorological Organisation is applicable when the daily maximum temperature of more than five consecutive days exceeds the average maximum temperature by 5° C, the normal period being 1961-1990.

As per the India Meteorological Department, heat waves are not to be considered as serious till maximum temperature of a station reaches at least 40° C for plains and 30° C for hilly regions. In a station with normal maximum temperature of less than or equal to 40° C, if the prevailing maximum temperature is 5 to 6° above the normal, then heat wave is presumed to exist there. If the departure from normal is 7° or more, then the term severe heat wave is used. Where the normal maximum temperature of a station is more than 40° C, heat wave is declared when departure from normal is by 4 to 5° and severe heat wave is declared when departure from normal is by 6° or more. When actual maximum temperature remains at 45° C or more irrespective of normal maximum temperature, heat wave is declared. Heat waves develop in May and June in northern and central India. Rajasthan and Punjab experience heat waves due to their being in the interior. The strong north-westerly winds along the land trajectory over hot regions inhibit the setting in of the sea breeze over the eastern coastal belt. Thus, there is high incidence of heat waves and their persistence over coastal Odisha and Andhra Pradesh. Chennai becomes another centre of heat waves in July and August.

Excessive heat affects the development of field crops like rice, wheat, maize, potato and soybean, and also many fruit crops like apples, grapes, *etc.* Yield of many crops may be reduced by high heat when it occurs at a critical time in the plant's development. Blowing of hot winds leads to pollen injury and premature fruit drop. High temperatures, especially during both day and night, occurring during the pollination of maize can significantly reduce yields. Soybeans exposed to heat stress during flowering can result in pollen sterility and reduced seed set. Heat stress during the ripening stage of wheat can affect grain quality and yield. Shade structures may be made to protect vegetable crops grown on sandy soils during summer. Windbreaks can also reduce the effect of heat wave by decreasing the velocity of the hot winds.

Livestock heat stress is a serious concern for livestock producers. Livestock such as poultry are severely impacted by heat waves. Milk production and cattle reproduction also decrease during heat waves. Livestock producers need to be proactive before and during a heat wave to prevent the effects of heat stress. Electric fans and coolers can be used in the shelters during summer to save the animals from heat wave.

COLD WAVES

Cold waves are defined with respect to the normal minimum temperature experienced over a given area. According to India Meteorological Department, if the normal minimum temperature of a station is equal to or more than 10° C, then cold waves and severe cold waves are defined when there is a marked fall of temperature by 5 to 6° and by 7° or more, respectively. At the station with normal minimum temperature less than 10° C, cold waves and severe cold waves are defined when there is a marked fall of temperature by 4 to 5° and by 6° or more, respectively. Nearly 75% of cold waves in the country occur during January to February. Excluding the extreme south peninsula, the country is susceptible to cold waves. The north western part of the country and areas further north are more favourable regions for the genesis of cold waves and the incidence of 5 to 20 days of frost in each month during the cold season is common (Patra, 2012). The damage by cold waves is more in the low lying areas, where cold waves settle and remain for a long time on the ground.

Ground frost which adversely affects various crops is experienced under cold waves. Cold waves that bring unexpected freezes and frosts during the growing season in mid-latitude zones can kill plants during the early and most vulnerable stages of growth, resulting in crop failure as plants are killed before they can be harvested economically. Night irrigations can be applied to the crops like potato and tomato to mitigate the effect of frost and severe cold. Smokes and heaters are used in the fruit orchards to reduce the effect of cold and frost. Straw mats, screens of dry grass netting, plastic covers can be placed over small plants during late afternoon and removed early in the morning for protection against frost. A cold wave can cause death and injury to livestock and wildlife. Electric heaters can be used to elevate the shelter temperature during strong cold.

CONCLUSION

The frequent occurrence of hydro-meteorological hazards such as drought, floods, cyclones and floods significantly limit agricultural productivity in India which in turn affects the socio-economic prospects of farmers and food security. Risks associated with natural hazards cannot be minimized successfully through application of isolated management measures. However, hazard preparedness, coupled with appropriate mitigation actions and programmes, can reduce and, in some cases, eliminate many of the impacts associated with hydro-meteorological hazards. Short to medium range weather forecasts and early warning systems can be useful ele-ments for the agricultural decision-making process, leading to reduced risks and increased opportunities. Immediate attention should be given to contingency crop planning and integrated cyclone and flood management strategies for reducing the extent of damage. The crops can be protected from floods caused by cyclonic rainfalls through improvement of drainage systems by strengthening of bunds all along canals and tanks; de-silting of water reservoirs, canals and drains; widening and deepening of drains and canals; keeping reservoirs and canals weed free; and diversion of existing drains and canals and alignment of new canals and drains keeping in view that water will be flowing out freely during disaster periods.

REFERENCES

Attri, S.D. and Tyagi, A. (2010): Climate Profile of India. India Meteorological Department, Ministry of Earth Sciences, Government of India, New Delhi, pp: 248.

Dracup, J.A., Lee, K.S. and Paulson, E.G. Jr. (1980): On the Definition of Droughts. *Water Resource Research* 16 (2): 297-302.

Gupta, A.K. and Nair, S.S. (2012): Environmental Extremes Disaster Risk Management - Addressing Climate Change. National Institute of Disaster Management, New Delhi, pp: 33.

Gupta, A.K., Nair, S.S. and Sehgal, V.K. (2009): Hydro-meteorological Disasters and Climate Change: Conceptual Issues and Data Needs for Integrating Adaptation into Environment - Development Framework. *e-Journal Earth Science India* 2 (2): 117-132.

http://www.mapsofindia.com/top-ten/geography/india-flood.html

http://www.nrdc.org/health/climate/drought.asp

http://www.nw-weathernet.com/wx_terms.

http://www.unisdr.org/we/inform/terminology

https://en.wikipedia.org/wiki/Meteorological_disasters

https://www.nws.noaa.gov

Kumar, A., Brahmanand, P.S. and Nayak, A.K. (2014): Management of Cyclone Disaster in Agriculture Sector in Coastal Areas. Directorate of Water Management, Bhubaneswar, pp: 108.

NDMA. (2008): National Disaster Management Guidelines: Management of Flood. A publication of National Disaster Management Authority, Government of India, New Delhi, pp: 134.

NDMA. (2008): National Disaster Management Guidelines: Management of Cyclones. A publication of National Disaster Management Authority, Government of India, New Delhi, pp: 156.

NDMA. (2010): National Disaster Management Guidelines: Management of Drought. A Publication of National Disaster Management Authority, Government of India, New Delhi, pp: 78.

Patra, P.K. (2012): A Text Book on Climatology. Kalyani Publishers, Ludiana, pp: 255.

Pages: 108-137

WATER RESOURCES MANAGEMENT: *MONITORING AND ASSESSMENT*

Edited by: Dr. Sandeep Gupta; Dr. Pawan Kumar 'Bharti'

ISBN: 978-93-5056-799-9

Edition: 2016

Published by: Discovery Publishing House Pvt. Ltd., New Delhi (India)

8

Farmers' Method of Fry and Fingerling Production of Major Carps and Propagation of Threatened Indigenous Catfishes

Subrato Ghosh

ABSTRACT

Fry and fingerling production of major carps in village ponds taken on lease have become established as a sustainable source of livelihood for many small- to medium-scale fish farmers. Since long past, farmers have been relying upon usage of Mohua oil cake in eradication of unwanted fishes during pond preparation but presently it is sold in adulterated form. Alternatively Aluminium phosphide tablets are being used in ponds, which is expected not to cause health hazards after consumption of toxicised fishes. It has been experienced that farmers are emphasizing on inherited wisdom, skill, ingenuity and ITK in their production method of fry and fingerlings. Remarkably use of unboiled hen eggs has been noticed as initial feed for growing spawn, which, according to farmers, increases their survivability. The farmers' version of approach of production has been comprehensively narrated in this communication and newly-developed seed production and farming techniques of three threatened indigenous freshwater catfishes have been dealt in detail.

Keywords: fry, fingerling, Aluminium phosphide, catfish, seed production, farming.

Fishery Field Assistant (Government of West Bengal), Kushmandi Development Block, PS Kushmandi, Dist. Dakshin Dinajpur, (West Bengal), (India)

INTRODUCTION

Freshwater fish farming in commercial terms in village ponds plays an important role in the socio-economic development of rural India by creating sustainable livelihood options for the inhabiting people, income generation, improved food and nutritional security and thereby reducing the extent of malnutrition-related health disorders among households. Scientific inputs, advancement and refinement of economically viable technologies over the years have made fish farming sector eminently suitable, profitable and significantly contributory to rural economy for poor persons having less water resource, those with adequate resource and rich farmers/entrepreneurs.

Renowned fish farmer and hatchery expert Late Sri Nilratan 'Nilu' Ghosh used boiled extract of a mixture of the plant products catechu nut *Acasia catechu* and myrobalan *Terminalia chebula* in order to prevent untimely hatching and premature rupture of shell of fertilized eggs of major carps in water column of hatching-cum-incubation pool, which has been regarded as the most outstanding example of Indigenous Technological Knowledge (ITK) applied in fisheries and aquaculture sector. We have also learnt how simply elderly village farmers harvest grown-up stinging catfish *Heteropneustes fossilis* in submerged earthen pots from culture ponds, which normally appears to be a difficult task. Elderly hatchery technicians have incorporated lentil flour "musur daler besan" and wheat flour "moida" into formulated supplementary feed meant for broodstock of major carps and other cultivable fishes, which has led to enhanced reproductive capability of male fishes with superior milt quality. Many farmers are aware that if seeds of Subabul *Leucena lecocephala* drop down from trees into fish ponds, then the ponds become more fertile, growth of fish food organisms increase and remarkably oil content of fish body muscle increases. Many farmers apply potassium permanganate solution @ 175-200gm per 33 decimal fish pond to bring up the dissolved oxygen content to its desirable level. $KMnO_4$ is used along with sand to increase DO content in pond bottom. Farmers in Ramsagar block of Bankura district in West Bengal have used branches of 'Lankasij' tree (Jhupigachh) in ponds to eradicate the ectoparasite fish lice *Argulus* sp. Many farmers have successfully used liquefied composted mixture of soyabean dust, mustard oil cake, rice husk and wheat chaff to increase plankton density in major carp broodstock ponds.

In Kakdwip and Namkhana of South 24 Parganas district, West Bengal, hatchery owners have successfully used a liquefied paste mixture of garlic, edible salt, $CuSo_4$ and $KMnO_4$ in carp broodstock ponds as a prophylactic measure against bacterial fish diseases and Epizootic Ulcerative Syndrome; it is believed to contain antimicrobial compound. Fish farmers keep pieces of banana logs in floating-to-immersed state in pond water to maintain pH balance and minimize protozoan and *Lernaea* sp. infection in fishes (Goswami *et al.*, 2006). Likewise, inconnection with commercial fish culture in freshwater ponds, other examples of ITK can be put up (feeding of dried and cultured duckweed *Azolla* sp. to grass carp and *Labeo rohita*, use of treated and BOD-reduced domestic wastewater in large fish culture water bodies to increase productivity therein and bring down cost relating to procurement of supplementary feed, use of neem *Azadirachta indica* oil cake in controlling WSSV and bacterial infections in tiger shrimp and *Clarias batrachus* respectively), which have been inherited and successfully put into effect by many elderly fish farmers in India. Along with Sri Nilratan Ghosh, name of Sri Premtosh Ghosh also deserves special mentioning. Regarding maintenance of fish health, 1kg neem seeds are powdered, mixed in 2lit water, kept overnight; it is filtered and 20lit water is added to it to get 5% neem seed extract. About 200gm washing powder is added to the extract and spread in a haul of fish at one corner of pond after netting.

Total annual fish seed (fry) production (2006-2007) in West Bengal has been recorded to be 13200 million. In West Bengal villages, professional fish farmers practice fish farming mainly in ponds (5-15nos.) taken on lease from individuals or Government bodies for a period of 4-5 years. In Dakshin Dinajpur district, during 2009-2010, the amount payable for ponds located beside good approach road (beside metalled/non-earthen road where buses can ply) of 33 decimal area that will be taken on lease for fish culture for one year was Rs. 10,000/-. In interior far-away remote areas and ponds located beside narrow road with mud top, payable lease amount for such ponds was Rs. 7000/-. For a nearby-located 33 decimal pond, amount stands Rs 50,000/- for five years. In 2014, lease amount for such a pond has increased to Rs. 15,000/- for one year. Generally fish farmers take pond of 66 decimal in area (supposedly) on lease by paying Rs. 1,25,000/- for five years (@ Rs. 25,000/- for one year). Farmers prefer to raise fingerlings instead of table-sized fishes as they opine that they will be able to utilize the ponds for more than one time in a year by raising 3-4 crops of major carp fingerlings.

According to scientists of CIFA, Bhubaneswar, fry reach to a size of 8-10cm (10gm) within 60-90 days of rearing, which is the fingerling stage. Officials of KVK Nimpith in West Bengal have observed the size of IMC fingerling to be 5-10cm (weighing 15-20gm) from stocked fry stage within 90 days. It has been noticed by the author that fish farmers maintain their own ingenious way of raising spawn and fry of major carps to fry and fingerling stage respectively. Interaction has been made with few professional and progressive fingerling producers in Kushmandi Block of Dakshin Dinajpur district and their ways of approach have been noted; which are interestingly much deviated from the package of practices developed in scientific institutions as well as from the recommended fish pond management methods.

Figures mentioned and processes described in this present write-up on carp fry and fingerling production are a compilation of the opinions and statements given by the six fish farmers in their own words during on-site personal conversation. Traditional and inherited wisdom, popularly known as ITK as well as science are given importance in their mode of approach. It is very surprising to know and understand how renowned elderly fish farmers of past days could detect the physico-chemical condition of fish pond water just by taking palmful of water and smelling it or by placing drops of water upon tongue. If any rectification and management measures are to be done, they could give proper advice also. In the absence of modern technologies, agro-farmers and fish farmers often experiment with their limited resources and traditionally accumulated knowledge and come up with practices/technologies that are appropriate which in turn become popular to the farming community in similar agro-climatic zones. The farmers' innovations need to be nurtured, promoted and complemented with scientific inputs where necessary. ITKs have existed since generations but there is a concern that these will cease to exist if these are not documented and preserved (Gupta, 2012; Sharma *et al.*, 2011).

USE OF ALUMINIUM PHOSPHIDE TABLETS IN FISH PONDS

(a) Importance of raising carp fingerlings

Fry and fingerling production of major carps in commercial terms in small to medium-sized village ponds is undoubtedly a lucrative proposition. Major carp culture in ponds is basically a three-tier culture system where the first step begins with the rearing of spawn upto fry (2-3cm) stage for 2-3 weeks in nursery ponds followed by rearing of 2-3 weeks' old fry for about three months upto fingerling stage (8-12cm) in rearing ponds, before they are finally released in stocking ponds for growing upto table-size fish.

Efficient management practice with special attention towards preparation of nursery and rearing ponds before releasing the live material to be stocked (spawn and fry of 3 days and 15-18 days in age respectively) is extremely necessary for successful rearing of spawn (7-8mm stage) of commercially important major carps *Labeo rohita, Catla catla* and *Cirrhinus mrigala* obtained from hatchery facilities to fry (25mm) and of fry to fingerlings (100-120mm). Spawn and fry are delicate miniature versions of adult fish that require special nurturing. Eradication of naturally-occurring and already-existing predatory and weed fishes is a prime step commonly adopted towards preparation of nursery and rearing fish culture systems by converting perennial ponds that cannot be drained completely. Farmers stocking spawn and fry in ponds with harmful predators and competitors (for food, space and oxygen with cultivable fishes) will experience total loss as the stocked early-stages of fishes will be devoured by large fishes already in pond. In unprepared ponds, voracity of predatory fishes and competitive nature of uneconomic small fishes is a major cause of large-scale mortality of spawn and fry.

Production of fry and subsequently fingerlings is a farming period of three weeks and total three and a half months respectively; above 80% of fish farmers prefer this practice instead of producing marketable-sized adult fishes as the latter is a continuous practice of around ten months duration. They raise healthy fingerlings in ponds upto 0.5 hectare and are able to raise four crops in a year, which is more profitable to them. Those are harvested, loaded in mini-trucks and transported in live condition during night (with water replacement every 15-20km and presence of 2-3 water beaters on truck overhead, who manually keep up DO content of loaded water) and sold in distant auction markets. Also the process of raising adult fishes is an unsafe affair as competitive envious farmers in neighbourhood may kill the entire lot of almost-grown-up fishes in successful farmer's pond by applying poisonous chemicals and capture those without the knowledge of the farmer. Farmers of Uttar Dinajpur and Dakshin Dinajpur districts in West Bengal have experienced that there is a very good market and customer demand all round the year for live fingerlings of major carps of size 12-15cm weighing 40-80gm in North Bengal, which includes places like Darjeeling, Siliguri, Kishanganj, Dhupguri, Chopra, parts of eastern Bihar like Purnia and eastern Nepal; as the local people there prefer to buy live fishes with preference to major carps which is very much superior in food/nutrient value and best for health. A net profit of Rs. 1900/- is expected in the enterprise of fingerling production of major carps with an investment on variable cost of Rs. 7100/- in a 0.2hectare pond (Source: Aquaculture Extension Manual, CIFRI, 1985).

(b) Preference of 'Gas tablets'

Scientists of Central Institute of Freshwater Aquaculture (ICAR) and different Krishi Vigyan Kendra at district level have recommended the use of oil cake prepared from fruits of Mohua tree *Bassia latifolia* or root powder of derris tree *Derris trifoliata* at their specified doses for killing undesirable naturally-occurring fishes efficiently in ponds where farming operations, particularly fry and fingerling production of major carps will be undertaken. During 1961-1962, the importance of application of Mohua oil cake in pre-stocking fish pond management was first elucidated in West Bengal and its dosage was standardized. Undoubtedly it is very effective in its function and commercial fish farmers have been relying upon its usage since long past. Commercial grade bleaching powder is another effective and usable piscicide; all these fish toxicants render the dead fishes suitable for human consumption. Fishes die within 4-6 hours of application of Mohua oil cake and early stages of fishes meant for farming can be stocked in pond after 20-21 days of its application. But recently commercial fish farmers in West Bengal have reported adulteration of this plant-derived poison available in 30-50kg sacks (Rs. 13-14/- per kg) where wood dust of saw mills and low priced rice husk powder remain mixed with the cake in considerable amount, lessening its effectiveness as piscicide. Good quality Mohua oil cake (Rs. 18-20/- per kg; popular as Ranchi and Kanpur product) with its distinguishing pungent odour is no more available in these two districts. Presence of saw dust is realized when the oil cake is kept immersed in water; saw dust does not get mixed up, also its presence is felt when wet and semi-solid oil cake is taken on palm and rubbed with fingers. Even fish farmers have stated that bottom mud-dwelling predatory fishes do not die after application of bleaching powder. It has to be applied only during late evening to nighttime to maintain its effectiveness. Moreover labour cost is involved in application of these piscicides. Alternatively under such circumstances, they have started using Aluminium phosphide tablets (popular to farmers as 'Gas tablets') for the purpose of eradication of such fishes during pond preparation.

Commercially and readily available Aluminium phosphide (AlP) tablets are mainly used as pest control measure for stored cereal grains; toxicity of the compound is attributed to the liberation of highly toxic phosphine gas (Hydrogen phosphide; PH_3) having foul odour, which is the active pesticidal as well as piscicidal component. AlP is very effective as an indoor fumigant at crop storage, transport or processing facilities for both food crops, non-food crops and animal feed stored in bulk. It repels away small mammals like rats, mice, rabbits and moles, even snakes and is also toxic to all stages of insects. It kills mites, imago, pupae and larvae of insects. In Government storehouses, 2-4 AlP tablets kept covered with soft cotton cloth pouches are applied in each of 2-3 layers over grains inside each of 50-60kg sacks of rice, wheat, oilseeds, hardnuts, tobacco, tea, wheat flour and pulses. Infestation of insects is thus avoided. Tablets of AlP release PH_3 upon contact with water and even atmospheric water, i.e., moisture/moist air. If the tablets covered with cotton cloth are kept on floor of crop storage rooms, it will be completely filled with the gaseous pesticide PH_3; as a result pests within are suffocated/poisoned. AlP is free from toxic residues, leaves very little non-hazardous residue on food grains. Sometimes two AlP tablets in cloth pouches are applied in each of 2-3 layers inside sacks containing seeds of paddy, wheat or pulses that will be sown in agricultural fields to prevent infestation of insects. Phosphine gas is free from toxic residues and does not affect seed viability (Chugh, 1992). Due to its extreme volatility, any release of phosphine to surface water would quickly evaporate to the surrounding air.

(c) Use of AlP by fish farmers

AlP is commercially sold in 1kg aluminium bottles as containers (total 1100gm including weight of container) with the brand name Celphos and Quickphos in the form of tablets. Quickphos is available in cylindrical tin containers. Each of the tablets weighs about 2.5-3.0gm, dark-brown or grayish in colour, not readily soluble in water and contains Aluminium phosphide and Aluminium carbonate in the ratio 56:44. The name of second compound is not displayed on the cover wrapper of containers and is mentioned as 'inert ingredient'. Some fish farmers describe the tablets as 2.0-2.5 times bigger in size than the digestive tablet 'Hajmola' and similar in appearance. According to others, it is 1.5cm in diameter, similar to naphthalene balls but dark ash coloured and less thick. Some fish farmers explain it as similar in appearance to the human digestive tablet 'Digene', only pinkish-red colour replaced by dark gray. Each 3gm tablet releases 1gm of PH_3 gas on exposure to moisture or water. In the farmed coldwater fish rainbow trout, LC_{50} value of AlP has been estimated to be 4.1microgram/litre, indicating very high toxicity.

AlP is sold in fertilizer shops in towns and villages. In some shops, the wrapper of container is first tear off by shopkeeper (since AlP is veterinary chemical and not permitted to be sold to fish farmers), then sold as 'Gas tablets' in partial amounts according to the need of farmers. In Uttar Dinajpur and Dakshin Dinajpur districts, about 14-15 days prior to stocking of spawn and fry, fish farmers customarily use two containers (bottles) of AlP (Celphos brand) of 1kg each in ponds of 100 decimal in areahaving 3.0-3.5 feet water depth. If the depth of water is 5.0-6.0 feet in the middle of such a 1 acre pond, then total 2kg and another three-quarter of a bottle will be required. Most farmers use 1kg container of AlP for ponds of 33-40 decimal and total 1kg and another half of a container for ponds ranging between 50-75 decimal in area having 3.5-4.0 feet water depth. There is no strict dosage in its use in ponds, neither prescribed on the wrapper of container nor recommended by any fishery professional. Farmers have experienced that if a 1kg AlP container is used for a pond of 100 decimal having 3.0-4.0 feet depth, then bottom dwelling fishes like *Monopterus cuchia, Channa marulius, C. gachua, Mastacembelus* sp. do not get killed, which will prey upon growing spawn and fry. Price of 1kg container (Celphos brand AlP) varies between Rs. 480-500/-. In Howrah district, shopkeepers advice fish farmers to use 750gm AlP tablets for every 100 decimal pond. Many farmers in North 24 Parganas district are using three AlP bottles of 1kg each for 1 acre ponds of 3.0-4.0 feet depth.

(d) Effect of AlP in ponds

In ponds, AlP will rapidly react to form PH_3 gas which is somewhat soluble in water, but will mainly bubble up into the air. Before use, a pungent fume is ejected as soon as the lid of container is opened, which is intolerable and somewhat harmful to human beings, so the lid seal is broken and opened after immersing the container in pond water. Then the tablets are taken handful and thrown into pond water from embankment. Within ten minutes, AlP tablets swell up and PH_3 is released.

Within 40-50 minutes of application of tablets, strong foul odour (like that of decaying fish) emits out from pond; it will be difficult to stand on the western bank of the pond at that point of time if wind is blowing from eastern side. Uneconomic small fishes like *Puntius sophore, P. ticto, Colisa fasciatus, Esomus danricus, Amblypharyngodon mola* will be found in restless condition, struggling for survival. They will die within next 10-20 minutes, i.e., within a period of 1 hour 10 minutes from application of tablets. Victims of AlP, i.e., toxicised/poison-addicted fishes comes upto surface of water frequently, become erratic and swim upside down restlessly. At the moribund state of being, these small fishes are harvested from pond using drag nets all along the width of pond. Predatory fishes bigger in size start to succumb after 30-40 minutes of death of weed fishes. Within 5-6 hours of application of AlP, every kind of finfishes (those even dwelling in bottom mud) will die. Mud-dwellers die in the end.

Common predatory fishes present in pond include four species of murrels *Channa* sp., two species of eel-like fishes *Mastacembelus* sp. and *Monopterus cuchia*, two species of featherbacks *Notopterus* sp., catfish *Wallago attu, Nandus nandus, Glossogobius giuris*, etc. Fish farmers catch these predatory fishes in drag nets from 2nd to 2.5th hour of application of tablets, *i.e.*, in their moribund condition before death (gasping for breathe, behaving abnormally, coming upto surface). If not caught, they will die and settle down at pond bottom. Those are sold in auction and retail fish markets in fresh condition. Sometimes the small fishes will be found in restless condition with ventral side up within 20-25 minutes of application of AlP on sunny days. If it is felt that considerable quantity of predatory and weed fishes will be obtained from a medium-sized pond after application of AlP, which will be having good market demand and can be sold at high price, then AlP is applied in between 1.00-1.30am (midnight). When the fishes start responding abnormally, drag net is kept ready in proper position to be operated to harvest moribund fishes. Within 4.00-4.30am, the moribund and immediately-died fishes are caught from pond, loaded in transportation vehicles and sent to auction markets in towns and sub-urban areas, which begins at daybreak time.

(e) Observation of fish farmers

If Mohua oil cake is used to eradicate undesirable fishes, then farmers have to use the commercial product 'Supercleaner' @ 20ml/bigha separately to kill aquatic insects present in pond. But AlP brings about mortality of different kinds of aquatic insects (water beetles, water bugs, dragon fly nymphs, surface swimming ones) also along with the fishes. Fish farmers have stated that if limestone powder is applied by throwing chunks of dry lime into ponds @ 300-350kg/hectare water body just prior to application of AlP, then the reaction of the fumigant in ponds becomes more vigorous, water temperature rises and AlP becomes functional even at low doses (1kg container for 50-75 decimal ponds). It quickens the time of death for both predatory and weed fishes, *i.e.*, shortens the interval between application of

AlP and death of fishes. But in such conditions, dead fishes acquire a reddish tinge on body, sold in fish markets at a low price as the taste of such fishes after cooking becomes inferior.

According to some elderly farmers, in cloudy days with dim sunshine, predatory fishes in ponds start to react desperately for life within 90-120 minutes in response to the toxicity of AlP but in summer days with strong sunshine, these big fishes start to react within one hour of application of the chemical. During April-June, within 7-8 days of application of AlP, spawn and fry can be stocked in nursery and rearing ponds respectively; by this time, toxicity of AlP fades away. But generally after 3-4 days of eradication of undesirable fishes and insects, lime is applied, subsequently the pond is made productive with sufficient growth of plankton by applying liquefied mustard oil cake or a mixture of mustard oil cake, cow dung and single super phosphate in recommended proportion and dosage and finally, the 'pond preparation' phase is completed. AlP drastically brings down the dissolved oxygen content of pond water to its minimum. During winter months, with mild sunshine, toxicity of AlP in ponds extends for a longer time; early stages of fishes can be stocked only after 18-20 days of application of the fumigant. In shallow ponds, sunlight penetrates almost upto bottom and toxicity of AlP fades away more quickly than in deeper ponds.

Fish farmers mentioned that if ducks are released in pond within 2.0 hours of application of AlP, they will die. Also an adult cow will succumb if it drinks pond water within 1.5 hours. A thin ash-like/gray coloured layer is produced over pond water surface within 20 minutes of application of AlP. When drag netting is done after 2.0-2.5 hours to harvest moribund and immediately-died fishes, the layer disappears. On the 5th day post-AlP application, if spawn and fry are stocked, then it has been observed that early stages of bottom-dwelling cultivable fishes *Cirrhinus mrigala, Labeo bata* and *Cyprinus carpio* do not survive. At this time, instead of stocking fish seed, the pond bottom mud (topsoil) is thoroughly raked using bamboo or brick and rope so that accumulated phosphine gas inside bottom mud is eradicated. It ensures complete detoxification of AlP and phosphine from pond water and soil. Many farmers have stated that AlP smells like commercial carbide (which is used to ripen mango and papaya artificially and untimely) after AlP is applied in ponds.

Use of AlP tablets, particularly of Celphos brand is entirely a new technique that many fish farmers in West Bengal have adopted during pond preparation, due to its highly potent characteristics and easy availability. Presently fish farmers in Howrah, Hooghly, West Midnapore and East Midnapore districts in West Bengal are also using this chemical compound. It has been observed that undesirable fishes ('undesirable' in context of major carp culture only, but very much desirable in context of biodiversity conservation) that have died due to AlP poisoning remained fresh for a longer time in fish markets, in comparison to those that have been illegally killed by application of insecticides Thiodane and Endosulfan. Residues of AlP and phosphine are not left on fish body muscle. Application of AlP suddenly depletes the DO content in pond to almost zero point, which is the major cause of death of fishes. For a 1 acre pond, 120-140kg bleaching powder or 1000kg Mohua oil cake will be required to eradicate predatory and weed fishes, but only as little as 2-3kg AlP will serve the purpose. Demand for AlP among fish farmers is increasing day by day. In Bangladesh, the perennial ponds are prepared for stocking spawn and fry by dewatering or by applying toxins such as rotenone, phostoxin and Celphos to kill carnivorous or unwanted fishes. In Kushinagar district, Uttar Pradesh, in carp fry and fingerling production ponds covering an areaof 1ha, there is a report of a successful farmer treating the ponds with Celphos brand AlP @ 10kg/ha to eradicate predatory and weed fishes. Five days after treatment, ponds were used for seedrearing. Application of Celphos needs to be avoided because frequent application of aluminium may adversely affect the pond environment (Radheyshyam *et al.*, 2012). Although there is no problem with PH_3 as it is volatile and will not reside in fish flesh, but Aluminium hydroxide that is produced may acidify pond soil; also aluminium is non-biodegradable and will accumulate in pond bottom.

SRI ABDUL KARIM AND HIS FINGERLING PRODUCTION METHODS

Sri Abdul Karim is the Group Leader of Uttar Karanji Fish Production Group in Kushmandi Block of Dakshin Dinajpur district and an elderly fingerling producer, leading 15 members. He releases *Dimpona* (spawn) of 7-8mm size in 0.5-1.0 acre nursery ponds and rears them for two months. He applies limestone powder after 5-7 days of application of Gas tablets, two packets in 0.5 acre pond (50 decimal) with each packet weighing 32-35 kg. Drag netting is done after one day all along the width of pond, with an intention of thorough mixing of lime in water in its three vertical layers, with the entire water spread area and water column.

After 10-12 days of application of Gas tablets in pond, surface dwelling *Catla catla* or silver carp is stocked (5-6 pieces stocked of 80-100gm size) and those are allowed to remain for a day; this is done to test whether the poisonous effect, *i.e*, toxicity of AlP in pond water has got completely eliminated or not and to ensure that the about-to-be stocked major carp spawn survives. Cowdung is not applied in this pre-stocking phase. He uses Metacid-50 (organophosphorus insecticide methyl parathion) to kill small insects. After 24 hours of its application, 8-10 *bati* (spawn measuring aluminium cup; 160ml capacity, 80,000nos./cup) spawn/Dimpona comprising a mixture of IMC {roughly 14 (Mrigal + Rohu) : 2 Catla} is stocked in 0.5acre or 50 decimal pond. On the 48th hour of stocking, mustard oil cake (MOC) is soaked in water overnight; 3kg is meant for application as supplementary feed in the 0.5acre pond. On the next morning, 500gm mustard oil is mixed with the liquefied oilcake to make it thin and undense. Generally 2kg MOC is diluted with 5-6 litres of water, after that oil is added. It is applied in the marginal areas of pond. From 4th day onwards till 12th day, a mixture of 4kg MOC and 400-500gm oil is applied daily. The carefully liquefied feed containing only dust-like particulate matter is sprinkled uniformly over water surface, particularly in pond margin where mostly spawn aggregate.

Drag netting (mosquito net cloth) is done on 11th-12th day. From then onwards, 5kg liquefied MOC is applied till 21st day on every alternate day. On 21st-22nd day, fishes reach 1.0 inch size. Feeding is continued and after three weeks, quantity of MOC is increased to 10kg, then 15kg and finally 20kg on every 10th day; the liquefied oil cake (without mustard oil) is applied every 2 days interval. Drag netting is done at an interval of ten days. Rice dust or rice bran is not applied as feed; it is feared that it may contain minute particles of rice husk, which may clog up the throat of growing spawn. Fishes reach 2.5-3.0 inch size at the end of two months, with 150-160 fishes weighing one kilogram. Further stocking of this stage (advanced fry) in larger ponds (1.0-2.0acre) is done @ 200kg fish/acre water area. Thus 30,000-32000nos. advanced fry are stocked in 1acre pond, which comes to 80000nos./ha. Fishes are reared for next three months.

In this bigger pond, before stocking the fishes, Gas tablets are applied, followed by lime (70kg/acre). Aquatic insects are not purposefully eradicated, Metacid not applied. A quantity of 140kg MOC (2 bags) is applied in 1 acre pond once in a month; it is applied either in dry and pulverized state over water surface or in liquefied state, the latter method is preferred. A mixture of 200kg single super phosphate (4 bags) and 75kg urea (1.5 bags) is applied monthly in this 1 acre fingerling production pond; it is sprinkled in dry state over pond water. Raw cowdung is kept heaped covered with polythene cloth at one corner on pond embankment; total 30 quintals is applied in three split doses at ten days interval. Drag netting is done twice a month. In three months, IMC reach 6-7inches size with 70-80gm body weight. It is believed that due to lesser stocking density of fry (as scientists recommend to stock 2.0 lakh IMC fry in 1 hectare pond), fingerlings attain high body weight in a short time (within 90 days) in this farmer's pond.

SRI SIREN SARKAR AND HIS FARMING METHODS

Another noted and experienced fish farmer Sri Siren Sarkar of Kushmandi Block stock spawn in nursery ponds at a much low density, i.e., 2 *bati* (1,00,000-1,10,000 Nos.) in each of 30 decimal ponds. Considering the pre-stocking phase, he applies 30kg lime stone powder in the pond and subsequently the bottom soil is raked. This is done after a week of application of Gas tablets. After 12-13 days of lime application, the liquid aqua-product 'Jackpot' is applied to kill aquatic insects @ 25gm/33 decimal water area (considering water depth 1mt). A 100gm container of it costs Rs. 30-35/-. A roughly estimated quantity of semi-decomposed cow dung is applied in pond before spawn stocking.

After stocking of spawn, from 3rd day onwards, a mixture of 1.5kg MOC (liquefied), 100gm mustard oil and four raw poultry eggs is applied in the 33 decimal pond as spawn feed all along the pond margin (gently applied on water surface). It is applied everyday till 6th or 7th day. From 7th day, a mixture of 2kg liquefied MOC and soyabean dust is applied everyday till 11th day, quantity of MOC is increased to 3kg till 16th day and upto 5kg till 22nd day. On 22nd day, fry are harvested which attains about 1.5 inch length. Those are stocked in bigger ponds (1 acre). According to the farmer, from 50,000-60,000 spawn (1 *bati*) stocked in nurseries, 120kg fingerlings can be produced within 60 days. Drag netting is done once in a week to 'exercise' the early stages. In preparation of liquefied MOC, it is paid attention that particles of MOC are fine enough and smaller than gape of mouth of spawn.

In rearing ponds, about 100kg fry (1.5 inch size) is stocked in ponds of 1 acre (100 decimal) in area. Before stocking, 100kg lime is applied in the pond (3 packs of 35kg each). After 8-10 days of fry stocking, 50kg urea and 100kg single super phosphate is applied in the pond. A high dosage of these two fertilizers is maintained by many farmers in commercial fingerling production. Supplementary feed in the form of liquefied MOC is applied at an interval of 2-3 days. For 100kg fry, 10kg MOC is applied initially, continued till end of first week, increased to 15kg, again maintained till 20th day. If natural productivity (plankton biomass) is felt insufficient, then it is increased to 25kg from 3rd week onwards. In this way, quantity of MOC is increased to 45-50kg during 5th-6th week. On the 25th day of fry stocking, liquefied compost manure comprising 1000kg raw cow dung, 70 kg mustard oil cake, 50kg SSP and 10kg urea is prepared in pits and applied in the pond. At the end of 45 days, fingerlings attain 2.5-3.0 inches body length, with 150 pieces weighing 1kg. At the end of 45-50 days of rearing, 400-450kg fingerlings can be harvested from this 1 acre pond. If rearing is continued for 100 days, at final harvest, fingerlings reach almost 6 inches size, with 25-40 pieces weighing 1kg. Mostly it comprises *Labeo rohita, Labeo bata, Cirrhinus mrigala* and silver carp, with lesser numbers of *Catla catla* and big head carp.

SPAWN PRODUCTION ACTIVITIES OF SRI MISIR MIYA

Sri Misir Miya is a progressive fish farmer in the Block who was selected for State-level training at Kalyani Fish Farm, Dist. Nadia during November 2014. He has taken about ten ponds on lease. In a nursery pond of 75 decimal area, he applies Gas tablets fifteen days prior to spawn stocking. After four days of application of tablets, 75kg lime is applied in the pond. About ten days prior to seed stocking, 150kg semi-decomposed cow dung is applied therein. After 3-4 days of cowdung application, Metacid is applied to kill *sujipoka* (larger zooplankton of Copepoda group, which may reside in the gill lamellae and cause respiration problems of fishes). Three days prior to seed release, 40kg MOC is applied in the same 75 decimal pond. To eradicate aquatic insects, he applies 'Supercleaner' in ponds @ 50gm per 50 decimal area following four days of MOC application.

After necessary pre-stocking management phase, 10 *bati* Dimpona is released in the 75 decimal pond. According to him, smaller size *bati* of 125ml capacity holds 50000-55,000nos. of spawn. After spawn stocking, a mixture of 80nos. raw/unboiled poultry eggs and 5kg mustard oil is applied over pond margin daily as supplementary feed in this 75 decimal pond. Feed particles remain in floating state. For 1st 3 or 4 days after stocking, unboiled eggs are used. From 4th day onwards and till 5th day of stocking, 3kg liquefied MOC is provided everyday as feed, sprinkled over water surface using *hundi* or plastic tub. Size of particles of oilcake in the diluted form must be smaller than the gape of mouth of spawn. On 6th day and 7th day, 4kg MOC is applied; on 8th, 9th and 10th day, 5kg is applied. Drag netting is done on 11th day, harvesting done on 12th day of rearing when spawn attain about 1inch (20-25mm) body length. It takes 35-40 days to get almost 2.0 inch sized fishes.

Relating to the test on neutralization/detoxification of Gas tablets in pond water, in between 10-12 days of its application, pond water is poured into a rectangular cemented chamber constructed on embankment and few *Dhanipona* (major carp fry) are released into it. Their survivability is noted in 30 minutes period. If no mortality or abnormality occurs, then the pond water is considered suitable and safe for stocking seeds.

SRI MOSHTAQ HOSSAIN AND HIS FINGERLING PRODUCTION METHODS

Another farmer Sri Moshtaq Hossain uses liquefied MOC @ 20kg/ha area generally from 3rd day of seed stocking in nursery ponds daily till 15th day. In rearing ponds where 1.5-2.0 inch sized fishes are to be stocked, 7-10 quintals of raw cow dung is kept dumped at one corner of pond before seed release and within next 30-45 days, the entire material is channelized in partial amounts into pond. He uses compost manure in rearing ponds, prepared in a (4.5 x 5.0) square feet pit, having 2 feet depth. It comprises a mixture of 1000kg cowdung, 40-45kg MOC, 100kg rice dust, 25kg urea and 50kg SSP. Water is applied over mixture, kept covered for 8-10 days. The wet material is further diluted and applied in pond using Hundi.

In rearing pond, he stocks IMC fry (*Dhanipona*) in high density, i.e., 7-8 lakh per hectare. After 2-3 days after seed release, MOC is applied as feed. This feeding schedule is an arbitrary one, done in his own way unmethodically. Many farmers like him remain involved in professions like agricultural labours in distant places, so are unable to maintain routinewise feeding of fishes. Diluted MOC is applied in the quantity 40kg in 1 hectare pond. The entire gunny bag (not untied) containing the material is kept immersed in pond water; it gets softened, semi-solid and is further diluted after untying the bag and made thin before application using plastic tub. In same time, a dry mixture of 20kg rice dust and 20kg maize dust is broadcasted over pond and provided to fishes as feed. Further feeding is done as such:

Fifteen days interval is kept after first time feeding
On 15th day, MOC applied 70kg in previous manner, in addition to 35 kg rice bran/dust and 35kg maize dust
Fifteen days interval is kept
On 30th day, MOC applied 50kg; suitable pores are made on gunny bag wall and the bag is kept submerged in pond with the support of rope and bamboo in inclined position. Separately 25kg rice bran/dust and 25kg maize dust is applied
Fifteen days interval is kept
On 45th day, MOC applied 50kg; suitable pores are made on gunny bag wall and feed provided in same manner. Separately 25kg rice bran/dust and 25kg maize dust is applied
Fifteen days interval is kept
On 60th day, MOC applied 60kg, and a mixture of 30kg rice dust and 30kg maize dust (rice dust and maize dust are applied irregularly)
Fifteen days interval is kept
On 75th day, MOC applied 60kg, and a mixture of 30kg rice dust and 30kg maize dust (rice dust and maize dust are applied irregularly)
Fifteen days interval is kept
On 90th day, MOC applied 150-160kg; in addition to 75kg rice bran and 75kg maize dust (rice dust and maize dust are applied irregularly)
Fishes are harvested after 25-30 days

According to the farmer, fingerling production from fry stage is a 110-120 days' crop. According to such farmers who do not apply daily feed to fishes and also in improper quantity, stocking is done during monsoon at 2 inch size (4-5gm) and in almost four months, it reaches 50-60gm (6-7 inches). After 15 - 20 days of seed release, 200kg single super phosphate and 50kg urea are applied in the one hectare pond. Those two are applied separately in dry form. On the 60th day of culture, 200kg lime is applied in the same pond. Among fish farmers, it has been a trend of using SSP and urea in a high dose in fingerling production ponds.

FINGERLING PRODUCTION PROCESS OF SRI KAMALAKANTA SARKAR

Sri Kamalakanta Sarkar is a widely-experienced farmer and was chosen also for the State-level training programme from Kushmandi Block; a beneficiary covered under the FFDA Block-level Demonstration Centre (DC) scheme of Fisheries Department. He stocks 5-7 *bati* spawn (each aluminium *bati* of 120ml capacity, he described it as having the shape and size of bell of ladies bicycle, holding 50,000 spawn) in every 33 decimal nursery pond. Each mass of 50,000 spawn costs Rs. 200-220/-, but during early season (May-mid June), it costs Rs. 700-750/-. He further stated that each such *bati*/'spawn measuring cup' will contain 25,000-30,000 spawn if purchased from dishonest hatchery owners, where, in such cases, the *bati* will contain much water. In the pond preparation phase, before stocking fish seeds, he uses Gas tablets for killing undesirable fishes and insects and within 7-8 days post AlP application, water turns transparent. After 4 days of its application, lime ($CaCO_3$) is applied @ 50kg/33 decimal pond. About 15 quintals of raw cow dung is brought to pond site and kept heaped at one corner on bundh. After 3-4 days of lime application, semi-decomposed and semi-diluted cow dung is slowly allowed to enter into water column.

After 14-15 days of its application, spawn are stocked. He observed low growth if spawn are stocked in higher density, i.e., @ 10-12 *bati*/33 decimal pond. In his ponds, spawn attain 32-37mm size within 20-25 days of rearing and at time of harvest. In 33 decimal pond, on the first day of stocking, he uses a mixture of four raw/unboiled chicken eggs and 500gm mustard oil as feed for the spawn; the watery mixture is gently spread gently over water surface at the margin of ponds. Likewise, six, nine, twelve and fifteen unboiled eggs are used on the 2nd, 3rd, 4th and 5th day respectively in addition to oil. On 4th and 5th day, quantity of oil is increased to 800gm. On the 6th day, 1.5kg yellow-type mustard oil cake is applied in pond in diluted form. It is continued and on 8th day, 2.0-2.5kg oilcake is applied. From 9th day till 25th day, a mixture of 1.0-1.5kg maize dust and 1kg rice dust (rice polish) is applied as feed in addition to oil cake; quantity of oil cake is increased to 4.0-4.5kg on 10th day and an increase of 1kg is made on every subsequent day till 25th day. Quantity of maize dust and rice polish is increased upto 5kg each, but truly speaking these two are irregularly applied. On the 12th day, spawn reaches 15-16mm size, when it can be distinguished into specific major carp species. On 25th day, almost 1.5 inch size is obtained (about 750 pieces weighing 1kg), which can be called as fry. Then fry are harvested in shifted to bigger (rearing) ponds.

According to him, from such a 33 decimal nursery pond, 14-15kg major carp fry is obtainable from the quantity of 5-7 *bati* spawn (2,50,000-3,50,000nos.) within 14 days. At the end of 25 days, fry stage is stocked in rearing ponds @ 400kg fry in 200 decimal pond. Like him, some farmers stock IMC fry @ 30-40kg (about 25,000nos., 1.5inch size)/33 decimal pond. In his pond, within the next 55 days period, fry reach to such a stage when 125 pieces weigh 1kg and within 100-110 days, they reach the 40-50gm size (fingerling; 15-16cm size) individually when 20-25 pieces weigh 1kg. Those are harvested and in live condition are transported to long distances of 200km and more during nighttime in parts of northern-most West Bengal, border of Nepal, Assam and eastern Bihar. Fingerlings of silver carp and big head carp are sold at Rs. 70-90/- per kg, whereas those of Indian major carps are sold at Rs. 110-120/- per kg.

GENERAL TREND OF POND MANAGEMENT - FARMERS' PERSPECTIVE

From 8th day till 22nd day, some farmers apply 8-10kg liquefied MOC in nursery ponds at one day interval, but mostly feeding is done everyday. Many farmers maintain the lesser density of stocking of spawn, *i.e,* 2 *bati* (1,00,000-1,10,000nos.) in a 30 decimal pond and those attain 2cm size within 8-10 days, with proper feeding. The practice of application of a mixture of 2kg MOC, four unboiled poultry or duck eggs (increased if stocking density is increased) and 250gm mustard oil daily from 3rd day till 6th or 7th day has become a general one. It ensures higher survivability rate of growing spawn. Members of the Chandipur Fish Production Group, a well-established tribal group in Kushmandi Block are stocking 9-10 *bati* major carp spawn (capacity: 50,000nos./*bati*) in each of 1 acre nursery ponds and from the 3rd day of stocking, a mixture of 30 unboiled hen eggs, 500gm mustard oil and 1kg wheat flour is provided as feed to the growing spawn daily for continuous one week. The feed once applied slowly extends wider along its circumference, as if a stone thrown in pond water from a nearby distance. Many farmers are using the commercial aqua-product 'Supercleaner' @ 20ml per bigha for killing superficial and submerged aquatic insects present in pond, which may prey upon the stocked early stages of fishes.At time of harvest, weight of fingerlings varies between 50nos./kg (20gm size) to 25nos./kg (40gm size) in farmers' ponds. In a lesser stocking density, fingerlings reach 40-50gm size within 90 days of rearing. In rearing ponds *i.e,* fingerling production ponds, generally a basal dose of MOC, cow dung and single super phosphate is applied before fry stocking to maintain the plankton production in pond and irregular feeding is done with liquefied MOCduring rearing period. But fish farmers normally maintain the everyday feeding schedule in nursery ponds. Considering the farmers' perspective of commercial major carp fingerling production practices, quite a high dosage of inorganic fertilizers is applied in rearing ponds.

Sri Alok Chauhan, another progressive fish farmer (fingerling producer) of Kushmandi Block who has taken about ten ponds on lease, applies Gas tablets in ponds ten days prior to spawn stocking. After 5-6 days, the bottom soil is raked considerably so that accumulated harmful gas inside bottom soil is eradicated. Before five days of spawn stocking, MOC is applied @ 5kg/33 decimal pond which influences the development of light green colour of pond water, indicating good primary productivity. Before spawn stocking, he applies 50kg lime in every 33 decimal pond and after that, drag netting is done throughout the water column for uniform mixing of lime in water. He stocks 3 *bati* major carp spawn (according to him, each *bati* of 125ml capacity holds 45,000-50,000 spawn) in every 33 decimal nursery pond. From the 24th hour of spawn stocking, for every one *bati* spawn, he applies a mixture of one unboiled hen egg and 60gm mustard oil daily as feed. The material is mixed and yellow colour is produced, and then gently applied over water surface. This feed is applied for successive four days. From 6th day till 30th day, at every one day interval, a mixture of 10kg MOC and 2kg wheat flour is applied as feed in every 33 decimal pond. Before application, the raw MOC is soaked in water for about 48 hours so that the strong pungent odour is eradicated, otherwise which may be harmful for growing spawn. In its semi-decomposed form, wheat flour is added and applied as feed. Bigger fry stage (2 inches) is obtained at the end of one month in his pond, whereby 300-350 pieces weigh 1kg.

The bigger fry stage is stocked in rearing ponds, @ 10-11 quintals of bigger fry per 7 acre pond. According to the farmer, it will be better if bigger fry of almost 3 inches in length are stocked (250 pieces weighing 1kg). Feeding with MOC is done irregularly but once in a month, after fry stocking, a mixture of 35kg single super phosphate and 15kg urea is applied per 33 decimal water area. In addition to this, monthly application of 50kg lime and one pack MOC of 60kg weight is done in 33 decimal ponds. Within next 100 days of rearing, major carp fingerlings reach 5-6 inches size, with about 25 fingerlings weighing one kilogram. In lesser stocking density, farmers have reported about growth of IMC fingerling to 6-7 inches in three months from initial 2 inch stage, with 15 fingerlings weighing 1kg at harvest.

RECOMMENDED FEEDING SCHEDULE IN REARING PONDS

In fingerling production ponds, aquaculture experts and scientists recommend the stocking density of 2 lakh fry/hectare water body; a mixture of rice bran and mustard oil cake (1:1) should be applied as supplementary feed. In 1st month, it is applied in dry pulverized form and from 2nd month onwards in dough ball form. A single 15-18 dayold fry of 1 inch size weighs about 0.4-0.5gm (according to KVK Nimpith officials, it is between 0.5-1.0gm, lengthing 25-30mm). Thus about 2000nos. early fry will weigh 1kg. If 30,000 fry is stocked in 33 decimal pond, then total weight will be 30,000 x 0.5 = 15kg. If 0.4gm is considered, then total weight becomes 12kg. During the 90-100 days of rearing, feed is applied @ 20-3% of total body weight everyday. For the first 10 days, quantity of feed to be applied will be: 20% of 15kg = 3kg.

SC Farmer Stocking Fish Seed (1)

Tribal Farmer Stocking Fish Seed (1)

Tribal Farmer Stocking Fish Seed (2)

Harvested Major Carp Fingerlings

SC Farmer Stocking Fish Seed (2)

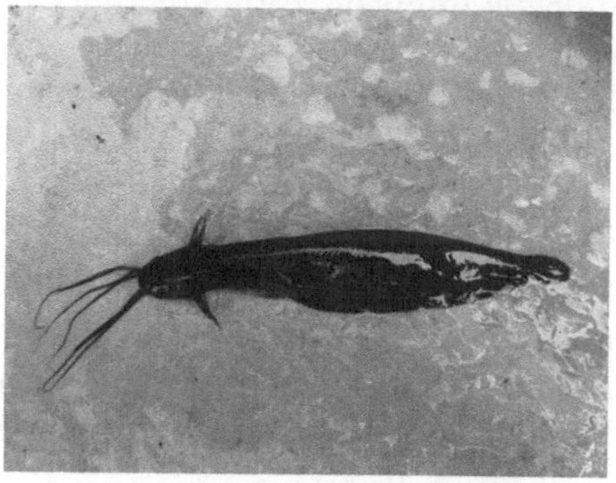

Heteropneustes fossilis (singhi)

The feeding schedule is mentioned below:

Period (in days)	Quantity of Feed to be Applied Daily
First 10 days	2kg 400gm - 3kg
Second 10 days	3kg 60gm - 3kg 800gm
Third 10 days	3kg 700gm - 4kg 600gm
Fourth 10 days	4kg 400gm - 5kg 500gm
Fifth 10 days	5kg 200gm - 6kg 500gm

(Contd...)

Sixth 10 days	6kg - 7kg 500gm
Seventh 10 days	6kg 800gm - 8kg 500gm
Eighth 10 days	7kg 700gm - 9kg 600gm
Ninth 10 days	8kg 600gm - 10kg 800gm

Scientists at CIFA, Bhubaneswar have recommended feed application to be 10-8% of stocked biomass of fry during first month, followed by 8-6% and 6-4% during the second and third month. Ingredients like fish meal and soyabean dust can be incorporated into the feed to improve its quality. On an average, a 16cm Mrigal fingerling weighs 40gm, 17cm Catla weighs 70gm while 15cm and 18cm Rohu fingerling weigh 50gm and 70gm respectively. A 10cm and 20cm Catla have been found to weigh 18gm and 160gm respectively.

RECOMMENDED FEEDING SCHEDULE IN NURSERY PONDS

According to aquaculture experts, in nursery ponds, 72-hour old spawn can be stocked @ 30-40 lakh/hectare water body. For optimum growth and survival, it is recommended to restrict the rearing period for 12-15 days. Within 20 days, they reach 25mm size. One million spawn weigh about 1.5kg. For every 1,00,000 stocked spawn, 560gm supplementary feed should be applied daily for the first seven days and 1120gm feed should be applied daily for the last 7-8 days. Feed will comprise a finely pulverized and finely sieved dry mixture of mustard oil cake and rice polish (1:1).Particle size must be uniform. Supplementary feed is broadcast on the surface of nursery ponds in the form of fine powder daily in the morning hours. Feeds incorporating vitamins, minerals and micronutrients ($CoCl_{3;}$ 0.1mg per kg diet)) have shown better growth and survival of fry. Soyabean milk can be spread evenly in nursery ponds 2-3 times daily. According to aquaculture expert Dr Asish Panigrahi, for every 5 lakh stocked spawn, feed should be applied accordingly: 1800gm daily for the first five days, 2600gm daily for the second five days and 3200gm daily for the last five days. It has been observed that instead of pulverized and dry MOC, fish farmers are using MOC in liquefied state; a combination of it with rice bran or rice polish is very rarely used.

CIFE scientists have recommended the following feeding schedule in rearing period of spawn to fry:

Period	Feed per day in terms of weight (gm) of spawn at the time of stocking
1st to 5th day after spawn stocking	Equal to double (two times)
6th to 10th day after spawn stocking	Double to three times
10th to 15th day after spawn stocking	Three times to four times

At a stocking density of 10-20 lakh spawn per hectare water body, 20,000-40,000 fry can be obtained by conventional methods. For the first two days after stocking in nurseries, spawn do not take supplementary feed and depend upon planktonic food.It has been observed that IMC fry of 4.7-5.5cm in length weigh between 1.1-1.8gm. A Catla fry of 18.5mm length has been found to weigh 65mg and a Rohu fry of 19.5mm length weigh 70-75mg. A 15-day old Mrigal fry generally becomes 18-19mm in body length.

OTHER METHODOLOGIES ON CARP SPAWN FEED AND FEEDING

In villages of Orissa, raw cattle dung is applied as basal manure in nursery ponds. To enhance its fertilization effect, liming is done. For sustained production of natural fish food organisms, a mixture of de-oiled rice bran, cattle dung or bio-gas slurry, single super phosphate and a multiplex pre-mineral mixture and vitamins are used in liquid forms before 4-5 days of spawn stocking. Fry are harvested and/or thinned in phases according to the local demand, allowing an extended period of rearing of 14-44 days in rural areas. Ponds had been stocked @ 30-50 lakh spawn per hectare. Fry are harvested after 30-45 days with a recovery of 15-30%. In rural Orissa, fish seed production includes egg to spawn production for 3 days, spawn to fry nursing for 15-20 days, fry to fingerling rearing for 60-90 days and fingerling to yearling (stunted and old fingerlings) rearing for 8-9 months. In case ponds are used for fry rearing, fry areharvested by repeated netting on day 15-20 of spawn stocking (Courtesy: Dr Radheyshyam, Retd. Principal Scientist, CIFA).

There is a report of providing semi-boiled microfine half yolk of chicken egg everyday *ad libitum* to Mrigal spawn one hour prior to giving morning ration of powdered rice polish and groundnut oil cake (Jain, 1989). During 48th-72nd hour in hatching pool, supplementary spawn feed in the form of hard-boiled egg yolk or powdered milk can be applied on the water surface. Growing carp spawn in nursery ponds can be fed with milk, wheat flour or boiled egg yolk by spreading it on the water surface. This feed can be supplemented with rice bran, bread crumbs or fish meal. A formulated supplementary feed has been evaluated for fry and fingerlings of Indian major carps; it consisted of groundnut oilcake, roasted soyabean meal, rice polish, fish meal and vitamin-mineral mixture with a crude protein level of 31% (Courtesy: Dr P.K. Mukhopadhyay, Retd. Principal Scientist, CIFA). A mixture of finely powdered oil cake (soyabean, mustard, etc.), rice or wheat bran and powdered and sieved fish meal in the ratio of 5:4:1 can be supplied to fry @ 200gm divided into several portions per day. Spawn can be stocked @ 60,000-70,000 hatchlings/200 square metre area of 4-5 days in age (total weight: 200-250gm) (Courtesy: Md. Golam Azam Khan). A suspension diet was developed by renowned scientist Late Dr. K.H. Alikunhi using rice bran, groundnut oil cake and small shrimp. The ingredients were mixed, cooked and passed through a 300-400 micrometer sieve and the filtrate was fed to carp spawn in nursery ponds several times a day.

In Jessore, Mymensingh, Comilla and Rajshahi districts of Bangladesh, from 48th hour of hatching, Indian major carp fry are fed hard-boiled chicken egg yolk that is mixed with water and spread over the surface waters of hatching pool. The 5-day old spawn (120 hours old) are stocked in nurseries. In addition to thenatural food, supplemental feed is provided on a regular basis to spawn stocked in nursery ponds. Farmers fed hard-boiled chicken egg-yolk to the stocked spawn for the first three days after stocking. Three to four eggs are required for each kg of growing spawn (It should be remembered that the stocked spawn were of bigger size). Sometimes 0.5-1.0kg of cooked and diluted wheat flour is mixed with the egg-yolk. Subsequently the spawn are fed wheat flour (1kg wheat flour/kg of fish) for three to four days. The wheat flour is mixed with water and broadcasted across the pond surface. When the fry areseven days old, mustard oil cake is provided at the rate of 2kg feed per kg fry. Prior to feeding, it is soaked in water for at least 24 hours and further diluted with water before being broadcasted over the water surface. This feedingschedule is used for the next seven days.

After two weeks, most of the farmers in Bangladesh switch to mustard oil cake, and continued feeding the same ration until the spawn attained fry stage, which are sold at 4-5gm, some 30 to 40 days after hatching. Some farmers add rice polish to the mustard oil cake when the fry were about 1.2cm, and the fry could ingest small food particles. In general, during first 7 to 14 days of rearing the fry are fed to satiation. At the end of this period the fry reach 0.5 inches (1.27cm). Between 14 and 21 days, the fry are fed at 60% of body weight per day. The ration is reducedto 40% between 21-30 days of rearing. At 2-3gm size, the ration is reduced to 15-20% of body weight per day. Farmers rear the initially stocked spawn for a maximum of 30 to 40 days, then fry are obtained and start to sell those from 30 days onwards, when they reach approximately 1.0-1.5 inches (2.5-3.8cm), *i.e.*, the fry stage. Some farmers, who have grow-out ponds, rear the fryfor seven to eight months in their own rearing ponds and stock them out into their large pondsas juveniles/sub-adult fishes/very large fingerlings (10-15 inches/25-38cm; 70-100gm) (Courtesy: Dr. M.R.I. Sarder, Faculty of Fisheries, Bangladesh Agricultural University).

According to late Dr V.G. Jhingran, food and feeding behaviour of the hatchlings and fry of the Indian major carps differmarkedly from those of the fingerlings and adults. With the development of science-based fish culture and its practices, farmers havebecome aware of the need to provide supplementary food to the fish. Earlier in this article, it has been mentioned about adulteration of Mohua oil cake. But surprisingly MOC, *i.e.*, mustard oil cake is also available in markets of West Bengal in adulterated form where considerable amount of saw dust remains mixed with it. To bring up its familiar pungent odour, farmers have reported about mixing of red chilly dust in MOC. This edible oil cake is sold at Rs. 1940 per quintal but a fish farmer has to be careful while buying it. Many dishonest businessmen in West Bengal are adulterating MOC in the oil mills.

PROPAGATION OF THREE THREATENED FRESHWATER CATFISHES

Small indigenous fishes are our valuable heritage resource naturally occurring in the still freshwater bodies of West Bengal. Presently concerns have arisen about many fishes that have exhibited declining trend in availability. Since last few decades, lentic-type freshwater ecosystems of West Bengal have been exposed to serious stress, posing threat to sustenance of many indigenous freshwater fishes. There has been a noticeable reduction in biodiversity of such fishes. These are source of good quality protein and other nutrients for rural poor, offering similar or even larger benefits in terms of nutritional security to the people in comparison to the conventional cultivable fishes. Revival of threatened and endangered freshwater fishes calls for adoption of quick conservation efforts. Captive breeding programmes and mass seed production *via* administration of exogenous inducing hormones have been initiated in research institutions to attempt to propagate these fishes artificially for conservation and aquaculture production. Catfishes are included under different families of Order Siluriformes, possessing maxillary and mandibulary barbels and their skin is devoid of scales.

In south-western Bengal, there has been an average population decline of 35.3% over a period of four decades (1960-2000) for *Ompak pabda*; the average decline per decade since 1980 has been about 69%. From the early 1980s, sharp falls in its catches were observed in North Bihar and West Bengal (Chakrabarti *et al.*, 2009). Natural population of *O. pabda* is greatly reduced in Indian waters and its restricted occurrence with smaller population size has been noticed in North-eastern India (Banik *et al.*, 2012). A decline of 34.3% in catch for *Mystus vittatus* in south-western Bengal during 1960-2000 has been reported (Mishra *et al.*, 2009). Although in early 1970s, it supported a strong fishery in West Bengal, but in 1980s and onwards sharp fall in catches was observed. There has been a growing concern over exploitation and depletion of the stock of *M. vittatus* in some open water bodies and wetlands (Source: CIFRI, Barrackpore Newsletter January-June 2008). In natural water bodies of the state, availability of *Heteropneustes fossilis* has severely diminished, very rarely to be found in city fish markets (Bhattacharjee, 2012). Due to rough water management policy for irrigation, over exploitation and various ecological changes in its natural habitat, *H. fossilis* is threatened now

(Chakraborty and Mirza, 2008). Successful laboratory and on-farm investigations on broodstock conditioning, induced breeding, larval rearing and pond farming of three threatened indigenous freshwater catfishes of the state, i.e., 'pabda' *Ompak pabda*, 'singhi' *Heteropneustes fossilis* and 'desi tengra' *Mystus vittatus* have been discussed in the following portion of this write-up.

SHRINKING FISHERY RESOURCE OF DAKSHIN DINAJPUR DISTRICT

There was a time when undivided Dinajpur district was famous for the repository of freshwater fishes. According to the epic Mahabharata, Dinajpur was familiar to people as *'Matsya-desh'*. When Bangladesh established itself as a separate country, then a part of the district by the name 'Paschim Dinajpur' came under our country's jurisdiction; again during 1990-1991, Paschim Dinajpur got further divided into Uttar Dinajpur and Dakshin Dinajpur. Important and productive rivers namely Nagor, Mahananda, Tangon, Atreyee, Kulik, Chiramoti, Punarbhaba flow through these two districts. Here 80% of the inhabitants are agriculture-dependant. DakshinDinajpur district is particularly famous for the presence of many resourceful large-sized beels/natural wetlands, namely Saraidighi, Maliandighi, Aaltadighi, Gourdighi, Tapandighi, Karandighi, Mahipaldighi, Kaaldighi, Dhamdighi, Chopradighi, Tutuliadighi, Rangadighi, Pransagardighi; some other beels are known by the names Nehali, Hatiya, Bajargaon, Kachan, Kachnagoch, Bura, Matiya, Taron, Chandanpur, Raygachhi, Raypur, Bhlimadaha, Bhodra, Azadpurbeel, Fakir, etc. All these perennial water bodies are valuable heritage resources to the people of the district. Along with the familiar cultivable freshwater fishes, different kinds of nutrient-rich small indigenous fishes, known by the local names mourola, punti, bele, meni/nados, kholse, daarke, chanda, kakles, saati, shol, gajar, baan, folui, singhi, magur, koi, raikhoira, banspata, chela, tengra, sarpunti, kursa, teenkaata, loch, khoira, piyali, pabda, phesa, gangkoi are noted not only as the 'poor man's protein source', but also came under demand of elite consumers gradually. According to Fisheries Mapping Project (Govt. of West Bengal) officials, in Dakshin Dinajpur district, total number of water bodies between 8-50 decimal in area is 31,245, those between 50-125 decimal in area is 13,156 and those above 125 decimal in area is 4,113. There are total 48 beels in Dakshin Dinajpur district. In this district, 8500 hectare of ponds are presently being utilized for fish farming.

Unfortunately many of the resourceful wetlands have considerably shrunk in area with progress of time. Resources of many naturally-occurring fishes have diminished, inland fishermen have been losing their profession, conversion of water bodies into agricultural lands and human settlements have become evident. Siltation, infestation of aquatic weeds, jute retting processes has been deteriorating their natural entity. Fishes like bacha, banspata, kursa, meni, bele, sarpunti are very rarely to be found nowadays in the district. Experienced and progressive fish farmers namely Sri Dipak Roy in Maldah district, Sri Ashis Sarkar in Uttar Dinajpur, Sri Anisur Rahaman and Sri Jibananda Singha in Dakshin Dinajpur have been putting efforts in seed production of some threatened fishes and raising them to marketable size in captivity under controlled conditions.

SEED PRODUCTION AND FARMING

(a) *Ompak pabda* (Hamilton-Buchanan)

In experiments conducted by West Bengal Fisheries Department, broodstock of *O. pabda* maintained throughout 10-12 months attained maturity after one year in May (body weight: 85gm). Breeding was carried out in bundh; such impoundments after a heavy shower in monsoon receive large quantities of rainwater from their catchment area and provide a large spawning ground. Sex ratio used was 2 free-oozing males: 1 ripe female. Dosages of inducing hormone pituitary extract were administered @ 3-4mg/kg and 8-10mg/kg body weight as 1st and 2nd injections respectively to females at an interval of five hours, and 2-3mg/kg body weight to males. Ovatide was administered @ 3ml/kg body weight of fishes in females only (Mukherjee *et al.*, 2002). In such situations, 50% and 70% success(s) in hatching of fertilized eggs was achieved with pituitary extract and Ovatide respectively. Injected brooders were kept in hapa cloth containers in bundhs for spawning. Egg incubation period was 22 hours. Larvae were fed with steam-cooked mixture of egg and mussel meat from third day of hatching. About 7500 hatchlings are obtainable from 20,000-30,000 fertilized eggs.

In CIFA (ICAR) ponds, brood males matured earlier than females, attaining 30-40gm body weight. Brooders were maintained on trash fish (alternatively live tubifex worms and ground silkworm pupae) and boiled chopped chicken viscera at about 5-10% of body weight per day. Ovaprim was used as inducing agent, applied @ 1.0-1.5ml/kg body weight for females and 0.5-1.0ml/kg body weight for males (Chakrabarti *et al.*, 2009). Females were stripped for spawning 8-10 hours after 2nd injection. Milt was obtained from males by surgically removing the testes, which were macerated to produce a suspension to be mixed with the eggs for fertilization. Fertilized eggs were transferred to fibreglass/cement tank for hatching. Newly hatched larvae obtained after 23 hours can be reared in fibreglass tanks, cement cisterns as well as in nursery ponds. Mixed zooplankton, tubifex worms and egg custard were provided as larval feed. Larvae became fry between 15th-18th day with 1.1-2.0cm in body length and 0.6-2.0gm weight. Fry can be reared in cement cisterns with both zooplankton and tubifex worms as feed on alternate days.

In fry stages and onwards, the fish can be fed with compound feed comprising rice polish, silkworm pupae and boiled egg at 100% of total body weight. After a rearing period of forty days, fry attained fingerling stage with a size 5.0-6.0cm and 3.0-5.0gm. These if stocked during October-November in grow-out ponds and maintained on a mixture of groundnut oil cake, rice bran and fish meal, will attain 40gm by May-June in the following year. During maturity stages, the male and female attains minimum lengths of 16.3cm and 17.0cm respectively (Banik *et al.*, 2012). Fertilized eggs may be spread evenly over round-meshed mosquito net stretched and fitted just below water surface in rectangular cemented cisterns. Aeration by sprinkling of water over eggs is done through a perforated PVC pipe. *O. pabda* can be grown along with major carps in composite culture system; a combination of groundnut oil cake, rice bran and fish meal (15-20%) is fed to the fish. Feed containing 40% rice dust, 30% mustard oil cake and 30% fish meal may be used in broodstock conditioning and grow-out ponds.

Moist supplementary feeds are dispensed to *O. pabda* fry and fingerlings at 2-3% of body weight. With good management practices, 800-1000kg/ha production of this fish can be achieved within 7-8 months. Fry of size 1.5-2.0 inches have been found to attain a marketable size of 50-60gm within 120-130 days of culture in grow-out ponds, and 75-100gm in ten months. Fry of *O. pabda* are normally fed tubificid worms, processed chicken viscera, isolated soya protein, silkworm pupae and plankton; they attain maturity in 10-11 months. Spawn of size 3-4mm and 2mg maintained on Daphnia-rich zooplankton, silkworm powder and chopped tubifex worms have been found to reach 30mm and 207-245mg after 15 days of rearing and 7.0-9.5cm and 2.5-4.2gm (advanced fry stage) after 100 days of rearing. This stage when stocked in grow-out ponds @ 30,000nos./ha and maintained on mixture of groundnut oil cake and silkworm pupae powder (1:1) @ 5% of body weight daily, have been found to attain 16.7cm length and 24gm body weight on average after 120 days of culture (Source: CIFA Annual Report 2007-'08: 62pp). Grow-out culture in earthen ponds (initial size at stocking: 8cm and 2.8gm) registered a production of 415 and 536kg/ha, stocked @ 0.3 and 0.5 lakh/ha respectively (Source: CIFA Annual Report 2010-'11: 81pp). *O. pabda* will feed upon the marine fish *Harpodon nehereus* if hanged down into pond water, but do not eat live trash fishes. *O. pabda* is a sweet and delicious fish, popular to almost every Bengalee and in Bengali cuisine.

(b) *Mystus vittatus* (Bloch)

In breeding programmes, tubifex worms have been given as live feed to brood fishes of *M. vittatus* and after two days of conditioning, they were used for induced breeding purpose. Males and females are 25-30gm and 40-50gm respectively in body weight. Dosages of pituitary gland extract with 4mg/kg body weight for males and 8mg/kg for females have been found to be effective in induced breeding of *M. vittatus*in breeding hapa cloth which may provide 80% and 56% fertilization and hatching success(s) respectively (Islam *et al.*, 2011). Spawning occurred within 16-18 hours of application of hormone injection at 28-30°C water temperature. Highest survivability rate of spawns till day-10 post-hatching was found to be 68%. Finely powdered feed is prepared using fish meal, rice polish, groundnut oil cake, soyabean meal, cod liver oil and vitamin mixture for feeding fry of *M. vittatus*, which is fed four times a day @ 3% of body weight (Mohanty, 2006).

In experiments conducted by WB Fisheries Department, sex ratio used was 2 males: 1 female, dosage of Ovatide hormone used was 8ml per kg body weight of fish for females only and in such a situation, 80% hatching success was achieved (Mukherjee *et al.*, 2002). Successful induced breeding of *M. vittatus* was done by administering synthetic hormone Ovaprim @ 3ml/kg body weight for female and 1ml/kg body weight in case of male in a single dose. Fertilized eggs remain adhered to the roots of water hyacinth. The percentage of hatching was 70-80% (Source: Directorate of Research, Assam Agricultural University). Fertilized eggs have been found to remain adhered to small cut-out bunches of palm tree leaves when kept inside hatching-cum-incubation pool.

Successful breeding and rearing of post-larva and fry of *M. vittatus* were achieved at CIFA, Kalyani, West Bengal. During early monsoon, male and female brooders weighing 15-20gm and 30-40gm respectively were chosen for induced breeding. Brood fishes of body length 9.6-13.9cm and weight 18.0-25.2gm had been previously maintained in 0.4ha brood stock pond and fed regularly with boiled chicken viscera. Ovaprim was applied as the inducing agent @ 1.0-1.5ml/kg and 1.0ml/kg body weight to females and males respectively. Injected brooders were kept in both 400lit capacity FRP tanks (filled with rainwater upto 8 inches height) and hapa containers in pond for spawning. Submerged aquatic weeds were kept inside the breeding environment. Spawning was found to occur in between 7-10 hours post-injection and larvae hatched out in 21-24 hours after fertilization of eggs. Success(s) in fertilization and hatching of eggs were recorded to be upto 80% and 60% respectively (Source: CIFA Annual Report 2007-'08: 60-61pp). The hatchlings have been reared in aerated fibreglass tanks with natural food (zooplankton). In a properly managed composite fish culture farm of 5.0ha in Nadia district, West Bengal, along with stocking of fingerlings of *Labeo calbasu* and six species of major carps, *M. vittatus* was also stocked in addition to *Notopterus chitala*, *Pangasius* sp. and two species of murrels. Catfish *M. vittatus* stocked @ 500nos./ha water area (biomass: 5kg) gave a production of 18kg/ha/year (Chakraborty and Das, 2012). From fry stage, *M. vittatus* takes almost one year to reach marketable size of 30-50gm. It has a good demand as a foodfish in fish markets as it has high nutritional value in terms of protein, micronutrients, vitamins and minerals (Ross *et al.*, 2003). Even *M. vittatus* of 3.0-3.5 inches size are sold above Rs. 300/- per kilogram in Kolkata markets.

In West Bengal villages, matured and gravid *M. vittatus* are found in weed-infested small beels and shallow wetlands during July-August and seeds of 1.0 inch size (400-500 pieces weighing 1kg) are available in nature during October. These enter into carp culture ponds via outlets channels when excess water in ponds is let off. During April-May of following year, when carps are harvested from ponds and water table recede; table-size *M. vittatus* of around 3.5 inch in length are obtained. Some farmers stock seeds of 1inch size @ 1500-2000 pieces per 33 decimal during September-October in carp culture ponds, those are fed chopped earthworms, fish meal and within next 7-8 months, those reach 4-5 inches in length with 25-30 pieces weighing 1kg. Chicken entrails may be composted and fed to them.

(c) *Heteropneustes fossilis* (Bloch)

Regarding brood stock maintenance, young male and female *H. fossilis* can be stocked in ponds of 100-200sqmt in area @ 10-20 fishes/mt^3 and a mixture of groundnut oil cake, rice bran, fish meal and soyabean meal is fed to them for 3-4 months. Single intramuscular injection of Ovaprim @ 0.60-0.90ml/kg and 0.30-0.45ml/kg body weight to females and males respectively has been found useful in induced breeding. Carp pituitary extract @ 90-150mg/kg body weight to females (two split doses at an interval of 5-6 hours) and 30-60mg/kg body weight to males can also be used. The routine dosage of CPE is 5-10mg/100gm body weight of female (may be injected in a single installment) and 4-5mg/100gm of male (CIFRI, 1982). Matured females are stripped on 11th-14th hour of hormone administration. Testes of males are dissected out, squeezed in muslin cloth with 0.8% saline solution and this sperm suspension is spread over stripped eggs. Fine-meshed nylon net is spread horizontally in a container 5-10cm under water level; fertilized eggs are spread over it and maintained under flowing water. Incubation period is 16-19 hours. Hatched-out larvae (2.72mm) are fed from the 3rd-4th day accordingly: mixture of minute rotifers and boiled egg yolk for first two days, rotifers and ciliated zooplankton from 3rd to 12th day and mixture of zooplankton and chopped molluscan meat during 13th - 21st day. Fry are produced in between 19th-21st day.

This stage may be stocked in cement cisterns having 25-30cm water level @ 200nos/m^2, and maintained on a diet containing finely ground trash fish, rice bran (1:1) and molluscan meat. Fry attain 4-5cm in one month of rearing and are suitable for stocking in ponds. *H. fossilis* may be induced bred during the months April to October. At CIFA, Bhubaneswar, with proper environmental and feeding regime in pre-vitellogenic phase, *H. fossilis* were administered with carp pituitary extract @ 5ml/kg body weight and bred in

April; the same fishes could be allowed to re-mature and induced to breed again successively in the months of June, August and November. Spawning of *H. fossilis* has been observed after 8-10 hours of PG extract injection in hapa cloth fixed in rectangular tanks. It is possible to induce this fish to breed 8-10 weeks ahead of peak spawning season by administering pituitary gland injections. Larvae measuring 2-7mm in length feed voraciously on zooplankton. It is suggested that before stocking the larvae, the nursery ponds have to be prepared to have abundant zoop-lankton to get better survival of hatchlings. Highest egg fertilization and hatching success(s) could be found upon injection of Ovaprim to both males and females @ 0.40-0.55ml/kg body weight (Source: NBFGR Annual Report 2011-'12: 15pp).

In small shallow ponds, a production level of 2625-2750kg/ha may be achieved in six months (50-75gm size) with a stocking density of 50,000 fingerlings (6-10gm size) per hectare water body, maintained on a mixture of dried and grinded marine trash fish and rice bran as feed. An optimum dosage of Ovatide @ 0.4ml/kg body weight to females has caused increase in number of eggs laid by a female from 1508 to 4358. Single dosage of injections of HCG (1000-3000IU/kg) and Ovaprim (0.3-0.7ml/kg) to males and females of 80-105gm and 90-115gm body weight have caused spawning in *H. fossilis* (Haniffa and Shridhar, 2002). Latency period was between 18-24 hours.

In monoculture system, rectangular ponds of 0.30±0.11ha in area were used, which were stocked with *H. fossilis* having initial length of 3.05±0.01cm and weight of 2.54±0.11gm. Stocking density was 2,47,000nos. fry/ha. Commercial fish feeds with 30% crude protein were supplied @ 100 to 5% of total biomass twice daily. At the end of 120 days of culture, fish production was recorded to be 10042.56±5.44kg/ha; final length and weight attained by each fish was 18.17±3.88cm and 46.44±3.11gm respectively (Chakraborty and Nur, 2012). Munshi (1996) recommended an ideal stocking rate of upto 50,000 fingerlings per hectare in semi-intensive grow-out culture operations. The culture of *H. fossilis* could be an alternative for farmers since they grow fast at high density. In village ponds, *H. fossilis* are harvested by keeping earthen pots in submerged state in pond margin and bana-tulsi plants are kept inside it. Attracted by the unique smell of the plants, fishes congregate quietly inside such pots. Because of its fast growth, tolerance to high stocking densities, high market value, ability to survive in oxygen-low waters, low fat, high protein and iron content and high medicinal values, *H. fossilis* is considered as an ideal fish species for aquaculture (Froese and Pauly, 2012). In a four-month culture of *H. fossilis*, stocking density of 60,000 individuals/ha has been recommended for farmers; from an initial length and weight of 5.13cm and 0.7gm respectively, mean weight of individuals was observed to be 51.84gm at time of harvest (Khan and Islam, 2003). Being a lean fish, it is very suitable for people who must not accept animal fats, as prescribed by physician. The species has high content of iron (226mg/100gm flesh) and fairly high content of calcium compared to many other freshwater fishes. In rice fields, *H. fossilis* has been found to grow to about 25gm during 60 days culture period.

As an end note, it can be stated thatfish and fisheries are inseparable from the culture and heritage of West Bengal and the fisheries sector plays an important role in the rural economy in terms of nutrition, income generation, employment and foreign exchange earning of the state. Having high consumer preference, catfishes are sold at high price in markets due to their soft meat texture, delicious taste, less intramuscular spines and medicinal properties. Other than *Clarius batrachus* and *H. fossilis*, induced breeding and farming technologies of other catfishes like *Mystus seenghala, M. aor, M. gulio, Pangasius pangasius, Horabagrus brachysoma* are also being experimented in our country. Along with the recommended species of major carps in composite culture ponds, many farmers are integrating some threatened fishes like *M. vittatus, Anabas testudineus, O. pabda, Puntius sarana* and *Amblypharyngodon mola*. Cultivation of small indigenous fishes, alone or in combination with carps will lead to increased nutritional and livelihood security of rural population.

Mystus vittatus (desi tengra)

Ompak pabda (pabda)

REFERENCES

Banik, S., Goswami, P., Acharjee, T. and Malla, S. (2012): *Ompak pabda*: An Endangered Catfish of Tripura - New Reports from Freshwater Environment of Tripura, *Journal of Environment*, 1(2): 40-44.

Bhattacharjee, Silanjan (2012): Banglaar Maachh (Bengali Version), *West Bengal Biodiversity Board*, Kolkata: pp. 36-37.

Chakrabarti, P.P., Chakrabarty, N.M. and Mondal, S.C. (2009): Breeding and Seed Production of Butter Catfish, *Ompok pabda* at Kalyani Centre of CIFA, India, *Aquaculture Asia* Jan-Mar: 33-35.

Chakraborty, D. and Das, S.K. (2012): Carp Pond Fertilization, In. Aquaculture Pond Fertilization, Ed. C.C. Mischke, *Wiley-Blackwell*: 236.

Chakraborty, B.K. and Nur, N.N. (2012): Growth and Yield Performance of *Heteropneustes Fossilis* and *Anabas Testudineus* in Bangladesh Under Semi-intensive Culture Systems, *Int. J. Agril. Res. Innov. and Tech.*, 2(2): 15-24.

Chakraborty, B.K. and Mirza, J.A. (2008): Growth and Yield Performance of Threatened Singhi, *Heteropneustes Fossilis* (Bloch) Under Semi-intensive Aquaculture of Bangladesh, *J. Fish. Soc. Taiwan*, 35(2): 175-183.

Chugh, S.N. (1992): Aluminium Phosphide Poisoning: Present Status and Management, *J. Assoc. Physicians India*, 40: 4011-4015.

CIFRI Workshop Report. (1982): All India Co-ordinated Research Project on Air-breathing Fish Culture, CIFRI Sixth Workshop Report: pp. 20-21.

Froese, R. and Pauly, D. (2012): Fishbase 2012. World Wide Web Electronic Publication, Available at: http://www.fishbase.org (Accessed on 23 June 2012).

Goswami, B., Mondol, S. and Dana, S.S. (2006). Indigenous Technological Knowledge in Fish Farming, *Indian Journal of Traditional Knowledge*, 5(1): 60-63.

Gupta, M.V. (2012): Message, In. Radheyshyam, G.S. Saha and H.K. De, Ed. Aquaculture Success Stories, *CIFA (ICAR), Bhubaneswar*: iii.

Haniffa, M.A. and Shridhar, S. (2002): Induced Spawning of *C. punctatus* and *H. Fossilis* Using Ovaprim and HCG, *Vertrinarski Archiv*, 72(1): 51-56.

Islam, Sk. S., Shah, Md. S. and Rahi, Md. L. (2011): Study on the Fecundity and Induced Breeding of *Mystus Vittatus*, *Bangladesh J. Zool.*, 39(2): 205-212.

Jain, A.K. (1989): Indoor High-intensive Rearing of Fry of *Cirrhinus mrigala* Versus Traditional Rearing, *Indian J. Fish.*, 36(1): 28-33.

Khan Noor, M. and Islam, A.K.M. (2003): Marginal Analysis of Culture of Stinging Catfish (*Heteropneustes Fossilis* Bloch): Effect of Different Stocking Densities in Earthen Ponds, *Pakistan Journal of Biological Sciences* 07/2003; DOI: 10.3923/pjbs.2003.666.670.

Mishra, S.S., Acharjee, S.K. and Chakraborty, S.K. (2009): Development of Tools for Assessing Conservation Categories of Siluroid Fishes of Freshwater and Brackishwater Wetlands of South West Bengal, India, *Environmental Biology of Fishes*, 84(4): 395-407.

Mohanty, S.N. (2006): Nutrition of Finfishes and Shellfishes, In. *Handbook of Fisheries and Aquaculture*, Ed. J.K. Jena, S. Ayyappan and Others, *ICAR*, New Delhi: pp. 503.

Mukherjee, M., Praharaj, A. and Das, S. (2002): Conservation of Endangered Fish Stocks Through Artificial Propagation and Larval Rearing Technique in West Bengal, India, *Aquaculture Asia*, 7(2): 8-11.

Munshi, J.S. Datta. (1996): Ecology of *Heteropneustes Fossilis*, an Air-breathing Catfish of South-east Asia, *Narendra Publishing House*, Delhi: pp. 174.

Radheyshyam, Shyam, T., Saha, G. S. and Sinha, S.K. (2012): Livestock-horticulture-grass-agro Forestry-fish Integration at Pokharbhinda Village, Kushinagar in Eastern Uttar Pradesh. In. Radheyshyam, G.S. Saha and H.K. De, Ed. Aquaculture Success Stories, *CIFA (ICAR), Bhubaneswar*: 1-21.

Ross, N., Islam, M. and Thilsted, S.H. (2003): Small Indigenous Fish Species in Bangladesh: Contribution to Vitamin A, Calcium and Iron Intakes, *Journal of Nutrition*, 133: 4021-4026.

Sharma, A., Debnath, B. and Mishra, S. K. (2011): Indigenous Technological Knowledge as Local Resource for Sustainable Development: Study of Cases in Fisheries and Aquaculture. In. Krishnan *et al.*, Ed. Farmers as Stakeholders in Commercial Aquaculture. Proc. CIFE Golden Jubilee Lecture Series, *CIFE, Mumbai*: 89-94.

Pages: 138-149

WATER RESOURCES MANAGEMENT: *MONITORING AND ASSESSMENT*

Edited by: Dr. Sandeep Gupta; Dr. Pawan Kumar 'Bharti'

ISBN: 978-93-5056-799-9

Edition: 2016

Published by: Discovery Publishing House Pvt. Ltd., New Delhi (India)

9

Adaptive Changes in Respiratory Movements in an Air Breathing Murrel Fish *Channa Gachua* Exposed Toendosulfan

Qaisur Rahman* and **D.N. Sadhu**

ABSTRACT

With the industrialization the water of the streams, lakes and rivers are receiving an increasing load of industrial wastes. Besides polluting water in many cases these water kills the fish and other aquatic organisms. Freshwaters are highly vulnerable to pollution since they act as immediate sinks for the consequences of human activity always associated with the danger of accidental discharges or criminal negligence. Primary effects such as fish kills can be detected but secondary effects may go unnoticed. The ability to detect identifies and properly respond to natural chemical stimuli is an important component of the environmental physiology of fishes. The classic eco-toxicology approach to testing aquatic toxicity is to measure the direct effect in simple experiments using death, more often than not, as the endpoint. In situations where no toxicity is available bioassays become extremely important. Development of acute toxicity bioassay data must be viewed as a necessary step for providing comparative toxicity information on different toxicants and species of organism. In the present investigation an attempt has been made to study the toxic effects of endosulfan in the freshwater air breathing fish *Channa gachua*. It was

University Department of Zoology, Vinoba Bhave University, Hazaribag - 825 301 (Jharkhand), (India)

observed that the sub-lethal (LC0) Median (LC50) and Lethal (LC100) concentration of endosulfan for 120hours were assessed as 190, 240 and 260 ppm respectively. From the 120 hours LC50value, the 1/3rd and 1/6th sub-lethal concentration were calculated as 80ppm and 40ppm respectively, to which the fishes were exposed. The pattern of changes in the respiratory movements of endosulfan exposed in *Channa gachua* were taken to suggest that the fish showed adaptive increase in its frequency of surfacing with a tremendous drop in its opercular movements during first hour of exposure to higher concentration of endosulfan. The reduced opercular movement is also considered adaptive for the fish to prevent itself. The details will be discussed in this paper.

Key words: Endosulfan EC50, Respiratory movements, *Channa gachua.*

INTRODUCTION

Pesticides belong to important class of chemicals that pose continuous liability to the stability of aquatic ecosystem. Indiscriminate, excessive and injudicious use of pesticides has resulted in pollution of general environment including water, air, soil and food. Water pollution by pesticides is a serious problem for aquatic flora, fauna and for us as fishes form important source of food for human beings. Pesticides are known to enter into the rivers and streams mainly through the aerial sprays operated to control the pests in forests and agricultural areas. Another source of entry of pesticides is rain water as reported by Qaisur *et al.*, (2014).Pesticides have recently been in the main focal theme and the volumes of published research works on the effects of pollution on aquatic organisms have increased enormously (Mckim *et al.*, 1975). The pesticides may reach the water bodies such as rivers, lakes and streams in a variety of ways. They may be applied deliberately into water bodies for the control of undesirable aquatic fauna affecting public health. They make an incidental impact as a result of aerial application of pesticide for control of terrestrial pests in agriculture and forestry in surrounding areas and also reach the lakes and rivers by aerial drift or by run-off from land. Finally gross impact of pesticides may occur from time to time as a result of accident or carelessness involving chemical depositions (Qaisur Rahman, 2011).

Most of the pesticides applied for the pest control in agriculture and forestry enter the aquatic environment through various routes, polluting the aquatic ecosystem. The persistence of these toxic chemicals in aquatic environment may be dangerous for the survival of fish (Johnson, 1968; Saunders, 1969; Mawdesley and Thomas, 1971). Therefore, the study of toxicity to organisms is an essential prelude concerning evolution of pesticide impact on the fresh water environment for achieving the objective, such as determination of safe concentrations and formulation of the safe application rate of pesticide concerned. The Pesticide pollution is known to affect a number of physiological systems of fish. Most organic environmental pollution taken up by organism undergoes extensive biotransformation before being excreted. The rate and extent of biotransformation as well as the chemical nature of the products can vary widely between species and even among individuals within the same species. Most information concerning xenobiotic metabolism has been derived from studies on liver. However, the ability to metabolize xenobiotics is not restricted to the liver. Endosulfan (thiodon - 6 - 7 - 8 - 9 - 10 - 10 - Hexachloro -1, 5, 5a, 6, 9, 9a-hexahydro 6-9 metano 2, 4, 3 benzodioxathiepin-3-oxide) a brown crystalline solid, is soluble in organic solvents and sparingly (20ppm) soluble in water. It is used in agriculture against a wide variety of insect including lepidopteran larvae, beetles and aphids. It has been especially effective against certain wood and stem bores such as peach tree borer, bronze birch borer and locust borer. Toxicology is the branch of biology dealing with the damages caused to the organism by any toxicant. These toxicants are generally pesticides, industrial chemicals, heavy metals and even drugs. Among these toxicants, pesticides are undesired highly dangerous pesticides are applied in the agriculture to kill various pests of which insects are the most important. Pesticides directed against the insects are called "Insecticides". Insecticides have been developed to affect specific target mechanisms in the insects. There are several major kinds of insecticides like organochlorines, organophosphates, carbamates and pyrethrioids etc., (Satake *et al.*, 1997). Like phosphamidan, dichlorovos and malathion are acetylcholinesterse (AchE) inhibitors (Sarin and Gill 1998).The AchE is an enzyme inthe post synaptic of neurons. It inactivates the excess quantum of acetylchloline released during the transmission of nerve impulse across the synapses. If AchE is not present to inactivate the excess acetyl choline, the post synaptic will continue to remain in the stimulated state. The consequent disturbance in the neural mechanism is responsible for the death of the insect (O' Brien, 1976). The technical endosulfan contains isomer α and β in a 4:1 ratio, which differ markedly in terms of their persistence and toxicity, the former being at least 20 times more toxic than the latter (Devi *et al.*, 1981). Although α- endosulfan disappear less than 100 days residues of the β isomer persist in the environment for as long as 2 years (Me Ewen and Stephanson, 1979). Respiration is one of the important parameters on which depend many of the vital functions like growth and reproduction of fish. One of the early symptoms of acute pesticide poisoning is alteration of failure of respiratory metabolism Holden (1972) respectively. A survey of literature on fish and pesticide pollution clearly indicates that same pesticides increase respiratory metabolism (Davis 1973; Brafield and Mathiessen 1976; Lunn *et al.*, 1976; Bakthavathasalam and Srinivasa Reddy, 1983). Some pesticides decrease the oxygen uptake fish (Ferguson *et al.*, 1966; Lee 1969; Gopalakrishna Reddy and Gomathy 1977; Gopalakrishna Reddy *et al.*, 1977; Qaisur and Sadhu 2014) respectively. To supplement the information available on the increase and decrease of oxygen uptake of fish exposed to different pesticides an attempt is made in the present study to examine the changes in the respiratory movements in anair breathing fish *Channa gachua* upon exposure to different concentration of endosulfan.

Channa gachua is known as air breathing murrel fish belonging to the family Channidae of the order Channiformes. It is found in estuaries and freshwaters of India. It has a very good flavour and is popular as food. This fish has dual mode of gas exchange mechanism as it extracts oxygen consumption from water through gills and from air by accessory respiratory organs. The accessory respiratory organs comprise one pair of suprabranchial chambers.

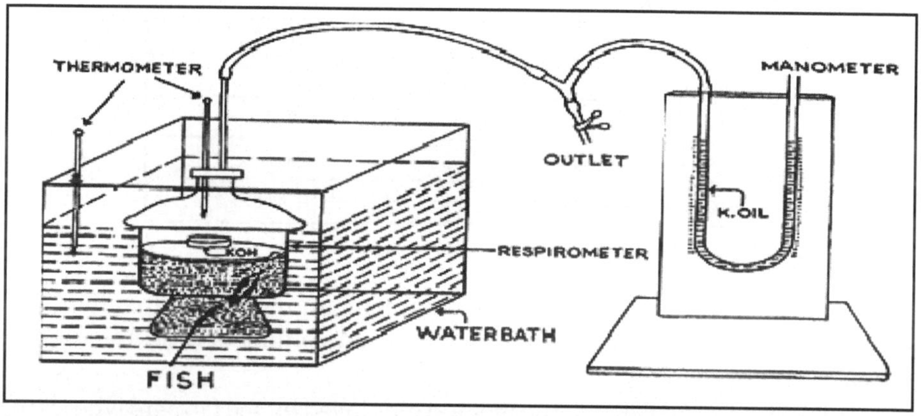

Fig. 9.1: Experimental set up for the measurements of oxygen uptake in *Channa gachua*

MATERIALS AND METHODS

Live specimens of *Channa gachua* were procured from local fish dealers at Hazaribag (Latitude 25° 59′N & Longitude 85° 22′E) and maintained in large glass aquaria size (90 x 60 x 60cm) with continuous flow of water. The specimens were fed on chopped goat liver daily during a minimum acclimation period of 15 days in the laboratory. Routine oxygen consumption from air and still water was measured in a closed glass respirometer containing 3 litres of water (initial O_2 content = 6.5 mg O_2/litre; pH = 7.2) and 0.51 mL of air. The fish had free access to air through a small semicircular hole (10 cm diameter) in a disc float. Carbosorb (B.D.H) or KOH in a petridish placed on the float absorbed CO_2. Thus the fish could exchange gases with water by way of its gills as well as with the air using the supra branchial chamber. The air phase of respirometer was connected to a differential manometer. Movement of the manometer fluid follow uptake of oxygen when the CO_2 is absorbed by Carbosorb (KOH). The fish were acclimated to the respirometers for at least 12 hours before the readings were taken. The experiments were conducted at 29.0 ± 1.5° C. The pH of the ambient water was measured by an electronic pH meter systronics. The respiratory chambers were thermostated by immersion in a temperature controlled water bath by Qaisur Rahman (2011). Fishes from 70-100g were used during the experiment. Feeding was stopped two days prior to experimentation to reduce additive effects of the animal's excreta. In the test medium as suggested by Arora *et al.*, (1984).The chlorine free water was used as test water in all experiments. The conditions of test water maintained at contrast characterization as recommended by committee on water quality criteria Ramakrishnan and Sivakumar (1993) throughout the test were depicted in the following.

Table 9.1: Showing Different Water Parameters in *Channa gachua*

Parameters	Values
Temperature	29.0 ± 1.5°C.
Salinity	2.7±1.3
pH	7.2±1.3
Dissolved oxygen	7.7±0.2Mg/L
Free carbon dioxide	1.5±0.01 Mg/L

ACUTE TOXICITY TESTS

In the present investigation, the commercial grade of endosulfan 35EC were selected and used by diluting it in required volume or any other organic solvents.

This is in accordance with the method employed by the farmers who simply dilute the grade with water and apply in paddy fields. Acute toxicity tests were conducted to determine the impact of toxicant on aquatic animals within a short period of 2 hours, simultaneously the toxicity of pesticides on the test fish *Channa gachua* 6, 12, 24, 48, 72, 96 and 120 hours were determined. The (LC50)is statistical estimate of the concentration of the toxic materials in water that kills 50 percent of the test animals under experimental conditions at specific time intervals Sprague (1973). The value is ideally suited for toxicity studies as it gives a more acceptable and reproducible concentration required to affect 50 percent of the fishes that any other value Pickering and Henderson (1966) respectively.

RANGE FINDING TEST

In the toxicity evaluation studies to avoid delay expense and to save time and effort, the preliminary exploratory tests were conducted. These tests determine.

An appropriate range of pesticide concentration which should be covered in the full scale tests endosulfan was first prepared over acute solution. The range of concentration from 100ppm to 400ppm with an interval of 25ppm endosulfan small plastic trough having 5 liters capacity were used in which 3 liters of the endosulfan solution of the different concentrations were taken separately.

TOXICITY EVALUATION

For assessing the toxicity the concentration of the pesticide in the test solution was selected on the basis of previous tests (preliminary test). About 7 fishes were exposed in 3 liters of solution taken in a plastic trough. To maintain the pesticide concentration and DO level of water and to avoid the accumulation of excretory wastes during the experimental period, the test solution in the trough was renewed after every 24 hours with least disturbance to the fishes the control experiments were also carried out simultaneously. The rate of mortality was observed at an interval of 1, 6, 12, 24, 48, 72, 96 and 120 hours and the fishes showing no respiratory movements. The responses to tactile stimuli were considered dead and were removed immediately to avoid concentration of the medium. The concentration at which 100 percent mortality was observed within 120 hours was considered as lethal concentration (120 hours, LC100) and the concentration having 100 percent survival till 120 hours was considered as sub-lethal concentration (120 hours, LC0) respectively.

ENUMERATION OF OPERCULAR MOVEMENT

Control and endosulfan exposed fishes were kept in glass jars either pesticide containing free tap water for control fish or a particular concentration of endosulfan exposed fish and acclimated for 10minutes. After 10 minutes the number of operculum beat was enumerate for 10minutes using a stopwatch. Enumeration was repeated for 10 times and mean value was calculated to get the opercular movement of particular fish. Similarly enumeration of opercular movement was made in control and endosulfan exposed *Channa gachua* after different periods of exposure of opercular movements of the fish was expressed as number of beat per minute. Enumeration of frequency of surfacing after a period of acclimatization .The frequency of surfacing per hour it was also carefully observed and enumerated in control and endosulfan exposed fishes for different periods of exposure. Frequencies of surfacing in control endosulfan exposed fish were represented as frequency of surfacing per hour changes in opercular movements and surfacing frequency either increase or decrease of endosulfan exposed from those of control levels were calculated as percentage and tested for their significance.

RESULTS

Toxic impact of the pesticide endosulfan of *Channa gachua* was recorded from the mortality value of the experimental animals in relation to different concentration level of the pesticides. The impact of the toxicity of endosulfan in *Channa gachua* was assessed and presented in the form as sublethal median lethal and lethal concentration. The (LC50) value of endosulfanin *Channa gachua* for 120hours was found to be 240 ppm as 50% of mortality. But the concentration of 190 ppm of endosulfan no mortality was recorded till the end of 120hours. At the same time the concentration of 280 ppm of pesticide, all the exposed experiments fishes died showing 100% mortality with in 120 hours, indicating it as the lethal or most toxic to the animal. Thus, it is evident from the present study that the sublethal 0% mortality, 50% median lethal mortality and 100% lethal mortality in *Channa gachua* occurred at 190, 240 and 280ppm ofendosulfan respectively.

The opercular movements are expressed in terms of number of beats per minute of control and exposed fish *Channa gachua* together with percent change in opercular movements of endosulfan exposed fish from control fish. *Channa gachua* a control level of opercular movement of about 36 ± 2 beats per minute clearly indicates that endosulfan caused unequivocal changes in opercular movement of the fish. When exposed to (190ppm). The endosulfan for first 1hour the fish showed a spurt in its opercular movements. However following prolong exposure for sublethal concentrations of 1/3rd and 1/6th of (LC50) value of endosulfan (80ppm and 40ppm). The fish showed a tremendous reduction in its opercular movement. A progressive inhibition of opercular movement up to 120 hours followed by slight recovery after 96th hours of endosulfan exposure could be observed in fish exposed to sublethal concentraction, whereas under higher concentration the fish showed progressive inhibition even up to 120 hours of exposure respectively.

It provides surfacing frequency of control and endosulfan exposed *Channa gachua* along with the percent changes in frequency of surfacing of endosulfan exposed fish from that of control fish. The patterns of changes in frequency of surfacing of endosulfan exposed *Channa gachua* were found to be different from those of opercular movements witha frequency of surfacing of about 46 per/10minutes in control fish. Unlike opercular movement, surfacing frequency is formed to be increased first 24 hour ofexposure in all the concentration of endosulfan studied, when exposed to sublethal 1/3rd and 1/6th concentration of (LC50) value of endosulfan the fish showed progressive reduction in the frequency of surfacing up to 96 hours of exposure. A progressive inhibition was observed in the frequency of surfacing of fish exposed to sub lethal concentration up to 120 hours exposure. A progressive reduction up to 96hours followed by a slight recovery after 120 hours of exposure could be seen in endosulfan exposed fish.

DICUSSION

In the present study, the 190, 240 and 280ppm of endosulfan was found as sublethal, median and lethal concentrations for 120 hours. However the fishes were exposed to 80ppm, which is 1/3rd of (LC50) value of endosulfan is sublethal to fishes. The same view that the time and concentration dependent mortality has been reported of Agarwal (1971) in *Channa punctatus* exposed to mercuric chloride, Similarly Maruthanayagam and Sharmila (2004) have reported that the (LC50) value of monocrotophas to *Channa punctatus* and also Singh (1984) have reported the (LC50) value of dimethoate to *Barbus stigma*.

Table 9.2: Showing Opercular Movement of Control and Exposed Fish *Channa gachua* Treated with Endosulphan

Conc. of Endosulphan	Control	24 Hours	48 Hours	72 Hours	96 Hours	120 Hours	144 Hours
Sublethal (190) ppm	36 ± 0.2	39 ± 0.1	32 ± 0.2	28 ± 0.3	23 ± 0.2	30 ± 0.2	31± 0.2
LC 50(80) ppm of one third	36 ± 0.2	40 ± 0.1	136 ± 0.1	31 ± 0.1	29 ± 0.2	30 ± 0.3	30 ± 0.5
LC 50(40) ppm of one sixth	36 ± 0.2	29 ± 0.1	24 ± 0.1	21 ± 0.1	30 ± 0.1	29 ± 0.2	30 ± 0.2

* N=7, ± Standard deviation.

Table 9.3: Surfacing of Control and Endosulfan Exposed *Channa Gachua* Expressed Frequency of Surfacing per Hour

Conc.of Endosulphan	Control	24 Hours	48 Hours	72 Hours	96 Hours	120 Hours	144 Hours
Sublethal (190) ppm	46 ± 0.5	64 ± 0.6	51 ± 0.5	33 ± 0.2	29 ± 0.2	35 ± 0.2	38 ± 0.1
LC50(80) ppm of one third	46 ± 0.5	63 ± 0.6	45 ± 0.4	35 ± 0.3	32 ± 0.2	33 ± 0.3	38 ± 0.2
LC50(40) ppm of one sixth	46 ± 0.5	64 ± 0.2	45 ± 0.4	35 ± 0.3	32 ± 0.2	33 ± 0.2	36 ± 0.2

* N=7, ± Standard deviation.

Table 9.4: Mortality of *Channa Gachua* Exposed to Different Concentrations of Endosulfan at Different Hours of Exposure

Conc. in ppm	Exposed Fishes	6 Hours	12 Hours	24 Hours	48 Hours	72 Hours	96 Hours	120 Hours
180	35	0	0	0	0	0	0	0
190*	35	0	0	0	0	0	0	0
200	35	0	0	2	4	4	6	6
210	35	0	2	5	5	5	6	6
220	35	5	5	6	6	8	10	10
230	35	6	6	8	8	10	13	13
240**	35	6	8	11	14	14	15	15
250	35	10	10	16	16	18	18	19
260	35	10	15	20	22	22	24	24
270	35	12	15	22	24	26	26	30
280***	35	15	22	22	24	26	26	30

* Sub Lethal conc. ** LC 50 (Median Lethal) conc. *** Lethal conc.

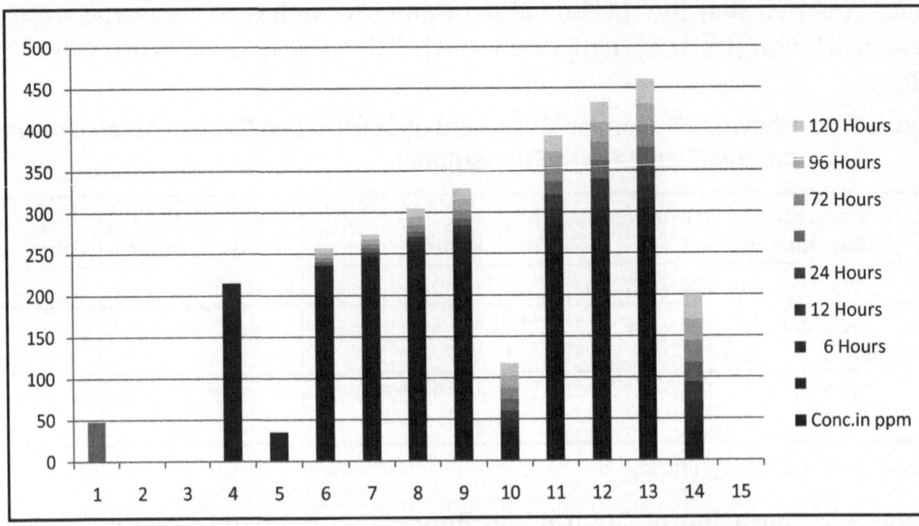

Graph 9.1: Showing Mortality of *Channa Gachua* Exposed to Different Concentrations of Endosulfan

Pesticides are known to affect the oxygen uptake of fish. A depression in oxygen consumption to about 50% has been reported in *Colisalalia* following exposure to sublethal concentration of a-BHC (Uthaman 1977). *Mystusvittatus* when exposed to thiodon showed a 50% decrease in its oxygen consumption Gopalakrishna Reddy and Gomathy (1977). Gopalakrishna Reddy *et al.*, (1977) also reported a similar decrease in oxygen uptake of *Colisalalia* exposed to disyston. *Sarotheredonmossambicus*, when exposed to thiodon concentration showed drop in oxygen uptake to about 36-40% by Vasanthiand Ramaswamy (1987) Natarajan (1981) and Qaisur *et al.*, (2014) in *Channa gachua* also studied reduced oxygen uptake. A reduction is haemoglobin content and erythrocyte population resembling in hypochromatic microcytic anaemia have also been suggested as reasons for drop in oxygen uptake in fish exposed to pesticides (Natarajan 1981; Srivastava *et al.* 1977).

In the present study *Channa Gachua* show unequivoral changes in its opercular movements and surfacing frequency following exposure to endosulfan concentrations for different periods. The initial increase in opercular movements upto 1 hour of exposure to sublethal concentration of 1/3rd and 1/6th concentration indicates that the fish adaptively increased its opercular movement to increase its oxygen uptake to meet the pesticide stress. Perhaps the low concentration of endosulfan brings about a triggering mechanism for an increased oxygen uptake. Onthe other hand, higher concentration of endosulfan caused inhibition effect on opercular movement even from the first 24 hours of exposure. In particular those drops in opercular movement of fish exposed to higher concentrations of endosulfan and corresponding increase in frequency of surfacing of the fish clearly indicate that the fish adaptively shifts more towards aerial respiration by obtaining atmospheric oxygen by surfacing to meet its energy demand by reducing its opercular movement. The fish perhaps, tries to avoid intimate contact (through the gill opening) with the pesticide. Qaisur Rahman (2011) in *Channa Gachua* reported that an increase oxygen uptake, to meet the energy demand during early period of pesticide exposure, in spite of reduced opercular movement could be possible only in air breathing fish where truly could adaptively employ their extra route of respiratory mechanism air breathing organs to increase theiroxygen uptake more effectively under pesticide stress, as seen in *Channa Gachua* in the present study respectively. Progressive decline in opercular movement of fish exposed to endosulfan concentration upto 120 hours and in frequency of surfacing indicates the severe inhibitory effect of the endosulfan on the respiratory movements of the fish. Investigator like Qaisur and Sadhu (2014) reported that the decreased respiratory movement may be the result of inhibition of enzymes associated with the metabolic activity respiratory movements under endosulfan toxicity. However, recover of different magnitudes observed in opercular movement following 120 hours of exposure to different concentration of endosulfan and in frequency of surfacing following 96 hours and 144 hoursof exposure indicates the reversible, inhibitory nature of the pesticide endosulfan on the respiratory movements of *Channa Gachua* which is similar with the finding of other workers respectively.

CONCLUSION

The analysis of data from the present investigation that endosulphan is highly toxic and hadprofound impact on behaviour and respiration in *Channagachua*. The Variation in the oxygen consumption in treated fish is probably due to impaired oxidative metabolism and endosulphan induced respiratory stress. Inthe present study, copious mucous secretion andbulging of gills were also observed. The drop in theoxygen consumption rate of *Channa Gachua* exposed can also be attributed to clogging of gills bymucous. Gills are vital respiratory and osmoregulatoryorgans and cellular damage induced by the pesticides might impair the respiratory function of the fish by reducing the respiratory surface area. These findings clearly suggest decreased respiratory surface area which can also account for the drop in the metabolic rate of the fish. Hence, dysfunction of behaviour and respiration can serve as index of pesticides toxicity.

REFERENCES

Agarwal, S.K. (1971): Bioassay Evaluation of Acute Toxicity Levels of Mercuricchloride to an Air Breathing Fish *Channapunctatus* (Bloch) Mortality and Behavioural Study. *J.Environ. Biol.* 12: 99-106.

Arora, M. Neelan, S. and Kulshrestha, A.K. (1984): Histopathological Effects Induced by Sublethal Doses of Carbaryl and Endosulfan on the Fish.*Comp. Anim. Physiol.* 25: 250-253.

Bakthavasalam, R. and Srinivasa Reddy, R. (1983): Changesin Bimodal Oxygen Uptake of an Obligate Air Breather *Anabas testudineus* Exposed to Lindane. *Water. Res.* 17: 1221-1226.

Brafield, A.E. and Matthiessen P. (1976): Oxygen Consumption by stickle Backs *Gasterosteusacculeatus J. Fish. Biol.* 9: 359-370.

Davis, J.C. (1973): Sublethal Effects of Bleached Kraft Mill Effluents on Respiration and Circulation in Sockeyesalmon *Onchorhynchusnerka. J. Fish. Res. Bd. Canada.* 30: 369-377.

Devi, A.P., Rao, D.M.R., Tilak, K.S., and Murthy, A.S. (1981): Relative Toxicity of the Technical Grade Material Isomers and Formulation of Endosulfan to Fish *Channapunctatus. Bull. Environ. Contam.Toxicity.* 27: 239-243.

Ferguson, D.E., Ludke, J.L. and Murphy, G.G. (1966): Dynamics of Endrin Uptake and Release by Resistant and Susceptible Strains of Mosquito Fish. *Trans. Amer. Fish. Soc.* 95: 335-344.

Gopalakrishna Reddy, T. Palaniappan, S.P. and Pillai, K.P.S. (1977): Respiratory and Histopathological Effects of the Pesticide Disyston on the Anabantid fish *Colisalalia*. All India Symposium of Environmental Biology, Universityof Kerala.

Gopalakrishna Reddy, T. and Gomathy, S. (1977): Toxicity and Respiratory Effect of Pesticide Thiodon on Catfish *Mystusvittatus. Indian J. Environ. Hlth.* 19(4): 360-363.

Holden, A.V. (1972): Effects of Pesticide on Fish. (In): Environmental Pollution by Pesticide. (Ed.) C.A. Edwards, Plenum Press New York. pp. 213-253.

Johnson D.W. (1968): Pesticides and Fishes a Review of Selected Literature. *Trans. Amer. Fish. Soc.* 97: 398-424.

Lee E.L. (1969): Measurement of Pesticides Toxicity by Fish Respiration Rate *Diss. Abst.* 30B: 17-27.

Lunn, C.R. Tower, D.P. and Pree, D.J. (1979): Effect of Three Pesticides on Respiration, Coughing and Heart Rates of Rainbow Trout, *Salmogairdneri. Can. J. Zool.* 54: 214-219.

Maruthanayagam, C. and Sharmila, G. (2004): Sublethal Effects of Endosulfan onhae Matological Parameter and Biochemical Constituent of Different Tissue of *Channapunctatus. Nat. Env. Poll. Res.* 3: 250-254.

Mawdesley Thomas. L.E. (1971): Toxic Chemicals the Risk to Fish. *News Scientist.* 49: 74-75.

McEwen, F.L. and Stephensen, G.R. (1979): The Use and Significance of Pesticide in the Fish Environment Willington New York. pp. 1-379.

Mckim. J.M., Benoit. D.A., Biesinger K.E., Brunghes. W.A., and Slefert R.E., (1975): Effects of Pollution on Fresh Water *J. Water Poll. Cont.* 47 (6): 1711-1768.

Natarajan, G.M. (1981b): Effect of Lethal (LC50/48hr) Concentration of Metasystoxon Selected Oxidative Enzymes, Tissue Respiration and Histology of Gills of the Freshwater Air Breathing Fish *Channastriatus* (Bleeker). *Curr. Sci.* 50 (22): 985-989.

Natarajan, G.M. (1981a): Changes in the bimodal gas exchangeand some bloodparameters in the airbreathing fish*Channastriatus*(Bleeker) followinglethal (LC50/48hr) exposure to metasystox(Dimeton). *Curr. Sci.* 50 (1):40-41.

O'Neil, J.G. (1981): The humoral immune response to *Salmotrutta*and*CyprinusCarpio*(Linn.) exposed to heavymetals. *J. Fish. Biol.* 19: 297-306.

Pandian, T.J. and Muthukrishnan, J.M., (1988): Identification of Sex in Economically Important Fishes. In: DET Workshop on Research Methods for Chromosome Manipulation in Fish 1-5.

Panikkar N.K. and Thambi P.R.S. (1954): Studies on the Mouth Breeding cichlid *Tilapia mossambicus* (Peters) *Ind. J. Fish.* 1: 27-32.

Pickering, H.Q. and Henderson, C. (1966): The Acute Toxicity of Some Heavy Metalsto Different Species of Warm Water Fishes. *Int. J. Air. Wat. Poll.* 10: 453-463.

Qaisur Rahman (2011): Studies on Some Factors Affecting Aerial and Aquatic Respiration in an Air Breathing Fish *Channa Gachua* (Ham.) Ph.D. Thesis, Vinoba Bhave University, Hazaribag, Jharkhand, India.

Qaisur Rahman and D.N. Sadhu, (2014): Morphometric Partioning of the Respiratory Surface Area and Diffusion Capacity of Gills in an Air Breathing Fish *Channagachua*. *J. Res. Dev.* 14: 66-74.

Qaisur Rahman and D.N. Sadhu and Shamim Akhter Choudhary. (2014): Effect of Monocrotophos on Histopathological Changes in Gills of an Air Breathing Fish *Channa Gachua* (Ham.) *J. Res. Dev.* 14: 9-13.

Ramakrishnan, R., and Sivakumar. (1993): Effect of Insecticides Quinolphos on the Fish *Orechromismossambicus*. *J.Ecobiol.* 5 (1): 45 - 50.

Saunders, J.W., (1969): Mass Mortalities and Behaviourof Brook Trout and Juvenile Atlantic Salmon in a Stream Polluted by Agricultural Pesticides. *J. Fish. Res. Bd.Can.* 26: 695-699.

Singh, M.M., (1984): A Survey of Environmental Awareness in Gujarat In: Pesticides and Environmental Pollution. Himanshu Publications, Rajasthan. pp. 1-12.

Sprague, J.B. (1973): Measurement of Pollutant Toxicity to Fish.Vol. (II) Utilizing and Applying Bioassay Results. *Wat. Res.* 4: 3-32.

Sterba, G. (1962): Fresh Water Fishes of the World Vista Books Bangalore Press Ltd., London. pp. 172-185.

Srivastava, A.K and Mishra, S., (1977): Blood Degeneration in a Teleost *Colisafaciatum* Following Exposure to Sublethal Concentration of Lead. *J. Fish. Biol.* 14: 199-203.

Uthaman, M. (1977): Toxicity and Respiratory Effects of Pesticides, BHC in Ananabantid Fish, *Colisalalia*, M.Sc., Dissertation, Annamalai University.

Varadaraj, K. (1990): Endocrine and Genetic Studies on Sex Regulation in Tilapia Ph.D., Thesis, Madurai Kamaraj University, Madurai, India.

Vasanthi, M. and Ramaswamy, M. (1987): A Shift in the Metabolic Pathway of *sarotherodonmossambicus* (Peters) Exposed to Thiodonendosulfan. *Proc. Indian. Acad. Anim. Sci.* 95 (1): 55 - 61.

Pages: 150-183

WATER RESOURCES MANAGEMENT: *MONITORING AND ASSESSMENT*
Edited by: Dr. Sandeep Gupta; Dr. Pawan Kumar 'Bharti'
ISBN: 978-93-5056-799-9
Edition: 2016
Published by: Discovery Publishing House Pvt. Ltd., New Delhi (India)

10

Water Quality Trading

S. Ponmani[1*] and **C. Udayasoorian**[2]

INTRODUCTION

Globally, 532 coastal areas have been identified as experiencing some form of eutrophication or nutrient over enrichment. Of these, at least 405 coastal areas experience hypoxia (oxygen depletion) (Diaz and Rosenberg, 2008). Eutrophication affects the ability of lakes, rivers, streams and estuaries from supporting aquatic life and providing suitable drinking water.

Sources of water quality impairment are generally divided into two categories: point sources and nonpoint sources. Point sources are those sources that discharge pollutants into a water body via a discrete conveyance such as a pipe. Examples of point sources include sewage treatment plants and industrial facilities. By contrast, pollution from nonpoint sources is typically diffuse in nature, such as agricultural or urban runoff. Because the precise origin of pollution from nonpoint sources is difficult to identify, these sources are frequently not regulated for pollutant discharges.

To address the increasing occurrence of eutrophication in local water bodies, some government agencies are beginning to implement nutrient caps

1 Dryland Agricultural Research Station, Tamil Nadu Agricultural University, Chettinad - 630 102.

2 Department of Environmental Sciences, Tamil Nadu Agricultural University, Coimbatore - 641 003.

or limits for sources that discharge nutrients in waterways. In some cases, water quality trading is being proposed to reduce the costs associated with meeting nutrient caps, as well as to offset additional nutrient discharges that may result from urban or agricultural productivity growth.

Water quality trading can be a cost-effective, environmentally sound local solution to improving water quality. Generally, water quality trading (WQT) involves a party facing relatively high pollutant reduction costs compensating another party to achieve less costly pollutant reduction with the same or greater water quality benefit. Water quality trading can be a useful tool for water quality enhancement in the right circumstances and some dischargers will welcome the flexibility it can provide.

The United States Environmental Protection Agency (EPA) has supported the concept and implementation of water quality trading for several years. Several water quality trading markets are currently operating, with others under development. Most of these markets are focused on either phosphorus or nitrogen-based trading, though increasing interest has emerged for trading sediment runoff, biological oxygen demand and temperature.

BACKGROUND AND PURPOSE OF THE PROGRAMMES

The Clean Water Act (CWA) was enacted in 1972 in US to restore and maintain the chemical, physical and biological integrity of the nation's waters. It established a national policy that called for the discharge of pollutants to be eliminated and established interim goals for protecting fish, wildlife and recreational uses. The CWA also established a national policy for development and implementation of programmes so the goals of the Act could be met through controls of point and non point sources of pollution.

The purpose of this policy is to encourage states, interstate agencies and tribes to develop and implement water quality trading programmes for nutrients, sediments and other pollutants where opportunities exist to achieve water quality improvements at reduced costs. More specifically, the policy is intended to encourage voluntary trading programmes that facilitate implementation of Total Maximum Daily Load (TMDL), reduce the costs of compliance with CWA regulations, establish incentives for voluntary reductions and promote watershed-based initiatives. A number of states are in various stages of developing trading programmes. This policy provides guidance for states, interstate agencies and tribes to assist them in developing and implementing such programmes.

Total Maximum Daily Load (TMDL)

A total maximum daily load is a calculation of the maximum amount of a pollutant that a water body can receive and still meet water quality standards and an allocation of that amount to the pollutant's sources. TMDL determinations are critical to the attainment of water quality goals in watershed management. Watershed-based pollutant trading has gained more and more popularity as an innovative approach for TMDL allocation and implementation over the past several years.

BENEFITS AND LIMITATIONS OF WATER QUALITY TRADING

Benefits

All forms of market-based pollution reduction may yield similar economic, social and environmental benefits compared to traditional command-and-control regulatory programmes. Highlights of the benefits that effluent trading may provide include:

- Economic Benefits – reduces costs for individual sources and reduces overall costs of addressing water quality problems in a watershed; allows dischargers to take advantage of economies of scale and treatment efficiencies and provides incentives for innovations in pollution-reduction technology since investments in pollution control can lead to increased profits.
- Environmental Benefits – achieves equal or greater reduction of pollution at equal or lower cost, creates an economic incentive for dischargers to go beyond minimum pollution reduction; can reduce cumulative pollutant loading; improves water quality and prevents future environmental degradation; may lower political resistance to higher water-quality goals over time and if credits generated by nonpoint abatement can be sold, this creates an economic incentive for nonpoint source dischargers to reduce pollution even in the complete absence of regulatory standards.
- Social Benefits – encourages dialogue among stakeholders; fosters concerted and holistic solutions for watersheds with multiple sources of water-quality impairment and facilitates construction of social capital and trust.

Limitations

It is important to note that very few trading schemes for point and nonpoint source water pollution control have actually resulted in active markets. This lack of trading activity is due to a number of limitations of water quality trading. For example, the number of trades is influenced by the availability of trading partners and whether or not they discharge the same pollutants. Also, water quality trading is usually best suited for aggregate pollution problems, not pollutants with highly located effects and threshold damages, limiting the applicability to pollutants that have been less regulated historically.

Control of nonpoint sources is difficult because the effectiveness of technologies to reduce their loadings is uncertain and will be determined in part by random factors such as weather. Another limitation stems from the transaction costs required to implement and participate in a trading programme; these costs can be quite high and have repeatedly proven to be a barrier to a successful programme. Given these and other barriers, if resources for development, education and promotion are insufficient, the potential for success are severely limited. Overcoming the limitations of water quality trading is a major challenge for developers of future programmes and would require careful and creative planning and active agency promotion (Eiichiro Nishizawa, 2003).

Success in watershed scale trading markets will be influenced by several factors, including:

(a) Pollutant to be reduced and the physical characteristics of the watershed
(b) Cost of pollutant control for individual dischargers
(c) Mechanisms used to facilitate trading
(d) Ability and willingness of stakeholders to embrace and participate in trading

STATUS OF WATER QUALITY TRADING PROGRAMMES

In 2008, World Research Institute (WRI) undertook an assessment of water quality trading programmes worldwide. They identified 57 programmes; of these, 26 were active, 21 were under consideration or development and 10 were inactive. Of the programmes identified, all but six were located in the United States.

Table 10.1: Assessment of Water Quality Trading Programmes Worldwide

Sl. No.	Programme Name	State/Country	Types of Trades
	Active programmes/Pilots		
1.	Hunter River Salinity Trading Scheme	New South Wales, Australia	PS-PS
2.	South Creek Bubble Licensing Scheme	New South Wales, Australia	PS-PS
3.	Minnesota River Basin Trading Programme	Minnesota, U.S.	PS-PS
4.	Lower Boise River Effluent Trading Demonstration Project	Idaho, U.S.	PS-NPS
5.	Pennsylvania Water Quality Trading Programme	Pennsylvania, U.S.	PS-PS/NPS
6.	Virginia Water Quality Trading Programme	Virginia, U.S.	PS-PS/NPS
	Programmes/Initiatives in development or under consideration		
1.	Maryland Water Quality Trading Programme	Maryland, U.S.	PS-NPS
2.	Shepherd Creek Clearinghouse	Ohio, U.S.	PS-NPS
3.	Upper Little Miami River Basin	Ohio, U.S.	PS-NPS
4.	Portland Tradable Stormwater Credit Initiative	Oregon, U.S.	PS-PS
5.	Moreton Bay Nutrient Trading Scheme	Queensland, Australia	PS-NPS

(Table Contd...)

Sl. No.	Programme Name	State/Country	Types of Trades
	Inactive trading programmes/Completed pilot or demonstration programmes		
1.	Clear Creek	Colorado, U.S.	PS-PS
2.	Boulder Creek Trading Programme	Colorado, U.S.	PS-NPS
3.	Fox-Wolf Basin	Wisconsin, U.S.	PS-NPS
4.	Rock River	Wisconsin, U.S.	PS-NPS

(PS- Point source, NPS- Non point source)

COMPONENTS OF A TRADING PROGRAMME

The following table defines the key components and examples for establishing a state trading programme.

Table 10.2: Components of Trading Programme

Sl. No.	Key Component	Example
1.	*Water quality goals* are set by federal, state or local authorities based on public input and can be defined in terms of ecosystem restoration, improvement of fish population or public safety or as pounds of pollution load reduced.	The Clean Water Act's "fishable and swimmable" waters and the Chesapeake Bay Agreement's "Restoring and Protecting the ecosystem and the living resources of the Chesapeake Bay"
2.	*Pollution cap for a watershed* is a limit on the total pollution load from all sources to a water body. Usually the cap is set for an annual load of specific pollutants. The size of the cap is based on the public's water quality goals.	TMDLs and tributary strategies (i.e., regional and state designated pollution reduction goals that serve as caps)
3.	*Regulated baseline for point sources* is the numeric level of pollutant load allowed at a particular point in time.	National Pollution Discharge Elimination System (NPDES) permit provides an allowable pollution limit for industrial and municipal point sources. Group or watershed permits, which cover several point sources, also provide this limit.
4.	*Regulated baseline for nonpoint sources* is the numeric level of pollutant load allowed at a particular point in time.	A TMDL may set allowable pollution limits for nonpoint sources.
5.	*Unregulated baseline for agricultural nonpoint sources* is the minimum level of pollution abatement an agricultural operation must achieve before it can participate in a trading programme.	A set of Best Management Practices (BMPs) that create a minimum level of pollution abatement required by a specific trading programme.

(Table Contd...)

Sl. No.	Key Component	Example
6.	*Credits* are units of goods (pollution reduction) to be traded in the water quality market. Credits are generated for every unit of pollution reduction beyond the baseline level.	Implementation of agricultural BMPs beyond the baseline may generate credits. Point sources, both industrial and municipal, that implement new treatment technologies and reduce pollutants beyond their baseline may also generate credits.
7.	*Sellers* (credit suppliers) are the dischargers that reduce pollution below the baseline and generate credits for sale in the market. Credits can also be sold by intermediaries, if allowed by programme rules.	Farmers who implement BMPs; industrial point sources that install new abatement technologies; intermediaries such as credit banks or aggregators
8.	*Buyers* (demanders for credits) are the dischargers with regulated baselines for whom pollution reduction is expensive. For these sources, it is less costly to buy pollution credits from other parties and use these credits to help achieve their baseline loads. Credits can also be purchased by intermediaries and third parties, if allowed by programme rules.	Wastewater treatment plants with a regulated baseline and high abatement costs; third party buyers, like watershed groups, aiming at reduction of pollution by purchasing and retiring credits from the market; intermediaries, such as credit banks or aggregators
9.	*Credit price* can be determined from negotiations between the credit buyer and seller. Usually, the price cannot be lower than the costs of load reductions incurred by the seller, and it cannot be higher than the cost that of an abatement alternative for the buyer.	The lower the price of the credits offered by the seller (e.g., farmer), the more willing the credit buyer (e.g., wastewater treatment plant) is to purchase the credits. The break-even credit price for a farmer equals the ratio of the BMP implementation cost to the number of credits generated by the BMP. If the sale price is above the break-even level, the farmer would profit from the sale. If the sale price is below the break-even level, the farmer would not receive enough revenue to cover the costs of implementing the BMP.
10.	*Regulator* is the entity that determines the water quality goals, establishes caps for pollutants in a watershed, approves and administers the trading programme, and monitors and enforces the rules.	State, regional and federal agencies and local authorities.

(Table Contd...)

Sl. No.	Key Component	Example
11.	*Trading ratio* is the number of load-reduction credits from one source can be used to compensate excessive loads from another source.	A delivery trading ratio is set to ensure that trading among distant sources (e.g., upstream and downstream) does not violate an overall watershed pollution cap. Uncertainty trading ratio specifies the number of pollution reduction credits generated by the nonpoint source that should be purchased by the point source to offset one unit of their own discharge. The ratio is set to account for seasonal and daily changes in nonpoint source loading, and can be set greater, equal, or less than one.

(Eiichiro Nishizawa, 2003)

TRADING MECHANISMS

Identifying the Goal

The water quality goal needs to balance the benefits of improved water quality to the local and wider community, against the costs of achieving it. Consequently, efforts are likely to be made to improve the water quality but not in a manner which cripples the local economy. The decision regarding the water quality goal needs to be made using a combination of cost benefit analysis and political processes. This goal needs to be defined in terms of things people care about directly such as water clarity or the probability of algal blooms.

Water quality depends on the level of nutrients in the water body. Once the water quality goal has been identified, it needs to be related to the level of nutrients in the water body because these can be measured and more directly controlled, while having a strong relationship to the outcome in which we are really interested. We can identify the level of nutrients in the lake which will allow the water quality goal to be met, atleast on average. From a management point of view, it may be more useful to know what level of nutrients flowing into the lake will allow the water quality goal to be met. Thus, the water quality goal may need to be expressed in two ways: the level of nutrients in the water body and the amount of nutrients able to flow into the water body. The difference between the 'stock' of nutrients and the flow depends on the residence time of the nutrients in the water body.

Example - water quality goal can be achieved with 435 tonnes of Nitrogen and 35 tonnes of Phosphorus entering the lake each year, provided the water body is in equilibrium.

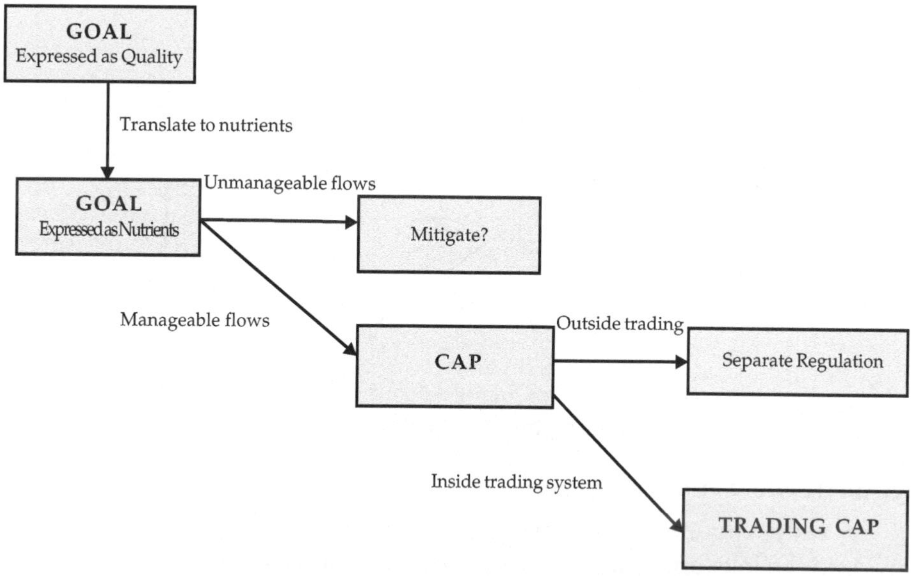

Fig. 10.1: The Relationship Between the Goal, Cap and Trading Cap for Water Quality Trading

(Donald *et al.*, 2005)

Setting the Cap

Once the goal is expressed in terms of nutrients, we can determine the amount of manageable nutrients able to enter the water body, or the cap (Figure 10.1). The goal provides a measure of the amount of nutrients able to enter the water body from all sources. However, some of these nutrients are going to be from 'unmanageable' sources and these will not be affected by any policy introduced now. This includes nutrients entering the water body from the sediment and nutrients that are already in the groundwater. Thus, to manage the nutrients entering the lake, we need to identify the amount of nutrients entering the water body from manageable sources. To do this, we need to realistically estimate the level of unmanageable flows. By subtracting the unmanageable nutrients from the level of nutrients defined in the goal, we can identify the nutrients able to enter the system from manageable sources, or the cap.

The level at which the cap is set determines the environmental effect of the system. If the cap is set too high, more nutrients will flow into the water body than the water body is able to support and the water quality goal will not be achieved.

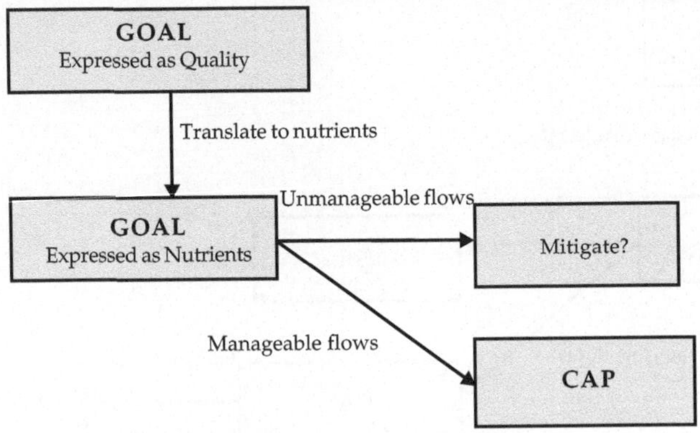

Fig. 10.2: Setting the Cap for Water Quality Trading

Scope of the Trading System

A water quality trading system is only one way of managing nutrient flow into the lake and may not be appropriate for all sources of nutrient loss. Thus, some sources may not be included in a water quality trading system. For example, it may be more appropriate for the nutrient loss from urban areas to be controlled under separate regulations.

Setting the Trading Cap

Once the scope of the trading system is identified, the trading cap can be determined. To do this, the nutrient loss from the sources outside of the trading system needs to be estimated. The remainder of the cap once the sources outside the trading system have been subtracted equals the trading cap. The trading cap must be expressed in a way that can be allocated to and monitored at the individual property level. This allows regulators to ensure that individuals are not exceeding their nutrient allowances.

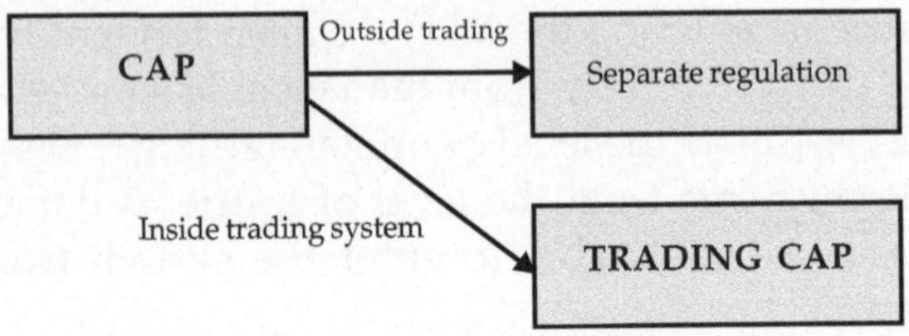

Fig. 10.3: Setting the Trading Cap for Water Quality Trading

Allocation of Allowances

One of the most difficult decisions when setting up a trading scheme is the initial allocation of the allowances. The allocation method used will not have any environmental effects. There are also no efficiency effects if the trading system works well. But there are large distributional effects associated with the allocation mechanism chosen. Once nutrient loss is limited, the resources devoted to controlling nutrient loss will rise and the allowances will become increasingly valuable. Those who must control nutrients will face high costs and those who are allocated allowances for free will receive something of high value. This makes it important to identify an acceptable mechanism for allocating allowances.

Monitoring

Regulator

Entity that determines the water quality goals, establishes caps for pollutants in a watershed, approves and administers the trading programme and monitors and enforces the rules.

The clean water act requires states to establish water quality standards that include designated uses for each water body in the state and water quality criteria, set at the level of water pollution that is permissible before there start to be significant effects on health or the environment. Every two years, states are required to identify waters which are not meeting water quality standard to the EPA.

For water bodies that do not meet the water quality standards or that are expected to fall short in the future, the state must establish a Total Maximum Daily Load of pollutants so that the water quality will not be worse than what is required by the standard. The process of setting up a TMDL is quite complicated. First, the state must determine the maximum amount of pollution that a body of water may receive and still meet the established water quality standards. That load must then be allocated to all sources contributing to the problem, including existing point sources, unregulated nonpoint sources and natural background sources of pollution. TMDLs are submitted by the state and approved by the EPA.

Legal and Regulatory Elements

Trading and other market-based incentive programmes must be consistent with the statutory requirements and water quality standards outlined in the federal clean water act and other federal laws. Trading and market-based transactions may be developed within any authorizing framework. The total maximum daily load (TMDL) process appears to be the preferred method of U.S. EPA for addressing non-attainment watersheds and it may offer the greatest opportunities for effluent trading. The regulatory agency must actively encourage effluent trading through information and education programmes. Eligibility and enforcement mechanisms must exist to ensure trading party performance.

Federal Agencies

1. The Regional U.S. EPA Office
2. U.S. Department of Agriculture

3. Natural Resource Conservation Service (NRCS)
4. Cooperative State Research, Education and Extension Service
5. U.S. Bureau of Reclamation (USBR)
6. U.S. Fish and Wildlife Service
7. National Marine Fisheries Service

State government

1. Department of Environmental Protection
2. Agriculture Departments
3. Department of Fish and Game
4. Department of Water Resources
5. Court-appointed water master
6. Tribal Councils

Local government

1. Municipal utilities
2. Wastewater treatment
3. Water suppliers
4. City or county government
5. Public Power Utilities
6. Resource Conservation and Development Councils
7. Soil and Water Conservation Districts

For example

Soil and Water Conservation Department served as a third party facilitator (broker) for the Red Cedar river water quality trading programme. The department negotiated with farmers and established trade agreements between participating nonpoint sources and the city of Cumberland.

Once a cap has been put in place and allowances have been allocated, monitoring is required to ensure that allowance holdings are not exceeded. Landowners are going to have an incentive to exceed their allowances if a binding cap is placed on the system restricting nutrient loss. If all nutrient loss is covered by allowances, the cap will be met (Walton, 2002).

Trading Partner

No trades can happen unless a producer has found a trading partner with the appropriate set of needs. Not every permitted industrial and municipal facility looking to buy pollutant reductions is an appropriate trading partner for a producer. Consider the type, amount and timing of pollutant reductions generated by the producer and determine if they match the type, amount and timing of pollutant reductions needed by a permitted industrial or municipal facility. Potential trading partner might need to offset its pollutant discharge with pollutant reductions in quantities that a single producer cannot provide. Instead, a group of producers together could provide pollutant reductions in the needed quantities and be a more suitable trading partner.

Trading

Water quality trading assigns economic value to the benefits generated by conservation practice implementation. Nitrogen and phosphorus in the soil are integral components of a producer's operation, but when excessive amounts of these substances run off fields, there is the potential to degrade water quality. Conservation practices reduce excess pollutants and improve water quality conditions. In addition to reducing pollutants, well-managed agricultural conservation systems can also mitigate elevated water temperatures and loss of wildlife habitat that can result from some land management practices. These improvements to water quality achieved through conservation practices are a valuable commodity that a producer can trade with an industrial or municipal facility that is required by law to reduce the amount of the same pollutants in its wastewater (Wu and Babock, 1999).

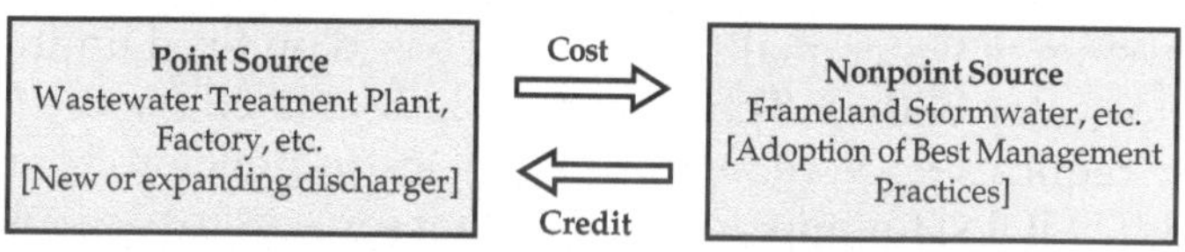

Fig. 10.4: Trading Between Point Source and Non point Source

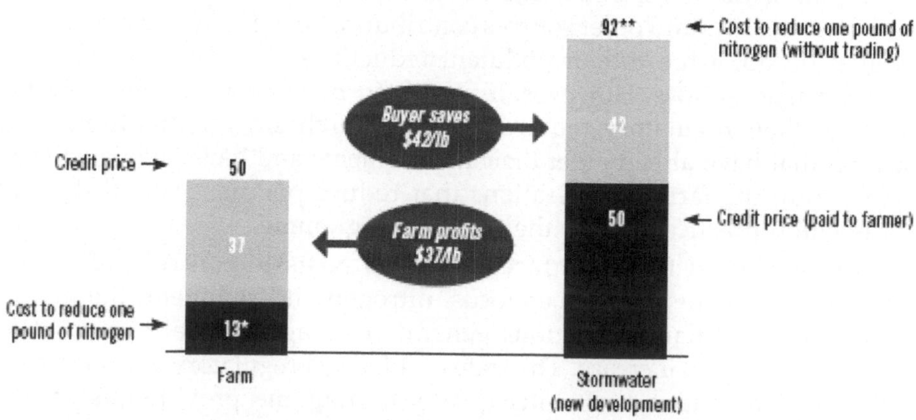

Fig. 10.5: Example of Nitrogen Trading

Types of Trade

Water quality trading has been classified into two broad categories:

1. Cap and trade
2. Field and trade

The cap and trade system is based on the regulations imposed by regulatory agencies. On the other hand, the field and trade system is designed to improve the quality of the entire ecosystem without any pre-defined limits. However, both systems are designed to help municipal waste and wastewater treatment plants, generally known as point sources, to meet their regulatory requirements. They can either buy credits from another point source or from agricultural producers referred to as non-point sources. The trade could involve a single pollutant such as nitrogen, phosphorus, or sediment; or the entire suite of services of a conservation activity such as a riparian buffer or a wetland. Such a trade is referred as ecosystem trading. Producers may be able to generate and sell credits to multiple markets from a single conservation activity. For example, the Great Miami River Watershed Water Quality Credit Programme encourages farmers to implement conservation measures, such as no-till farming, to generate phosphorus credits to sell through water quality trading programmes and carbon credits for sale through the Chicago Climate Exchange.

Cap and Trade

This system of water quality trading is based on fixed limits of pollutant discharge to water bodies. The discharge is regulated by the Clean Water Act, which requires state regulatory agencies to develop Total Maximum Daily Loads (TMDLs) for impaired waters that serve as road maps for meeting the water quality standards. TMDLs contain a maximum pollutant budget or load that impaired water can assimilate without hampering the designated water uses of the water body. TMDLs allocate portions of the total load to permitted facilities and other sources contributing to the load. If the permitted facilities do not achieve their pollutant reductions, they are in violation of state and federal laws. However, if permitted by state laws, these facilities can meet their regulatory requirements by purchasing credits from other facilities that have already met their requirements and have generated extra credits from the farming operations that reduce pollutant runoff through conservation practices within the trading programme.

As permitted facilities face increased costs to control pollutants, especially pollutants like phosphorus, nitrogen and sediment, the market demand for pollutant reductions generated by agricultural conservation practices is likely to increase. The state and federal regulatory agencies, such as the EPA, are supporting water quality trading and provide guidance to interested parties. However, it is important to note that the trading process must meet the over arching TMDL requirements and lead to nutrient reduction and improving the water quality (Horan *et al.*, 2002).

Field and Trade

In this trading model, farmers are paid to preserve the wildlife habitat, especially for an endangered species. The credits are earned for land preservation of the habitat. These credits can then be sold to land use industries or others who are required to mitigate the loss of habitat by the Endangered Species Act and other laws that restrict or prohibit development. The USDA would like to harness the market forces to change farmers' outlooks on endangered species protection from the three S's (Shoot, Shovel and Shut-up) to the three P's (Plan, Preserve and receive Payment) where they are paid for their stewardship in conserving and preserving wildlife and their habitat (Alberni and Segerson, 2002).

ELEMENTS FOR CONDUCTING WATER QUALITY TRADING FOLLOWED BY PRODUCERS

Many agricultural producers knew the benefits of implementing conservation practices in their operations. Better soil, cleaner water and greater profits are just some of the advantages. Water quality trading assigns economic value to the benefits generated by conservation practice implementation. Nitrogen and phosphorus in the soil are integral components of a producer's operation, but when excessive amounts of these substances run off fields, there is the potential to degrade water quality. Conservation practices reduce excess pollutants and improve water quality conditions. In addition to reducing pollutants, well-managed agricultural conservation systems can also mitigate elevated water temperatures and loss of wildlife habitat that can result from some land management practices. These improvements to water quality achieved through conservation practices are a valuable commodity that a producer can trade with an industrial or municipal facility that is required by law to reduce the amount of the same pollutants in its wastewater.

To help producers participate in water quality trading, one should have a general understanding of the elements involved in the process.

1. Assessing the potential goal for water quality trading
2. Determining what a producer can trade
3. Determining how much a producer can trade
4. Determining when a producer can trade
5. Finding a trading partner
6. Verifying and certifying conservation practice implementation
7. Tracking and reporting pollutant reductions and trades

Assessing the Potential Goal for Water Quality Trading

Trading is not suitable for every watershed. First, one should find out whether there is an opportunity for trading in a watershed. The catalyst for trading could stem from very specific, measurable goals to reduce the amount of pollutants entering the watershed. If these types of water quality goals exist, the catalyst for water quality trading might also exist (Greenhalgh and Faeth, 2001)

Pollutants of Concern

Use a TMDL, a wastewater permit or a watershed management plan to determine the pollutants of concern for a water body. The pollutants of concern identified in such documents usually will serve as the focus of water quality trading. For example, if a TMDL for nitrogen exists for a water body, water quality trading activities will likely focus on nitrogen. All pollutants are not suitable for trading. According to EPA's Trading Policy, EPA generally supports trading for total nitrogen, total phosphorus, and sediment. Other pollutants, such as temperature, might also be suitable for trading as long as the trading programme appropriately considers the water quality impact. TMDLs and watershed management plans that focus on nutrients, sediment and possibly temperature might provide the best opportunity for agricultural producers interested in water quality trading.

Amount of Pollutant Reduction

The TMDL, wastewater permit or watershed management plan that defines the goals for trading will not only specify the pollutants of concern, but also the amount by which the pollutants must be reduced to meet water quality standards. TMDLs, for example, include an overall pollutant budget for the water body and specific pollutant budgets for point and nonpoint sources that contribute the pollutant to the water body. This information will help you understand what pollutants and pollutant sources trading will address, as well as the amount of pollutants a producer or a group of producers might be able to reduce over time.

Determining what a Producer can Trade

Another important element in conducting water quality trading understands the commodity or service a producer can trade. By understanding the potential variations among trading programmes, able to help producers understand the different commodities and services that might attract potential trading partners (King, 2005).

Pollutant Serves as Commodity or Service

Water quality trading can involve a variety of commodities and services measured in units, such as pounds, acres or credits. Peoples were familiar with the idea of selling pounds and credits. Most trading programmes use pounds of pollutant removed (i.e., a pollutant reduction) or pollutant reduction credits as the commodity a producer will sell to permitted industrial and municipal facilities. In general, a producer will implement a conservation practice and then sell the pounds of a specific pollutant removed or reduced by implementing the conservation practice (Nishizawa, 2003).

Trading programmes that address the buying and selling of pollutant reduction credits use a calculation that involves the number of pounds of pollutant reduced and other factors established by the programme to account for issues, such as pollutant fate and transport or uncertainties with conservation practice effectiveness. The calculation translates pounds into pollutant reduction credits eligible for trading. Each of these approaches usually involves a producer implementing a conservation practice before trading and receiving payment at a later date for the pollutant reductions—measured either in pounds or as credits—generated through the conservation practice. So the commodity that the producer is selling is the actual reduced amount of a pollutant achieved by implementing a conservation practice. Instead of focusing on trading credits or pounds of pollutants reduced, some trading programmes provide compensation for the actual implementation and maintenance of conservation practices. This is especially true when a permitted industrial or municipal facility is required to take some action to offset its pollutant discharge.

For example, a permitted industrial or municipal facility might pay a producer a one-time fee for implementing a conservation practice. The permitted facility might even implement a conservation practice on a producer's land in exchange for a commitment by the producer to regularly maintain the practice. In this case, the producer is selling a service instead of a commodity—the service of implementing and/or maintaining a conservation practice to help a permitted facility meet its permit requirements.

Keeping in mind that there are different forms of the same pollutant, for example organic nitrogen and total nitrogen. A producer might have one form of pollutant reduction available for sale and a potential trading partner needs another form of that same pollutant. In these instances, a trading programme might recommend the use of a factor to convert different forms of a pollutant to the same form (e.g., a conversion factor used to convert organic nitrogen to total nitrogen).

It is important to know that one conservation practice, or a system of practices, might generate more than one commodity or service and might have the potential to earn a profit through other types of environmental trading programmes. For example, a conservation system that generates reductions in sediment and phosphorus might also (1) lower carbon emissions, (2) provide essential habitat for protected wildlife, and (3) lower water temperature to promote increased fish populations. It is possible that a producer could generate and trade multiple types of credits from this one conservation system through water quality trading, carbon trading programmes, and wetland banking programmes. The approach of using one conservation practice to generate a variety of credits for trading is referred to as multi-credit trading or credit stacking.

Conservation Practices Eligible for Trading

Conservation practices eligible for trading will vary from trading programme to trading programme. Some programmes might compile a list of approved or eligible conservation practices. Other trading programmes might not specify approved or eligible conservation practices and allow a producer to decide which practice is most appropriate according to the nature of the operation, the amount of pollutant removal desired, cost, and other factors. It is a good idea to consider a range of conservation practices to address the multiple pathways that pollutants might enter a water body from an operation (e.g., soil loss, runoff from a surface manure application, volatilization from fertilizer and manure).

Even if a trading programme provides a list of conservation practices, a producer will make some potentially challenging decisions about which practice is best. Producers select appropriate practices that provide conservation benefits and enable the producer to enter into water quality trading (Nishizawa, 2003).

Determining how much a Producer can Trade

The issue of how much a producer can trade is dependent on a number of factors, including eligibility requirements for trading, the amount of a pollutant reduced through conservation practice implementation, and discounts (trade ratios) established by a trading programme to account for challenges and characteristics unique to a trade, such as uncertainty in conservation practice performance.

Baseline

In water quality trading, producers must first meet a baseline, or a minimum requirement, to be considered an eligible participant in water quality trading. Using a baseline provides equity among producers and other entities wishing to sell pounds of pollutant removed, pollutant reduction credits, or conservation practice implementation. Baselines also help to ensure a certain level of water quality improvement in the watershed (Woodward *et al.*, 2002).

Trading programmes use a variety of approaches to express a baseline, including a specific pollutant reduction (in pounds), a percentage of a pollutant reduction, or a minimum required level of conservation practice implementation. For example:

1. Specific pollutant reduction: A producer is assigned a baseline phosphorus reduction of 20 lbs/day that implementation of a conservation practice must achieve before the conservation practice generates pollutant reduction credits. A producer generating any phosphorus reductions beyond 20 lbs/day can participate in trading by selling the excess phosphorus reductions or by receiving compensation to implement conservation practices that achieve the excess phosphorus reductions.
2. Percentage of a pollutant reduction: A producer is assigned a baseline sediment reduction of 20 percent from the current discharge before

conservation practices generate pollutant reduction credits. A producer generating any sediment reductions greater than 20 percent of the current discharge can participate in trading by selling the excess sediment reductions or by receiving compensation to implement conservation practices that achieve the excess sediment reductions.

Where a TMDL for a certain pollutant exists, trading programmes that address the same pollutant will most likely express the baseline for producers as the load allocation portion of the TMDL.

Total Pollutant Reduction

The total pollutant reduction is the amount of pollutants reduced through conservation practice implementation after achieving the baseline. The producer with assistance can determine the pollutant removal efficiencies of conservation practices or how much of a pollutant a conservation practice can be expected to remove. Trading programmes might provide this information with a list of approved conservation practices and associated pollutant removal efficiencies (Wu and Babock, 1999).

Trade Ratios

Water quality trading presents challenges in how to address unique environmental features, such as pollutant fate and transport through a certain type of water body and how to estimate pollutant reductions from agricultural operations using conservation practices. As a result, most trades incorporate a factor called a trade ratio to account for these features and challenges. The trade ratio affects how much pollutant reduction or pollutant reduction credits a producer has available to trade because it usually has a discounting effect.

Trading programmes use different terms to describe trade ratios. Commonly used trade ratios account for the location of the trading partners, the location of the impaired water body in relation to the trading partners, the type of pollutant being traded, and the uncertainty associated with pollutant reductions achieved by conservation practice implementation. The latter is referred to as an uncertainty ratio and is likely the type of trade ratio producers will most frequently encounter when participating in water quality trading (Horan *et al.*, 2002).

An uncertainty ratio compares the amount of pollutant reduction that a permitted industrial or municipal facility must buy from a producer to the amount of pollutant reduction the permitted facility can actually use. So, an uncertainty ratio of 2:1 means that a permitted industrial or municipal facility will buy either 2 pounds of a pollutant reduction or 2 pollutant reduction credits if it needs to actually use 1 pound or 1 credit to meet its permit requirements. Uncertainty ratios might range from 2:1 or as high as 5:1, depending on the rules of a trading programme. The higher the uncertainty ratio, the more expensive it is for a permitted industrial or municipal facility to trade with a producer. The better the understanding of a conservation practice's pollutant removal efficiency, usually through direct monitoring, the more likely it is a trading programme will use a lower uncertainty ratio.

Determining when a Producer can Trade

Many factors affect the time frame in which a producer can implement conservation practices, generate eligible pollutant reductions and sell the pollutant reduction, pollutant reduction credits or conservation practice implementation. The issues affecting timing will ultimately influence when a producer will receive payment for participating in water quality trading (Collentine *et al.*, 2002).

When a Producer can Trade

The period of time during which a producer generates pollutant reductions to trade and a permitted industrial or municipal facility can use those pollutant reductions to offset its pollutant discharge is referred to as a reconciliation period. A producer cannot sell pollutant reductions or pollutant reduction credits before the conservation practice actually generates them or after the reconciliation period ends. For example, if a permitted industrial or municipal facility must offset a pollutant discharge during the month of April, the facility must purchase pollutant reductions actually achieved during the month of April. Each trading programme will specify the appropriate reconciliation period and the process for ensuring trading partners trade during that time frame. It is likely that trading programmes will use reconciliation periods appropriate for the pollutant of concern and the timing of permit discharge limits for a permitted industrial or municipal facility. If a point source trading partner is required to meet a monthly discharge limit, the trading programme might also use a monthly reconciliation period.

Permits can express discharge limits on a monthly, seasonal or annual basis; therefore, a trading programme might use one or more reconciliation periods. Producers understand the function of a reconciliation period and determine if it is possible to generate pollutant reductions during the reconciliation periods established by a trading programme. In situations where a producer sells conservation practice implementation, a reconciliation period is not necessary because this type of transaction focuses on a one-time purchase of a service as opposed to the purchase and use of regularly generated pollutant reductions quantified as pounds or credits (Brain *et al.*, 2008).

Seasonal Variability Affect - Producer can Trade

Some conservation practices installed on agricultural lands are designed to control pollutants that leave an operation during wet seasons. A trading programme might limit a producer's ability to trade during dry weather if a conservation practice intended to operate during wet seasons is not generating pollutant reductions. Wet seasons produce runoff as a result of rainfall or snow melt. Irrigation practices might also generate runoff from an operation.

For conservation practices designed to address runoff during wet seasons or from irrigation practices, a trading programme might specify that a producer cannot generate a pound of pollutant reduction or a pollutant reduction credit when no runoff leaves the operation (Walton, 2000). For example, a farmer might implement a nutrient management system, including testing soil and manure to avoid applying excess nutrients to cropland, and immediately incorporating manure into soils to minimize nitrogen volatilization and surface runoff of nitrogen and phosphorus. The positive impact of this conservation practice will be realized primarily during wet weather because that is when much of the volatilized nitrogen and surface-applied nutrients would have been transported to surface water before the conservation system was implemented.

Limitations on a producer's ability to trade due to seasonal variability are dependent on state and trading programme rules. A trading programme will specify if a producer has anything to trade during irrigation and how to quantify associated pollutant reductions. For example, the trading programme might describe an irrigation schedule that is considered normal for our area and allow a producer to trade using pollutant reductions generated during those irrigation events.

Another consideration related to seasonal variability focuses on the timing of conservation practice implementation. Some conservation practices are appropriate for implementation only during certain times of the year. For example, producers in most parts of the country cannot establish vegetated buffer strips during the winter months. Keep in mind the potential for seasonal variability when helping producers determine when they can participate in water quality trading.

Life Span of Conservation Practices and Time Lags Affecting a Trade

Conservation practices might not generate pollutant reductions eligible for trading indefinitely. Some have a limited life span and most require some type of maintenance to ensure their effectiveness over time. Producers estimate the life span of conservation practices and select those that will generate the most pollutant reductions over the greatest period of time for the least cost (Alberni and Segerson, 2000).

A producer should also understand the potential time lags between when implements a conservation practice and the time when the conservation practice is considered fully functional. Conservation practices that are not yet fully functional cannot generate the full amount of expected pollutant reduction or pollutant reduction credits. If a lag time does exist, a producer still might have the opportunity to generate a prorated pollutant reduction eligible for trading before the conservation practice has reached its maximum pollutant removal efficiency.

For nonstructural conservation practices, you should consider how long it will take to develop the practice and how long it will take to implement. For example, if the selected conservation practice is to develop and implement a nutrient management plan, a producer might have to train employees and wait for an appropriate time to make necessary improvements to the operation's manure handling and storage structures or to sample soil and manure.

Finding a Trading Partner

Knowing what and how much a producer can trade is an important part of water quality trading, but no trades can happen unless a producer has found a trading partner with the appropriate set of needs.

Characteristics of an Appropriate Trading Partner for a Producer

Not every permitted industrial and municipal facility looking to buy pollutant reductions is an appropriate trading partner for a producer. To consider the type, amount and timing of pollutant reductions generated by the producer and determine if they match the type, amount and timing of pollutant reductions needed by a permitted industrial or municipal facility (King, 2005). For example, a producer might be selling pollutant reductions for a different form of the pollutant than the permitted facility needs to buy. Potential trading partner might need to offset its pollutant discharge with pollutant reductions in quantities that a single producer cannot provide.

Instead, a group of producers together could provide pollutant reductions in the needed quantities and be a more suitable trading partner. Timing is also another important characteristic to match between a producer and a potential trading partner. Keep in mind the time constraints of the specified reconciliation period. Also know that some potential trading partners might want producers to enter into a long-term agreement and guarantee that they can provide pollutant reductions for an extended period of time. This period of time might be at least five years because industrial and municipal discharge permits have a five-year term.

Mechanisms of Producers to Find Potential Trading Partners

Producers can use many mechanisms to find potential trading partners. The most obvious is independently researching and contacting permitted industrial and municipal facilities (Greenhalgh and Fateh, 2001). While this does not seem like a realistic option for most producers, it is possible with assistance from you or the state's NPDES permitting authority.

Other mechanisms for finding potential trading partners focus on the use of a credit exchange where a third party facilitates the exchange of pollutant reduction credits between buyers and sellers. There are several mechanisms you can consider under the category of credit exchange, including brokers, aggregators and central exchanges.

1. Brokers are third parties that bring together potential trading partners. Brokers can work independently or as part of a trading programme and they may charge a fee for their services. A broker does the footwork and research necessary to match buyers and sellers based on pollutant type, amount and timing. Buyers and sellers negotiate the terms of the trade directly, although the broker might facilitate the negotiation process. The broker does not actually transfer pollutant reductions or pollutant reduction credits between trading partners, however a broker might participate in evaluating and ranking bids or proposals from producers who apply for financial compensation for implementing conservation practices (Collentine, 2002).

   Brokers can help to facilitate trades and develop the necessary documentation to serve as a trade agreement between producers and their trading partners. To consider serving as a broker in water quality trading is to help producers find appropriate trading partners. Alternatively, some trading programmes use a virtual broker that advertises the needs of permitted industrial and municipal facilities using a Web-based tool so producers can easily identify potential trading partners. Existing trading resources, such as the Environmental Trading Network or the World Resources Institute can provide examples of brokers and brokering tools (e.g., Nutrient Net) to help establish a third-party broker in a watershed.

2. Aggregators are also third parties that collect pollutant reduction credits from several producers to sell in bulk to permitted industrial and municipal facilities. We might be familiar with the concept of an aggregator through existing carbon credit trading programmes like the Chicago Climate Exchange. Unlike a broker, an aggregator actually buys pollutant reductions or pollutant reduction credits from producers. As a result, trade agreements exist between producers and the aggregator. There are no agreements between producers and permitted industrial and municipal facilities. Aggregators will enter into separate agreements with the facilities that purchase the pollutant reductions compiled from several producers

   Aggregators benefit the water quality trading process by eliminating the need for a permitted industrial or municipal facility to contact several producers to find enough pollutant reductions to buy and by allowing producers to participate in trading without having to establish a relationship with permitted industrial or municipal facilities. Aggregators also might charge producers a fee for their services, but this cost is likely to be less expensive than the transaction costs of independently finding trading partners and negotiating trade agreements.

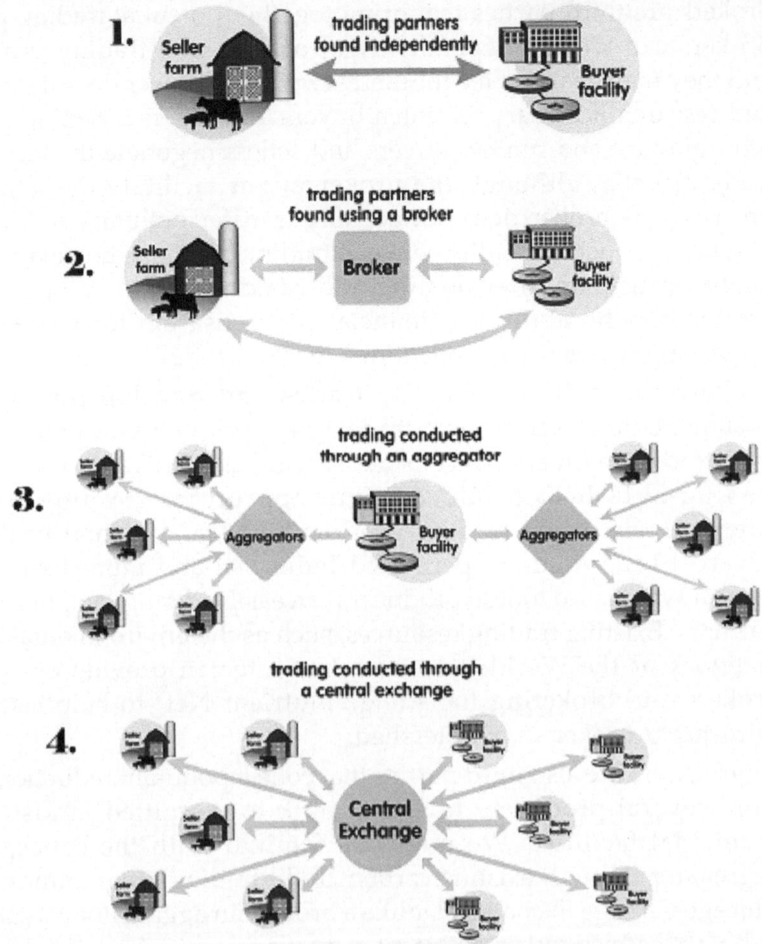

Fig. 10.6: Finding a Trading Partner

3. Central exchanges involve a third party that purchases pollutant reduction credits from one or more producers and then distributes the credits among buyers. The sellers and buyers who trade through the central exchange do not meet or negotiate trades directly with one another. A central exchange can buy pollutant reduction credits directly from producers and other entities that generate credits and then sell those credits to permitted industrial and municipal facilities during the appropriate reconciliation period. A producer does not negotiate directly with permitted facilities wanting to buy credits, only with the central exchange. The central exchange will likely have its own eligibility requirements and enter into separate agreements with each seller and buyer. The central exchange might also charge a service fee to help defray administrative and transaction costs.

From a producer's standpoint, a central exchange will perform the same function as an aggregator in terms of purchasing pollutant reductions from producers and selling them to permitted facilities. The primary difference between a central exchange and aggregators is that typically there will be only one central exchange in a trading programme, and the trading programme will be structured around the central exchange. In contrast, multiple aggregators may operate within a trading programme. The aggregators operate as free agents, and no one aggregator is central to the functionality of the trading programme (Shortle, 2007).

Verifying and Certifying Conservation Practice Implementation

Successful conservation practice implementation and maintenance is paramount to a successful trade. Therefore, it is imperative that all trades include a process for verifying and certifying that producers are properly implementing and maintaining conservation practices to generate the expected pollutant reductions (Wood ward, 2006). With an understanding of how this element works and why it is important to successful trading, you should be able to communicate this information to producers to alleviate their potential concerns about allowing trading partners or third parties to come onto their land to verify conservation practices.

Necessity to Verify and Certify Conservation Practice Implementation and Maintenance

It is difficult to measure actual pollutant reductions from conservation practice implementation. Many trading programmes use models or other calculations to estimate pollutant reductions from conservation practices. These procedures are inherently less certain than direct measurement. As a result, trading programmes often incorporate mechanisms to compensate for uncertainty related to quantifying conservation practice pollutant removal efficiencies. This is often accomplished by including requirements for conservation practice inspections and certification in trade agreements.

Information from inspections will help determine if conservation practices are achieving the expected pollutant reductions. Trading programmes often assume that as long as the conservation practices are properly implemented and maintained, they will achieve the expected pollutant reductions predicted by models or other tools. For such programmes, it is necessary to verify conservation practices to help refine the estimation methodology as the trading programme matures. In other words, if the predicted pollutant reductions were not achieved, the trading programme needs to know whether it was due to improper implementation or maintenance of conservation practices or incorrect estimates of pollutant removal efficiencies.

Verification and Certification Process

Trade agreements should define who is responsible for verifying and certifying conservation practice implementation and maintenance. This could be the producer, the permitted industrial and municipal facility or a conservation partner.

In addition to regular inspections to verify adequate implementation and maintenance, the trade agreement might also specify the need to certify the pollutant reductions generated by conservation practices. The trading programme will specify who is responsible for making this certification and the associated certification process. In some cases, a producer might self-certify by stating that all conservation practices are still functional. In other cases, the permitted industrial and municipal facilities or a third party might have to periodically inspect conservation practices to certify that they are still functional and that, over time, the conservation practice design and specifications remain appropriate for the site (Stavins, 1995).

Possibilities of a Producer to Fail or Compromise Conservation Practice

Factors like severe storms, drought, natural disaster or other events outside of a producer's control might impact the performance of a conservation practice. In selecting conservation practices and developing a trade agreement, it is important to carefully consider what contingencies are needed to deal with such events. Some trading programmes establish means to ensure that producers generate more pollutant reductions for a watershed than what permitted facilities actually need. If a trading programme purchases surplus pollutant reductions, it might allow a permitted facility to purchase from the surplus in the event one producer's conservation practices fail due to unforeseen circumstances. In any case, a producer should develop a plan for repairing or re-establishing conservation practices damaged by severe weather or other catastrophic events.

Tracking and Reporting Pollutant Reductions and Trades

Trade agreements might require specific tracking and reporting requirements to ensure that all trades are valid. The practice of tracking trades is particularly important to permitted industrial and municipal facilities because they will have to demonstrate to the NPDES permitting authority that they have purchased the required amount of pollutant reduction to offset their excess pollutant discharge. Some trading programmes use existing conservation programme tracking and reporting mechanisms, while others employ unique tracking and reporting processes (King and Kuch, 2003).

Type of Information is Tracked and Reported

To generate pollutant reductions eligible for trading, a producer will likely need to provide adequate documentation about conservation practice implementation and maintenance. In addition, trading programmes might require tracking and reporting of all financial transactions with a trading partner. This type of tracking will help trading programme administrators develop annual reports on the progress water quality trading has made toward achieving overarching pollutant reduction goals and at what cost. The trade agreement might also specify the need to complete and submit a certification form or a conservation practice pollutant reduction calculation form. This type of tracking and reporting will require detailed information on the producer's operation and the conservation practices implemented at that operation to generate pollutant reductions.

The frequency for tracking and reporting will vary from trading programme to trading programme, depending on the designated reconciliation period and the time frame necessary to review trade related forms and reports, develop required annual reports for the public and conduct an accounting of pollutant discharges and pollutant load reductions. Depending on details of the trade agreement, tracking and reporting activities might be the responsibility of the producer, the producer's trading partner, or the third party performing verification and certification services.

MEASUREMENT OF N LOSS

Since the quantification of N losses from agricultural fields is difficult (Delgado, 2002), computer models present an alternative to quantify and assess the effects of best management practices on reduction of N losses to the environment (Delgado, 2005; Shaffer and Delgado, 2001). The Natural Resources Conservation Service (NRCS), in cooperation with the Agriculture Research Service Soil Plant Nutrient Research Unit (ARS-SPNR), developed a prototype web-based Nitrogen Trading Tool (NTT) (Gross *et al.*, 2008; Fig. 10.7). The web-based prototype allows farmers to quickly determine how many potential N credits their farming operations can generate.

The Nitrogen trading tool estimates pollutant reduction under combination of field and farm level conservation practices also referred to as BMPs. The pollutant reduction can then be used to estimate tradable credits based upon the local conditions and regulations. Field level practices deal with fertilizer management (quantity, type, timing, method of application), irrigation management and tillage management for cropping systems of the region. On the other hand, the farm level practices are structural activities such as riparian buffers, wetlands, etc. that control pollutants flow to water bodies.

The NTT is a web-based system with an easy to use interface. The user starts by selecting the state, country and a weather station nearest and representative to the farm location. Based upon these selections, a list of cropping systems along with their tillage management, irrigation management and nitrogen input management are identified and presented to the user to choose the baseline and alternative options that trader wants to evaluate.

The management choices along with the site specific soil and weather information are inputted into the Nitrogen Leaching and Environment Assessment Programme (NLEAP) (Delgado and Shaffer, 1998) that simulates the flux of the nitrogen in the system to predict nitrogen losses through different pathways both for the baseline and alternative scenarios.

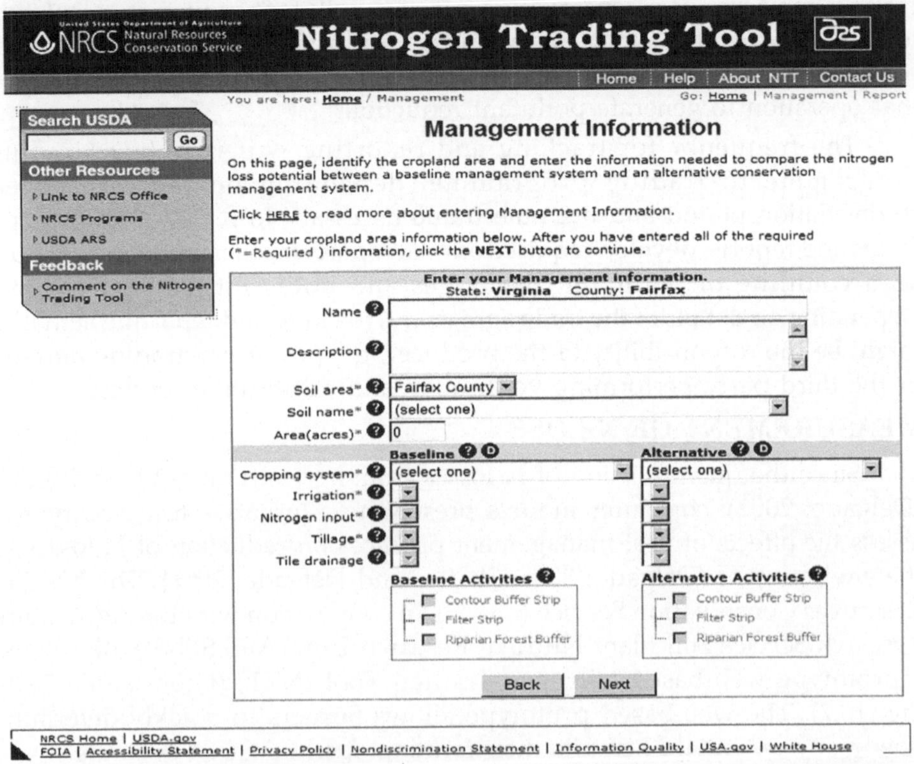

Fig. 10.7: Web-based Nitrogen Trading Tool User Interface (Gross *et al.*, 2008)

BEST MANAGEMENT PRACTICES

Silvopastural Practices

The tropical agroforestry systems (integration of trees in farmland and/ or rangeland) have indicated that tree and crop roots occupying different soil depths can enhance nutrient (specifically N) uptake and reduce nutrient losses from soils compared with monoculture crops that have more localized, shallow rooting depths (Nair *et al.*, 1999).

Recent studies in Florida's Panhandle region have demonstrated that Ultisols beneath pecan trees (*Carya illinoensis*) contained lower nutrient concentrations than those under cotton (*Gossypium sp.*) in a pecan + cotton alleycropping system (Allen *et al.*, 2006). These findings suggest that tree intercropping could be a means of addressing the problem of environmental impact of non-point source pollution resulting from addition of organic and inorganic fertilizers on soils. In a paired watershed study in north eastern Missouri, consisting of agroforestry (trees plus grass buffer strips), contour strips (grass buffer strips), and control treatments with a corn (*Zea mays*)–soybean (*Glycine max*) rotation, Udawatta *et al.* (2002) found that nitrate–N loss was reduced 24 and 37 %, respectively, by contour strip and agro-forestry treatments and the treatments also reduced total P loss by 8 and 17 % on contour strip and agro-forestry watersheds.

Reducing Nutrient Loss from Farms Through Silvopastoral Practices in Coarse-textured Soils of Florida, USA

Trees integrated into the range and pasturelands of Florida could remove nutrients from deeper soil profiles that would otherwise be transported to water bodies and cause pollution. Soil nitrogen and phosphorus concentrations were monitored in three pastures: a treeless pasture of bahiagrass (*Paspalum notatum*); a pasture of bahiagrass under 20-year-old slash pine (*Pinus elliotti*) trees (silvopasture); and a pasture of native vegetation under pine trees (native silvopasture).

Soil analysis from 10 profiles within each pasture showed that P concentrations were higher in treeless pasture (9.11mg kg^{-1} in the surface to 0.23mg kg^{-1} at 1.0m depth) compared to silvopastures (2.51 and 0.087mg kg^{-1}, respectively), and ammonium–N and nitrate–N concentrations were higher in the surface horizon of treeless pasture. The more extensive rooting zones of the combined stand of tree + forage may have caused higher nutrient uptake from silvopastures than treeless system.

The combined root systems of the pine and bahiagrass in the silvopasture may absorb soil nutrients more completely than in the grasses alone in the treeless system as indicated by the reduction in P in tree-based systems. In addition, the capacity of soils under silvopasture to receive additional P is greater than that under a treeless pasture. Thus, the silvopastoral association may be better than the treeless pasture in reducing nutrient loss from soil to surface water.

The potential of deep-rooted trees to capture nutrients from the lower soil depths has, however, not been explored as a means to remove excess nutrients from the soils and thereby reduce nutrient losses in this basin.

Riparian Areas

Riparian areas are lands directly adjacent to rivers and streams and can potentially buffer streams from the impacts of agriculture. The term riparian buffer refers to the management of riparian areas for water quality improvement. Riparian buffers can improve stream water quality by a combination of physical, chemical and biological processes and perform three key roles in minimising the impacts of agriculture on stream water quality.

Firstly, they help stabilise stream channel morphology (Thorne, 1990). Secondly, they help protect streams from upland sources of pollution by physically filtering and trapping sediment, nutrient and chemicals (Osborne and Kovacic, 2003). Thirdly, they can displace sediment and nutrient producing activities away from the stream.

Table 10.3: Nutrient Concentration in Different Pastures

Sl. No.	Depth (cm)	Location	WSP (mg kg^{-1})	NO_3–N (mg kg^{-1})	NH_4–N (mg kg^{-1})
1.	0-5	C-SP1	4.23	0.87	6.87
		C-SP2	1.72	1.26	6.36
		C-SP3	1.59	0.83	6.35
		Pasture	9.11	2.43	9.77
2.	5-15	C-SP1	2.09	0.74	5.15
		C-SP2	0.66	1.34	4.45
		C-SP3	1.28	0.55	5.41
		Pasture	2.79	0.50	4.07
3.	15- 30	C-SP1	0.78	0.49	3.86
		C-SP2	0.13	0.42	3.06
		C-SP3	0.12	0.23	3.32
		Pasture	1.52	0.32	2.98
4.	30-50	C-SP1	0.16	0.49	3.86
		C-SP2	0.00	0.42	3.06
		C-SP3	0.00	0.23	3.32
		Pasture	1.92	0.32	2.98

C-SP1: Silvopasture with 494 trees ha^{-1}; C-SP2: Thinned silvopasture with 309 trees ha^{-1}; C-SP 3: Native silvopasture; Pasture: Treeless pasture) (Nair *et al.*, 2007).

Before and After Riparian Management: Sediment and Nutrient Exports from a Small Agricultural Catchment, Western Australia

The study was undertaken in a small (5.9 km^2) agricultural catchment near Albany, Western Australia. The topography of the catchment is low gentle hills with one major granitic outcrop, Willyung Hill. Elevations range between 20 and 180 m above sea level.

The average sediment load prior to riparian management was 114 kg ha^{-1} yr $^{-1}$, although annual variability was large. After improved riparian management the average sediment load dropped to less than 10 kg ha^{-1} yr^{-1} and annual variability was reduced.

Total P exports from the catchment were similar throughout the monitoring period, generally between 0.2 and 0.6 kg ha^{-1} yr $^{-1}$.

Table 10.4: Effect of riparian areas in nutrient runoff (McKergow *et al.*, 2003)

Sl. No.	Time of Analysis (mg L^{-1})	Suspended Sediment	Phosphorus (mg L^{-1})	Total Nitrogen (mg L^{-1})
1.	Before	146.7	0.51	3.26
2.	After	9.9	0.48	2.51
3.	% reduction	93	6	23

In this catchment, water logging of riparian areas during the winter may further reduce the ability of riparian vegetation to filter sediment and nutrients from surface runoff. Riparian buffers may also remove the risk of direct fertiliser application to the stream and slow the transport between pasture and stream.

Cover Crops

A large reduction of soil loss with the cover crop treatment as compared to that with tillage has also been reported in previous studies; Francia *et al.* (2006) in their (Rye grass) cover crop plots measured 5.08 and 2.1 t ha^{-1} y^{-1}, compared to 41.6 and 5.7 t ha^{-1} y^{-1}, respectively.

Influence of Cover Crops and Tillage on Water and Sediment Yield, Nutrient and Organic Matter Losses in an Olive Orchard on a Sandy Loam Soil

One plot was devoted to conventional tillage (CT) consisting of regular chisel plough passes (2-3 times a year at 10-15 cm depth) depending on weed growth. The other treatment was a cover crop (CC) of Rye grass manually sown during early fall at 100 kg of seed per ha in the area outside the vertical olive canopy projection. The annual dissolved nutrient losses in runoff water are shown in Table 10.5.

Table 10.5: Effect of Cover Crops on Nutrient Losses in the Runoff

Year	NO_3-N kg ha^{-1} y^{-1}		Dissolved P kg ha^{-1} y^{-1}		Sediment (kg m^3)	
	CT	CC	CT	CC	CT	CC
2003/04	2.05	1.23	0.34	0.09	23.8	0.6
2004/05	0.46	3.67	1.08	0.16	16.0	3.6
2005/06	1.11	0.65	0.02	0.02	8.0	1.6
2006/07	9.51	1.43	0.25	0.13	21.3	1.6
Average	**3.28**	**1.75**	**0.42**	**0.10**	**17.3**	**1.9**

(CT- Conventional tillage, CC- Cover crop)

(Gomez *et al.*, 2009)

Lower runoff yield, but also of a lower sediment concentration in the CC treatment compared CT. The water infiltrated more easily into the soil under the protective plants and at the same time, the increased flow resistance dissipated the energy of the surface water and the aerial part of the plant intercepted part of the sediment particles carried by the water (Dunkerley *et al.*, 2001).

CASE STUDY

Water quality trading programme -reduces nutrient load in Chesapeake bay watershed

Projects: Dauphin, Chester, Bedford, Berks, Cumberland, Lebanon, Mifflin, Potter and Somerset conservation districts received grants to implement credit generating BMPs that can be sold and used toward permit compliance. 87,000 Nitrogen credits have been generated as a result of over 4,700 acres of no-till, cover cropping, buffer installation, stream bank fencing and rotational grazing. Additionally, 2 manure storage units and 3 mortality composters were installed; over 15,500 feet of farm lanes were stabilized and, nearly 800 tons of poultry manure was exported.

Results: Through the funding provided from the Pennsylvania Department of Environmental Protection grants, the conservation districts were able to assist the farming community to enhance local water quality, translating into the generation of pollutant credits.

Table. 10.6: Effect of Best Management Practices on Generation of N Credits

Sl. No.	BMP	Impact	N Credits
1.	No-Till	2,172 acres	16,727
2.	Cover Crops	2,478 acres	49,662
3.	Riparian Buffers	2.4 acres	86
4.	Stream bank Fencing	60 acres	3,377
5.	Rotational Grazing	13 acres	11
6.	Manure Storage	2	6,514
7.	Farm Lane Stabilization	15,542 feet	146
8.	Manure Export	794.43 tons	10,680
	Total		**87,000**

Table 10.7: Current Trading Programmes- in Pennsylvania's Chesapeake Bay Watershed

Sl. No.	Buyer	Seller	Date of Agreement (signature date)	Length of Agreement	N Credits*	Price	P Credits*	Price
1.	Mount Joy Borough Authority	Brubaker Farms	26-Feb-07	3 years	11,718	$3.81		
2.	Dunn Lake	Red Barn Trading Company	17-Oct-06	5 years	223	$9	3	$4
3.	Airy View Heights	Red Barn Trading Company	20-Feb-09	5 years	635	$10	48	$5
4.	Camp Iroqoina	Red Barn Trading Company	17-Mar-09	5 years	8	$15	11	$10

Appendix -1
Pollutant Reduction Certificate
EXAMPLE

VALID FOR POLLUTANT REDUCTION ACTIVITY FOR MONTH(S): ____________________ YEAR: _________
NAME OF FACILITY GENERATING CREDITS:
CONTACT NAME:
ADDRESS:
PHONE NUMBER:
BEST MANAGEMENT PRACTICE (BMP) IDENTIFIER: – Type of BMP: – Location of BMP:
VERIFICATION METHOD:
VERIFICATION FREQUENCY:
VERIFICATION RESULTS (POUNDS OF POLLUTANT REMOVED*) (A): *Not to include pollutant required by, or resulting from, trading baseline requirement
TRADE RATIO (B): ______________ = ____________ x ____________ x ____________ Trade Ratio = Ratio #1 (if applicable) x Ratio #2 (if applicable) x Ratio #3 (if applicable)
AMOUNT OF MARKETABLE CREDITS: Total Reduction Amount in Pounds Removed x Trade Ratio (A x B) = __________

CERTIFICATION

I certify that the above information is accurate and truthful to the best of my knowledge and is in accord with the state's trading programme.

Signature of Authorized Representative of Buyer:

....

Signature of Authorized Representative of Seller:

....

CONCLUSION

Water quality trading holds great promise as an effective market-based tool for achieving the water quality goals. The agricultural producers are integral to the success of water quality trading. Although water quality trading has been the focus of discussion for over a decade, in reality, it is just getting started. Momentum is growing, critical discussions are happening and pivotal decisions are shaping the future of water quality trading programmes and policies across the country.

As water quality trading success stories grow, demand for expertise in the area of water quality trading will also grow. Innovators in water quality trading will have unmatched expertise to offer producers interested in getting paid for their conservation efforts. Expanding the services to include water quality trading will not only help producers realize new economic opportunities, but also result in more conservation on the ground.

REFERENCES

Alberini, A and Sergerson, K. (2002): Assessing Voluntary Programmes to Improve Environmental Quality. *Environ. Res. Econo.*, 22 (1-2): 157-184.

Allen, S.C. Nair, V.D. Graetz, D.A. Jose, S and Nair, P.K.R. (2006): Phosphorus Loss from Organic versus Inorganic Fertilizers Used in Alley Cropping on a Florida Ultisol. *Agricult. Ecosyst. Environ.*, 117: 290-298.

Brain, M. Daniel, P and Los Huertos, M. (2008): Agricultural Non-point Water Pollution Policy: The Case of California's Central Coast. *Agricult. Ecosyst. Environ.*, 128: 151-161.

Collectine, D. (2002): Search for the Northwest Passage: The Assignation of NSP (Non-point Source Pollution) Rights in Nutrient Trading Programmes. *Water Sci. Technol.*, 45(9): 227-234.

Delgado, J.A and. Bausch, W.C. (2005): Potential Use of Precision Conservation Techniques to Reduce Nitrate Leaching in Irrigated Crops. *J. Soil Water Conserv.*, 60: 379-387.

Delgado, J.A. (2002): Quantifying the Loss Mechanisms of Nitrogen. *J. Soil Water Conserv.*, 57: 389-398.

Diaz, R and Rosenberg, R. (2008): Spreading Dead Zones and Consequences for Marine Ecosystems. *Science*, 321: 926-929.

Donald, I. Laura, S and Kostel, A. (2005): Nutrient Farming: The Business of Environmental Management. *Eco. Engg.*, 24: 279-287.

Eiichiro Nishizawa. (2003): Effluent Trading for Water Quality Management: Concept and Application to the Chesapeake Bay Watershed. *Marine Pollu Bull.*, 47: 169-174.

Francia, J.R. Dura, Z and Martinez, V.H. (2006): Environmental Impact from Mountainous Olive Orchards Under Different Soil Management Systems. *Science of the Total Environ.*, 358: 46-60.

Franklin, D. Truman, C. Potter, T. Bosch, D. Strickland, T and Bednarz, C. (2007): Nitrogen and Phosphorus Runoff Losses from Variable and Constant Intensity Rainfall-Simulations on Loamy Sand Under Conventional and Strip Tillage Systems. *J. Environ. Qual.*, 36: 846-854.

Gomez, A. Gema Guzma, M. Giraldez, V and Fereres, E. (2009): The Influence of Cover Crops and Tillage on Water, Sediment Yield, Nutrient and Organic Matter Losses in an Olive Orchard on a Sandy Loam Soil. *Soil Tillage Res.*, 106: 137-144.

Greenhalgh, S and Faeth, P. (2001): Trading on Water. *Forum for Applied Research and Policy*, 32: 71-77.

Gross, C.M. Delgado, J.A. McKinney, S.P. Lal, H. Cover, H and Shaffer, M.J. (2008): Nitrogen Trading Tool to Facilitate Water Quality Trading. *J. Soil Water Conserv.*, 63 (2): 44-45.

Horan, R.D. (2001): Differences in Social and Public Risk Perceptions and Conflicting Impacts on Point/Nonpoint Trading Ratios. *American J. Agricult. Econo.*, 83(4): 934-41.

Horan, R.D.. Shortle, J.S and Abler, D.G. (2002): Point-nonpoint Nutrient Trading in the Susquehanna River Basin. *Water Resources Res.*, 38(5): 126-131.

Horan, R.D. Shortle, J.S and Abler, D.G (2004): The Coordination and Design of Point-nonpoint Trading Programmes and Agri-environmental Policies. *Agricult. Res. Econo. Review.*, 33(1): 61-78.

King, D. M and Kuch, P.J. (2003): Will Nutrient Credit Trading Ever Work? An Assessment of Supply and Demand Problems and Institutional Obstacles. *Environmental Law Reporter News and Analysis*, 33(5): 10352-19368.

King, D.M. (2005): Crunch Time for Water Quality Trading. *Choices*, 20(1): 71-75.

Krutilla, K. (1999): Environmental Policy and Transactions Costs. In: J.C.J.M. Van Den Bergh (Ed.), Handbook of Environmental and Resource Economics. Edward Edgar Publishing Limited, UK. pp. 249-64.

Logan, T.J. (1990): Agricultural Best Management Practices and Groundwater Quality. *J. Soil and Water Conserv.*, 45(2): 201-206.

Malik, A.S. (1992): Enforcement Costs and the Choice of Policy Instruments for Controlling Pollution. *Economic Inquiry*, 30: 714-21.

McKergowa, A. David Weaver, M. Ian Prosser, P and Rodger Graysona, B. (2003): Before and After Riparian Management: Sediment and Nutrient Exports from a Small Agricultural Catchment. *Western Australia. J. Hydrol.*, 270: 253-272.

Nair, P.K.R. Buresh, R.J. Mugendi, D.N and Latt, C.R. (1999): Nutrient Cycling in Tropical Agroforestry Systems: Myths and Science. In: L.E. Buck, J.P. Lassoie and E.C.M. Fernandes (Eds)., Agroforestry in Sustainable Agricultural Systems. CRC Press, Boca Raton, Florida, USA, pp. 1-31.

Naira, V.D. Nairb, P.K.R. Kalmbacher R.S and Ezenwa, I.V. (2007): Reducing Nutrient Loss from Farms Through Silvopastoral Practices in Coarse-textured Soils of Florida, USA. *Ecol. Engg.*, 29: 192-199.

Nishizawa, E. (2003): Effluent Trading for Water Quality Management Application to the Chesapeake Bay Watershed. *Marine Pollu. Bull.*, 47: 169-174.

Osborne, L.L and Kovacic D.A. (2003): Riparian Vegetated Buffer Strips in Water Quality Restoration and Stream Management. *Freshwater Biol.*, 29; 243-258.

Shaffer, M.J and Delgado, J.A. (2001): Field Techniques for Modelling Nitrogen Management. In: R.F. Follett (Ed.), Nitrogen in the Environment: Sources, Problems, and Management, First ed. Elsevier Science B.V. pp. 391-411.

Shortle, J.S. (2007): Research Opportunities and Challenges. In: National Water Conference on Water Quality Credit Trading Symposium, January 29, Savannah, Georgia. pp. 91-97.

Stavins, R.N. (1995): Transaction Costs and Tradable Permits. *J. Environ. Econ. Manage.*, 29: 133-48.

Thorne, C.R. (1990): Effects of Vegetation on Riverbank Erosion and Stability. In: J.B. Thornes (Ed.), Vegetation and Erosion: Processes and Environments. Wiley, New York, pp. 125-144.

Udawatta, R.P. Krstansky, J.J. Henderson, G.S and Garrett, H.E (2002): Agroforestry Practices, Runoff and Nutrient Loss: A Paired Watershed Comparison. *J. Environ. Qual.*, 31: 1214-1225.

Walton, J. (2000): Should Monitoring be Compulsory within Voluntary Environmental Agreements? Sustain. Develop., 8(3): 265-273.

Woodward, R.T. 2006. Lessons About Effluent Trading from a Single Trade. *Review of Agricult. Econ.*, 25(1): 235-45.

Woodward, R. Kaiser, A and Wicks, A. (2002): The Structure and Practice of Water Quality Trading Markets. *J. American Water Res. Association.*, 38 (4): 967-979.

Wu, J.J and Babock, B.A. (1999): The Relative Efficiency of Voluntary vs. Mandatory Environmental Regulations. *J. Environ. Econ. Manage.*, 38(2): 158-175.

Index

❑ ❑ ❑ ❑ ❑